# My Samsung
# Galaxy Tab® 4

Eric Butow
Lonzell Watson

QUE®

# My Samsung Galaxy Tab® 4

## Copyright © 2015 by Pearson Education, Inc.

ISBN-13: 978-0-7897-5384-7

ISBN-10: 0-7897-5384-7

Library of Congress Control Number: 2014947249

Printed in the United States of America

First Printing: October 2014

## Trademarks

All terms mentioned in this book that are known to be trademarks or service marks have been appropriately capitalized. Que Publishing cannot attest to the accuracy of this information. Use of a term in this book should not be regarded as affecting the validity of any trademark or service mark.

Galaxy Tab 4 images are provided by Samsung Electronics America.

## Warning and Disclaimer

## Special Sales

For information about buying this title in bulk quantities, or for special sales opportunities (which may include electronic versions; custom cover designs; and content particular to your business, training goals, marketing focus, or branding interests), please contact our corporate sales department at corpsales@pearsoned.com or (800) 382-3419.

For government sales inquiries, please contact governmentsales@pearsoned.com.

For questions about sales outside the U.S., please contact international@pearsoned.com.

**Editor-in-Chief**
Greg Wiegand

**Acquisitions Editor**
Michelle Newcomb

**Development Editor**
Charlotte Kughen

**Managing Editor**
Kristy Hart

**Senior Project Editor**
Betsy Gratner

**Indexer**
Lisa Stumpf

**Proofreader**
Paula Lowell

**Technical Editor**
Christian Kenyeres

**Publishing Coordinator**
Cindy Teeters

**Cover Designer**
Mark Shirar

**Compositor**
Bumpy Design

# Contents at a Glance

# Table of Contents

# About the Authors

**Eric Butow** began writing books in 2000 when he wrote *Master Visually Windows 2000 Server*. Since then, Eric has authored or coauthored 24 other books. Those books include Addison-Wesley's *User Interface Design for Mere Mortals*, Amacom's *How to Succeed in Business Using LinkedIn*, Wiley Publishing's *Droid Companion*, Wiley Publishing's *Google Glass For Dummies*, Que Publishing's *My Samsung Galaxy Tab 3*, and Que Publishing's *Blogging to Drive Business*, Second Edition.

Eric lives in Jackson, California. He has a master's degree in communication from California State University, Fresno, and is the owner of Butow Communications Group (BCG), an online marketing ROI improvement firm.

Website: http://butow.net

LinkedIn: http://linkedin.com/in/ebutow

**Lonzell Watson** is the best-selling author of the *Teach Yourself Visually iPad* book series. His books have won the International Award of Excellence, the award of Distinguished Technical Communication, and Best of Show presented by the Society for Technical Communication. He is the author of other popular titles including *My Samsung Galaxy Tab 3, My Amazon Fire Phone, The Guide for Android Apps and Gear, My HTC EVO 3D, Teach Yourself Visually Digital Video, Teach Yourself Visually Final Cut Pro*, and the *Canon VIXIA Digital Field Guide*.

Lonzell is an instructional designer in the aerospace and defense industry and designs interactive training simulations for the Basic Engineering Common Core Studies of the United States Navy. He holds a master's degree in Instructional Design and Development, and is an Adjunct Professor at Bellevue University. Lonzell is also the owner of Creative Intelligence LLC, an instructional design and technical writing company.

Website: http://creativeintel.com

LinkedIn: http://linkedin.com/pub/lonzell-watson/6/b64/499

# Dedication

*To my literary agent, Carole Jelen. Carole, without you I wouldn't be the successful author I am today. I'm grateful for our relationship.*
*—Eric Butow*

*To my wife, Robyn Watson. Robyn, without you none of the amazing successes we have accomplished over the past year would have been possible. Thank you for your love, direction, and my incredibly fulfilled and happy life! I am forever grateful.*
*— Lonzell Watson*

# Acknowledgments

**Eric Butow:** My thanks as always to my family and friends. I want to thank my awesome literary agent, Carole Jelen, as well as Cindy Teeters, Christian Kenyeres, Charlotte Kughen, Todd Brakke, Greg Wiegand, and especially Michelle Newcomb. I'd also like to thank everyone who gave me permission to use their information, particularly the parents of my mother's daycare children for letting me take their pictures for the book.

**Lonzell Watson:** Thank you again to my wife, and thanks also to an old friend, Jennifer Sigman, and a new friend (who I am very fortunate to have made), John Tatum. I would like to give special thanks to Michelle Newcomb, without whom this project would not have been possible. I would like to thank Cindy Teeters and Greg Wiegand for the opportunity. Special thanks go to Laura Clor, Shannon Johnson, and Danya and Sean Platt.

# We Want to Hear from You!

As the reader of this book, *you* are our most important critic and commentator. We value your opinion and want to know what we're doing right, what we could do better, what areas you'd like to see us publish in, and any other words of wisdom you're willing to pass our way.

We welcome your comments. You can email or write us directly to let us know what you did or didn't like about this book—as well as what we can do to make our books better.

*Please note that we cannot help you with technical problems related to the topic of this book.*

When you write, please be sure to include this book's title and author as well as your name, email address, and phone number. We will carefully review your comments and share them with the author and editors who worked on the book.

Email:     feedback@quepublishing.com

Mail:      Que Publishing
           ATTN: Reader Feedback
           800 East 96th Street
           Indianapolis, IN 46240 USA

# Reader Services

Visit our website and register this book at quepublishing.com/register for convenient access to any updates, downloads, or errata that might be available for this book.

**Review the different
versions of Android**

**Meet the newest members
of the Galaxy Tab family:
the Galaxy Tab 4 7.0, 8.0,
and 10.1**

**Learn how the Galaxy Tab 4
compares to other Galaxy
Tab models**

In this chapter, you're introduced to the different versions of Android and the different models of the Galaxy Tab including the Galaxy Tab 4. Topics in this chapter include:

→ The three different versions of the Android operating system
→ The three models of the Galaxy Tab 4
→ A comparison of Galaxy Tab 4 and other models in the Galaxy Tab family

# The Galaxy Tab Universe

If you're brand new to the Galaxy Tab 4, start with this chapter so you can learn more about your new tablet and also learn more about the Android operating system that the Galaxy Tab 4 uses. If you want to get started right away, proceed to Chapter 2, "Meeting the Galaxy Tab 4."

## First, a Look at Android

The Galaxy Tab 4 runs the Android operating system that is produced and maintained by Google. As of this writing, the latest IDC report that tracked mobile operating system marketing share stated that in the first quarter of 2014 Android commanded 81 percent market share, well above the second place iOS used on iPhones and iPads (http://www.idc.com/prodserv/smartphone-os-market-share. jsp). As of May 2014, Samsung owns 22 percent of worldwide tablet market share, which is second only to Apple's 33 percent (https:// www.idc.com/getdoc.jsp?containerId=prUS24833314).

There are several versions of Android currently available that run on various smartphones and tablets. Each version is best known by the nicknames Google gives it. Since version 1.5, Google has given the name of a sweet treat to every new version; version 1.5 was known as Cupcake. (There were two previous versions before Cupcake that didn't have a nickname, so Google decided to give the third release of Android a nickname starting with the third letter of the alphabet.)

Galaxy Tab models run one of the following Android versions:

- Version 2.2, or Froyo (short for frozen yogurt), runs on the original Galaxy Tab 7.0. You can learn more about using Froyo on the Galaxy Tab 7.0 in Que's 2011 book *My Samsung Galaxy Tab* (ISBN 978-0-7897-4797-6).

- Version 2.3, Gingerbread, was the most widely used version of Android as of early July 2012. In addition to including user interface improvements, Gingerbread was designed for use on extra-large screen resolutions and provided improved network performance.

- Version 3, Honeycomb, was the first version optimized for use with tablets. It included more user interface improvements, support for video chat using Google Talk, and the ability to encrypt all user data.

- Version 4, Ice Cream Sandwich, included more improvements to the user interface, improved features, such as real-time speech-to-text dictation, and new apps, such as a photo editor. You can learn more about using Ice Cream Sandwich on the Galaxy Tab 2 in Que's 2013 book *My Samsung Galaxy Tab 2* (ISBN 978-0-7897-5038-9).

- Version 4.1, Jelly Bean, includes a new interface layout for tablets with smaller screens such as the Galaxy Tab 3 7.0, Google Chrome as the new web browser, and the Google Now personalized search app. This version of Jelly Bean was the most widely used version of Android as of early June 2014 (http://developer.android.com/about/dashboards/index.html).

- Version 4.2, which is also called Jelly Bean, includes everything in Version 4.1 as well as the ability to place widgets on your Lock screen, a redesigned Camera app, and a Gesture Keyboard that predicts what you're trying to type as you glide your fingers over the keys. You can learn more about using Android 4.2 Jelly Bean on the Galaxy Tab 3 in Que's 2014 book *My Samsung Galaxy Tab 3* (ISBN 978-0-7897-5193-5).

- Version 4.3, which Google decided to also call Jelly Bean, includes a new camera user interface, support for 4K resolution video, support for five more languages, and a restricted access mode for new user profiles.

- Version 4.4, KitKat (named for one of the Google employees' favorite chocolate candy bars), includes an updated interface, the ability to print wirelessly, and a built-in screen recording feature. The text and screen-shots in this book are based on the latest version of KitKat for the Tab 4 (as of this writing), Version 4.4.2.

You find out more about the versions each Galaxy Tab model uses later in this chapter.

## What About Android L?

As this book was being written in June 2014, Google unveiled the preview ver-sion of the next major Android release, called Android L. (L might be renamed Lollipop by the time you read this.) Your Galaxy Tab 4 automatically checks for operating system updates so you receive those updates when they're available. You should also check the Android website (www.android.com) often to see about upcoming versions. By the time you read this, Android L (or whatever Google decides to call it) might be available for your Tab 4.

When Android L is available, articles about the new version of Android and related articles will be available on the Que Publishing website at www.quepublishing.com.

# The Newest Members: The Galaxy Tab 4 Family

Before getting into all the Galaxy Tab models Samsung offers, it's important to talk about the subject of this book and the three newest additions to the Galaxy Tab family: The Galaxy Tab 4 7.0, 8.0, and 10.1. All three models were released at the same time, run KitKat, and play the latest audio and video files. However, each model has differences you should know about.

# The Galaxy Tab 4 7.0

The Galaxy Tab 4 7.0 has a 7" screen, which explains how it got its name. The Tab 4 7.0 only comes with 8GB of total data storage, but it does contain a microSD slot that can bring your total storage capacity to 32GB. The Tab 4 7.0 also includes

- Wi-Fi connectivity

- 1200 × 800 pixel screen resolution

- 1.3 megapixel front camera

- 3.0 megapixel rear camera

- 9.74 ounces (0.61 pound) total weight

- A 4,000mAh battery

## What Does mAh Stand For?

A milliampere-hour, better known by the acronym mAh, denotes the battery power capacity. A higher number indicates more capacity and thus longer battery life. However, the amount of time you can run the Tab 4 on a single battery charge is determined by the apps you run. For example, playing video takes up more battery power than checking your email messages.

If you prefer to hold a tablet in one hand comfortably but you also want more screen space than a smartphone then consider the Tab 4 7.0. Unlike some of the e-readers out there (such as Amazon's Kindle), the Tab 4 7.0 comes with the full version of KitKat as well as the Kindle app.

## The Galaxy Tab 4 8.0

The Galaxy Tab 4 8.0 has an 8.0" screen and has Wi-Fi connectivity. The Tab 4 8.0 also includes

- 1200 × 800 pixel screen resolution

- 16GB of data storage with a microSD slot that can bring total storage to 64GB

- 1.3 megapixel front camera

- 3.0 megapixel rear camera

- 11.11 ounces (0.69 pound) total weight

- A 4,450mAh battery

As with the Galaxy Tab 4 7.0 model, you can hold the Galaxy Tab 4 8.0 in one hand comfortably but you get more screen space than the Tab 4 7.0. You also get a higher screen resolution and more battery capacity in exchange for a larger and slightly heavier unit.

# The Galaxy Tab 4 10.1

The Galaxy Tab 4 10.1 is so named because of its 10.1" screen, which is one of the largest screens you can find on a tablet. The Tab 4 10.1 also includes

- Wi-Fi connectivity

- 16GB of data storage with a microSD slot that can bring total storage to 64GB

- 1200 × 800 pixel screen resolution

- 1.3 megapixel front camera

- 3.0 megapixel rear camera

- 17.28 ounces (1.08 pound) total weight

- A 6,800mAh battery

You can hold the Galaxy Tab 4 10.1 in one hand, but it's usually safer to hold it with both hands. If you want to have the most screen space available so you can use it for tasks that you've previously done on your laptop (such as taking notes or watching movies) then the Tab 4 10.1 might be the right tablet for you.

If you want to learn more about each Tab 4 model and the differences between them, skip ahead to Chapter 2.

# Comparing the Tab 4 to Other Tabs

There are now a total of seven different Galaxy Tabs, including the Tab 4 family. What's more, the Galaxy Note is a smartphone/tablet hybrid that's included in this discussion.

## Galaxy Tab 7.0

This is the original Galaxy Tab that Samsung produced. The Tab 7.0 was originally positioned as a smaller alternative to the iPad, which came in only one size at the time the Tab 7.0 was first released. Samsung decided that their Tab models would run various versions of Google's Android mobile operating system so the Tab would be compatible with other Android phones just as the iPad is compatible with the iPhone. The Tab 7.0 runs Froyo.

Though the Tab 7.0 Plus was designed to eventually replace the Tab 7.0, the original Tab 7.0 is still offered by AT&T, Sprint, Verizon, and T-Mobile. You can also buy a Wi-Fi only model. Prices vary between the carriers and the Wi-Fi version.

## Galaxy Tab 7.0 Plus

The Tab 7.0 Plus is a sleeker version of the original Tab 7.0 that runs Honeycomb and has some more hardware and software features than the original Tab. Therefore, the Tab 7.0 Plus doesn't have the buttons below the screen like the original Tab 7.0 or the Galaxy Note. Instead, the Tab 7.0 Plus works like its larger siblings, the Tab 8.9 and Tab 10.1. The Tab 7.0 Plus is only offered by T-Mobile or as a Wi-Fi model. If you choose the Wi-Fi model, there are several different online vendors that sell it.

## Galaxy Tab 7.7

The Tab 7.7 is not only a bit larger than the 7.0 models but it also boasts some interesting features. The screen is based on AMOLED technology with a 1200 × 800 pixel resolution. (AMOLED stands for active-matrix organic light emitting diode.) The Tab 7.7 includes a more powerful battery—5,100mAh compared to 4,000mAh on the 7.0 Plus—that results in longer usage times on a single charge. And unlike other Tab models, you can make and receive voice calls with the Tab 7.7.

## Galaxy Tab 8.9

The Galaxy Tab 8.9 not only has a larger screen and a larger footprint, it also has a 1280 × 800 pixel screen. Like the 7.0 Plus, 7.7, and 10.1 models, the 8.9 runs Honeycomb. The Tab 8.9 is only offered by AT&T with 16GB of memory, although you can also buy a 16GB or 32GB Wi-Fi model from several online vendors.

## Galaxy Tab 10.1

If you're looking for the largest Tab model, or a larger Tab that's offered by more carriers, then you should consider the Tab 10.1. Like the Tab 8.9, the Tab 10.1 includes a screen that has 1280 × 800 pixel resolution and a screen size of 10.1". This screen is not only larger than the iPad 2 screen but also has greater resolution. The battery (7,000mAh) is the most powerful of any Tab and provides 9 hours of usage on a single charge.

Like the Tab 8.9, you can buy a Tab 10.1 with 16GB or 32GB of memory. The Tab 10.1 is offered by Verizon and T-Mobile but also comes in a Wi-Fi model as well. As of this writing, the Tab 10.1 was not being sold because of a patent dispute between Apple and Samsung. What's more, the Tab 10.1 was effectively replaced by the Tab 2 10.1, which Samsung is selling as of this writing.

## Galaxy Tab 2 7.0 and 10.1

The Galaxy Tab 2 was the successor to the original Tab family, just as the Tab 4 family is the successor to the Tab 3 family. However, just as with the Tab 7.0, the Tab 2 7.0 and 10.1 models are still available on the Samsung website (www.samsung.com) if you want to purchase them. The Tab 2 7.0 is so named because of its 7" screen and you can purchase the unit from Verizon or in a Wi-Fi version.

The Tab 2 10.1 is so named because of its 10.1" screen. You can purchase the Tab 2 10.1 in a Wi-Fi version and also from a variety of carriers including AT&T, Verizon, Sprint, and T-Mobile.

You can get more information about the Tab 2 series on the Samsung website and in the Que book *My Samsung Galaxy Tab 2* (ISBN: 978-0-7897-5038-9).

## Galaxy Tab 3 7.0, 8.0, and 10.1

The Galaxy Tab 3 was the successor to the Tab 2 family. However, just as with the Tab 2 7.0 and 10.1 models, you can purchase the Tab 3 7.0, 8.0, and 10.1 models on the Samsung website (www.samsung.com).

The Tab 3 7.0 is so named because of its 7" screen, and you can purchase the unit from Verizon, Sprint, T-Mobile, or AT&T; you can also purchase a Wi-Fi version. What's more, you can even purchase a Tab 3 7.0 in a Kids version that has an interface friendly to kids, parental controls, and an optional stylus.

The Tab 3 8.0 is so named because it has an 8.0" screen. You can only purchase this version of the Tab 3 in a Wi-Fi version.

The Tab 3 10.1 is so named because of its 10.1" screen. You can purchase the Tab 3 10.1 only in a Wi-Fi version.

You can get more information about the Tab 3 series on the Samsung website and in the Que book *My Samsung Galaxy Tab 3* (ISBN: 978-0-7897-5193-5).

## Galaxy Note and Note Pro

In late 2011 and early 2012, Samsung released the 5.3" version of its Galaxy Note "phablet," which is a device that's larger than a phone but smaller than a tablet and has features of each. For example, the Note has buttons below the screen as the Tab 7.0 does because the Note runs Gingerbread. The Note comes with a stylus called an S Pen so you can manipulate screen elements, handwrite notes, and draw on apps created for use with the Note.

Samsung subsequently created the Note 8.0 and 10.1 models to replace the original Galaxy Note, but both new models still come with the S Pen. These new Note models are also available in 4G LTE versions from a variety of carriers, and the Android operating system version varies from model to model. For example, the AT&T version of the Note 8.0 runs Android 4.4 (KitKat) but the Wi-Fi version runs Android 4.1 (Jelly Bean).

In early 2014, Samsung released the Galaxy Note Pro 12.2 model that's sold alongside the Note 8.0 and 10.1 models. The Note Pro 12.2 has a 12.2" screen (hence the name of the device) with 2560 × 1600 pixel resolution, up to 64GB of memory, and an 8 megapixel rear camera in addition to the standard S Pen. The Note Pro 12.2 also runs Android 4.4 (KitKat), and is available in a Wi-Fi-only version as well in 4G LTE versions from AT&T and Verizon.

## Galaxy Tab Pro and Tab S

In 2014, Samsung introduced two high-end Galaxy Tab families: The Tab Pro and the Tab S.

Samsung introduced the Tab Pro series early in 2014 and has the same specs as the Note Pro with the exception that the Tab Pro doesn't include the S Pen. The Tab Pro comes in a 12.2" screen version as the Note Pro does, and the Tab Pro also comes in 8.4" and 10.1" screen versions.

In mid-2014, Samsung announced its top-of-the-line Galaxy S series that comes in 8.4" and 10.5" screen versions. Both models sport a high-resolution 2560 × 1600 pixel resolution, 8 megapixel rear camera, memory up to 128GB, and Android 4.4 (KitKat). The Tab S is also lighter than its Tab Pro brethren, and as of this writing both versions only offer Wi-Fi connectivity.

Choosing from all these models can be confusing or overwhelming, but you can't say that Samsung doesn't have an offering for nearly every potential tablet user. You can learn more about the Galaxy Tab and Note families and get updated information by visiting Samsung's website (www.samsung.com).

**See the differences between
the Galaxy Tab 4 7.0,
Galaxy Tab 8.0, and the
Galaxy Tab 4 10.1**

**Understand how to
manipulate the screen**

**Learn how to interact
with Android**

In this chapter, you discover the different hardware and the common screens on the Galaxy Tab 4. Topics covered in this chapter include:

→ Features on the front, back, and sides of the unit

→ Galaxy Tab 4 icons for manipulating the screen

→ Three important screens you need to know

→ Gestures for manipulating the Galaxy Tab 4 screen

→ Configuring email settings

→ Screen elements for interacting with Android

# Meeting the Galaxy Tab 4

This book covers two models of the Galaxy Tab 4: the 8" Tab and the larger 10" version.

Galaxy Tab 4 8.0

The 8" unit, called the Galaxy Tab 4 8.0, runs version 4.4.2 of Google's Android operating system, also called KitKat.

Galaxy Tab 4 10.1

The 10" unit, called the Galaxy Tab 4 10.1, also runs KitKat. Both models connect to the Internet and/or a network using a Wi-Fi connection. (As of this writing no cell phone carrier has offered the Galaxy Tab 4 with its data network plans.)

Many tasks throughout the book include information for one model or the other, and if there are any differences between the models then there are separate tasks for each. The headers for each section (or subsection) indicate in parentheses the model name, such as (Galaxy Tab 4 10"). If you don't see an area in parentheses in the section (or subsection) name, the information applies to both models.

### What About the Galaxy Tab 4 7.0?

There aren't many differences between the Galaxy Tab 4 7.0 and the other models. The Tab 4 7.0 has many of the same physical features (except for the screen size, of course).

# Investigating the Galaxy Tab 4 Unit

Before you work with your Galaxy Tab 4, it's important to take it out of the box and examine it so you can learn where all the controls and features are on the unit. If you've used (or tried) another tablet computer in the past, you might already be familiar with some of the features. If this is your first time using a tablet computer or the Galaxy Tab 4, though, take time to read this chapter and enjoy learning about it.

## It's Not All Good

**Why Do the Galaxy Tab Units Look Different Between Photos?**

Each of the three Galaxy Tab 4 models comes in two colors: White and Black. The figures show the two different colors of all the models (mostly the Tab 8.0 and 10.1) in photos throughout this book. Some screens may also look different because of app updates or the screen orientation. For example, when you read a message in the Email app, you see the message on the entire screen in vertical screen orientation, but in horizontal screen orientation you see the list of messages in the mail folder on the left side of the screen and the message you're reading on the right side of the screen.

## Physical Features of the Galaxy Tab 4 8"

The front of the Galaxy Tab 4 8" includes the LCD touch screen for viewing information as well as a camera so you can take photos and/or record video of yourself.

You learn more about using the cameras to take photos in Chapter 11, "Capturing and Managing Photos," and to record video in Chapter 12, "Playing Music and Video."

— **Camera viewfinder**

— **Touch screen**

The back of the unit has only one feature: a second camera that includes a flash so you can take photos and record video using your Galaxy Tab 4. (Otherwise, the function of the back is to rest in your hand, of course.)

**Camera**

There are four buttons included on both the Galaxy Tab 4 8" and the Galaxy Tab 4 10". Those buttons are covered later in this chapter's "The Galaxy Tab 4 Buttons and Switches" section. Aside from those four, the Galaxy Tab 4 8" contains a number of features on the sides of the unit:

- A headphone and microphone jack on the top side of the unit so you can either listen to audio privately or record audio into a microphone.

**Headphone/
microphone jack**

## Headphone/Microphone Jack on the Galaxy Tab 4 7.0

The headphone/microphone jack on the Galaxy Tab 4 7.0 model is on the top-right side of the unit.

- A MicroSD memory card slot on the right side of the unit.

MicroSD memory
card slot

- The audio speakers on the bottom side of the unit.

- A dock/charge and sync cable connector that is also on the bottom side of the unit. You learn more about docking, charging, and syncing your Galaxy Tab 4 in Chapter 3, "Setting Up the Galaxy Tab 4."

Speakers

Dock/charge
and sync cable
connector

- The Power button on the right side of the unit.

- The volume control slider also on the right side of the unit.

- An infrared (IR) blaster also on the right side of the unit. The IR blaster controls a device that accepts infrared commands from a remote device such as your television and your cable box.

Power button

Volume control slider

IR blaster

## Physical Features of the Galaxy Tab 4 10"

The front of the Galaxy Tab 4 10" includes the LCD touchscreen for viewing information and a camera so you can take photos or record video of yourself.

You learn more about using the cameras to take photos in Chapter 11 and to record video in Chapter 12.

**Camera
viewfinder**

**Touchscreen**

The back of the unit has only one feature: a second camera that includes a flash so you can take photos and record video using your Galaxy Tab 4.

**Camera**

There are three buttons included on both the Galaxy Tab 4 8" and the Galaxy Tab 4 10". Those buttons are covered later in this chapter's "The Galaxy Tab 4 Buttons and Switches" section. Aside from those three, the Galaxy Tab 4 10" contains a number of features on the sides of the unit:

- A headphone and microphone jack on the left side of the unit so you can either listen to audio privately or record audio into a microphone.

Headphone/
microphone jack

- The audio speakers on the left and right sides of the unit. The speaker on the left side of the unit appears below the headphone and microphone jack.

The speaker on the right side of the unit

- A dock/charge and sync cable connector that is on the bottom side of the unit. You learn more about docking, charging, and syncing your Galaxy Tab 4 in Chapter 3.

**Dock/charge and sync
cable connector**

- The Power button on the top of the unit.

- The volume control slider on the top of the unit.

- A MicroSD memory card slot on the top of the unit.

- An IR blaster at the top of the unit. The IR blaster controls a device that accepts infrared commands from a remote device such as your television and your cable box.

**Volume
control slider**

**MicroSD
memory        Power
card slot      button**

**IR blaster**

# The Galaxy Tab 4 Buttons and Switches

Both models of the Galaxy Tab 4 feature two touch buttons on either side of a physical Home button. All three are below the touch screen. The Power button and volume slider are on one side of the unit.

## Setting Up Your Galaxy Tab 4

When you start your Galaxy Tab 4 for the first time, you go through a series of steps to get your Tab 4 up and running including setting up your wireless connection. The four icons appear on your Home screen after you set up the Tab 4. This book presumes that you have already set up your Tab 4 using the documentation that came in your Tab 4 box. If you need help with setting up a Wi-Fi network then you can find that information in Chapter 3.

## The Three Galaxy Tab 4 Buttons

There are three buttons below the touch screen that you use frequently to manage the device and applications on it. They are (from left to right) Recent, Home, and Back.

**Recent   Home   Back**

- **Recent**—The Recent touch button opens the Recent Apps window at the bottom of the screen and displays a list of apps that are open currently. Show an open app on the entire screen by tapping the app's thumbnail image in the list. Close the menu by tapping the Recent touch button again.

- **Home**—The fact that the Home button is a physical button signifies its place of importance with regard to how the Tab 4 functions. It's probably the button you will use most often because it's the one you press to get out of a specific application, such as the Galaxy Tab 4 web browser, and move back to the Home screen so you can open another application.

  If you want to hide an application and go back to the Home screen, pressing the Home button is the way to go. Pressing the Home button hides the application you currently have open.

## What About the Task Manager?

The first two models of the Galaxy Tab had a separate Task Manager icon on the screen. On the Tab 4, you access the Task Manager screen by tapping the Recent touch button and then tapping Task Manager at the bottom of the Recent Apps window.

**Task Manager screen**

- **Back**—The Back touch button moves you back to the previous screen. For example, if you're on the Home screen and touch the Apps icon at the bottom right of the screen to bring up the Apps screen, you might decide that you don't want to open an app. Close the Apps screen by tapping the Back touch button.

# The Power Button

The Power button performs a number of important functions on your Galaxy Tab 4:

- Turns on the unit when you press the button. The Power button is on the right side of the Galaxy Tab 4 8" unit and on the top of the Galaxy Tab 4 10" unit. The Galaxy Tab 4 boots up and is ready for you to use in about 20 seconds.

- Turns off the unit when you press the button for about two seconds.

- If you press and hold the button for a few seconds while the unit is on, the Galaxy Tab 4 automatically restarts.

- If you press the button and immediately release your finger, the screen turns off and the Galaxy Tab 4 enters sleep mode.

**Power button on the Galaxy Tab 4 8"**

**Power button on the Galaxy Tab 4 10"**

## What Happens if I Don't Turn Off the Galaxy Tab 4?

If the Galaxy Tab 4 is idle for a long period of time, the unit goes into sleep mode automatically. Sleep mode drains very little battery power, so if the Galaxy Tab 4 is frequently in sleep mode, you don't need to recharge your battery as often. Refer to Chapter 18, "Troubleshooting Your Galaxy Tab 4," for information about expected battery life and strategies for extending that lifespan.

# Volume Control Buttons

There are two volume control buttons on the left side of the device—one that turns up the volume and one that turns down the volume. What device the buttons control depends on what you have connected to the Galaxy Tab 4.

Volume control buttons on the Galaxy Tab 4 8"

Volume control buttons on the Galaxy Tab 4 10"

If you're listening to audio through the Galaxy Tab 4 speakers, the unit remembers the volume settings for the external speakers and sets the volume accordingly. If you decide to connect headphones to the unit, the Galaxy Tab 4 adjusts to the headphone volume the unit has in memory. When you remove the headphones, the unit readjusts the volume to the speaker volume.

You might want to check your volume settings for your headphones and external speakers so you don't get any nasty surprises. You learn more about setting the volume in Chapter 3.

# Galaxy Tab 4 Screens

There are three important screens that are mainstays of your Galaxy Tab 4 experience no matter which Galaxy Tab 4 model you use.

## The Lock Screen (Galaxy Tab 4 8")

The lock screen is the default state of the Galaxy Tab 4 when it first boots.

The lock screen shows the current date and time as well as the Wi-Fi connectivity status and battery charge status in the upper-right corner of the screen. It also includes the Smart Stay feature icon (it looks like an eye), which indicates that this feature is on. Smart Stay detects whether you're looking at the screen. When the Tab 4 detects that you are looking at it, the device won't go to sleep.

All you have to do to unlock your Tab 4 is to hold your finger anywhere on the screen and then swipe your finger in any direction. If your Tab 4 is password-protected then you need to type your password in the password box. You learn more about password-protecting your Galaxy Tab 4 in Chapter 3.

## The Lock Screen (Galaxy Tab 4 10")

The lock screen is the default state of the Galaxy Tab 4 when it first boots.

The lock screen shows the current date and time, the current status of your Bluetooth and Internet connections, and the amount of charge you have in your battery. It might also include the Smart Stay feature icon (it looks like an eye), which indicates that this feature is on.

All you have to do to unlock your Tab 4 is to hold your finger anywhere on the screen and then swipe your finger in any direction. If your Galaxy Tab 4 is password-protected, the password box appears on the screen. You must tap the password box, type your password, and then tap the OK button to open the Home screen or the application you were working on before the unit went to sleep. You learn more about password protecting your Galaxy Tab in Chapter 3.

## What Is Smart Stay?

Smart Stay detects whether you're looking at the screen. When the Tab 4 detects that you are looking at it, the device won't go to sleep. If you stop looking at the screen and look back at it after a short period of time, you might see an alert in the Status bar that says, "Smart Stay cannot detect your eyes" before the screen turns off.

# The Apps Screen (Galaxy Tab 4 8")

The applications screen is your command center where you can access all the applications available on the Galaxy Tab 4. Tap the Apps icon to view the applications screen.

**The Apps icon on the Home screen**

When you tap an application icon, the application launches. If you have more than one page of application icons on the applications screen, bars appear at the bottom of the screen. You can scroll between pages by tapping one of the buttons or dragging or flicking left and right. You learn more about dragging and flicking later in this chapter.

**Two bars on the bottom
of the screen**

# The Application Screen (Galaxy Tab 4 8")

After you press an application button on the applications screen, the application launches and takes up the entire screen. For example, if you open the My Files application, a list of files and folders on your Tab 4 appears on the screen.

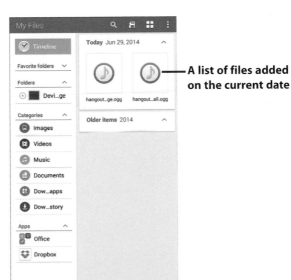

A list of files added
on the current date

# Manipulating the Screen

Like many tablets these days, the Galaxy Tab 4 doesn't come with a stylus (essentially a stick) for manipulating elements on the screen. Instead, you use your fingers and change the orientation of the Galaxy Tab 4 itself to make it do what you want. Although the examples in this section are for the Galaxy Tab 4 8", you manipulate elements on the Galaxy Tab 4 10" screen in the same way. If there are different instructions for manipulating the screen for the Tab 4 10" model, they are noted in a different subsection.

## Tapping an Element

Unlike a desktop or laptop computer, you don't have a mouse installed on your Galaxy Tab 4, so there is no cursor that you can see. However, when you quickly tap an element with your finger, the Galaxy Tab 4 performs an action. For example, when you tap an application icon, the Galaxy Tab 4 launches the application.

You can also double-tap, which is two quick taps in the same location, to perform a specific function. For example, you can double-tap an image to zoom in and double-tap again to zoom out.

## Pinching

Apple set the standard for multitouch screen gesture requirements with its iPad, and the Galaxy Tab 4 follows the same standard. A multitouch screen can recognize different gestures that use multiple finger touches. One such gesture is the pinching gesture.

You pinch when you touch the screen with both your thumb and forefinger and bring them together in a pinching motion. This is also called pinching in, and it has the same effect as zooming in. For example, you can get a closer view of a web page in the browser by pinching. You can also pinch outward, which has the same effect as zooming out, by touching the screen with your thumb and forefinger together and moving them apart.

# Dragging and Flicking

You can drag up and down the screen (or even left to right if an app allows it) by touching the top of the screen and moving your finger to drag content the length of the screen. If you want to move more content down the screen, remove your finger, touch the top of the screen, and drag your finger down the length of the screen again. You can drag a page of content up by touching the bottom of the screen and dragging your finger upward.

Dragging can become cumbersome, though, if you have to drag through a long document such as a web page or spreadsheet. The Galaxy Tab 4 makes it easy for you to drag through large chunks of content by flicking. That is, after you touch the top (or bottom) of the screen, move your finger quickly down (or up) and then lift your finger at the last moment so the content scrolls after you lift your finger. You can wait for the content to stop scrolling when you reach the beginning or end of the content, or you can touch anywhere on the screen to stop scrolling.

# Screen Rotation and Orientation

Your Galaxy Tab 4 has two screen orientation modes—vertical and horizontal—and it knows which way it's oriented. By default, the Galaxy Tab 4 screen orientation changes when you rotate the unit 90 degrees so the screen is horizontal, or you can rotate it another 90 degrees so the screen is vertical again. Nearly all default apps, such as the Browser, use both orientations. However, there might be times when you don't want the Galaxy Tab 4 to automatically change its screen orientation when you move the unit. For example, you might want to view a web page only in vertical orientation.

You can set the autorotation setting on or off as you see fit.

1. Open the Quick Settings and Notifications screen by holding your finger at the top edge of the screen and then swiping downward.

2. Tap the Screen rotation button. The button turns green to signify that orientation lock is on or gray when orientation lock is off.

3. Tap the Screen rotation button again to turn off orientation lock. The next time you rotate the unit 90 degrees, the screen rotates automatically.

**Hold your finger and swipe downward at the top edge of the screen**

**The green Screen rotation button indicates orientation lock is on**

# Interacting with Android

Android is a fun operating system to use; it includes a number of common elements, including sliders and switches, as well as the keyboard that you can use to enter and edit text in your Galaxy Tab 4.

## Sliders

A slider is a button that requires a bit of effort for you to activate. Android uses sliders to prevent you from doing something that can lead to unintended consequences. For example, if you open the Quick Settings and Notifications screen, you see the Brightness slider so you can adjust the brightness of the screen.

**The Brightness slider**

## Button Bar

You might see a button bar in different locations on the screen depending on the app you're using. For example, if you read a message in the Gmail app, you see some icon buttons in the bar at the top of the screen that enable you to perform certain tasks, such as putting the message in the trash.

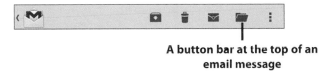

**A button bar at the top of an
email message**

## Tab Areas

Some apps have a Tab area that contains a set of buttons that control the app. The area location and buttons vary depending on the app; if the app doesn't have a Tab area, you won't see one. For example, if you tap the

Downloads app you see a Tab area in the center of the screen that enables you to view Internet downloads or any other type of download.

**A tab area that appears at the top of the Apps screen**

# Using the Keyboard

The Galaxy Tab 4 doesn't come with a physical keyboard like you find on many smartphones. Instead, you type in the text with something that looks similar to a computer keyboard. The keyboard appears at the bottom of the screen automatically when you want to enter text.

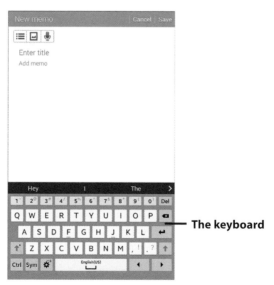

**The keyboard**

You can type a letter by tapping the letter's key. For example, if you tap the letter *a* on the keyboard, the lowercase letter *a* appears on the screen.

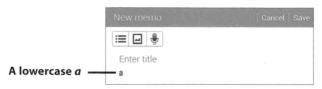

**A lowercase *a***

# >>>Go Further

## HOW DO I CAPITALIZE A LETTER?

There are two ways you can capitalize a letter:

- Tap one of the two Shift keys and then tap the letter you want to capitalize. Notice that after you tap the Shift key that all the keys on the keyboard become capitalized.

**The Shift keys**

- You can capitalize more than one letter by tapping the Shift key twice. The arrow on the Shift key turns blue; this denotes that the Shift key is locked. You can unlock the Shift key by tapping the key again. You know the Shift key is unlocked not only because the blue arrow on the Shift key is off, but also because all the letter keys on the keyboard are back to lowercase.

# Using Special Keyboards and Characters

It's not easy typing on a screen that's only 8" wide (or even 10"), especially with an onscreen keyboard, but Android has a trick to make it a bit easier to add information.

You can't access special characters from the standard Tab keyboard, but you can access those special character keys by tapping the Sym key to see a variety of symbols.

**The Sym key**

If the symbol you need isn't on the keyboard that displays then you can access an extended symbols keyboard by tapping the 1/2 key on the numbers and symbols keyboard. After you tap this key, the key label changes to 2/2, which signifies that you are on the second of two extended keyboards. When you're on the second extended keyboard, you can return to the numbers and symbols keyboard by tapping the 2/2 key.

The 1/2 key ———

## My Keyboard Doesn't Look the Same!

Your keyboard options might change somewhat depending on the app you're in. For example, if you're typing an email message in the Gmail app, you see the @ key to the left of the spacebar because that's a key that you use often when typing an email address.

If you hold down a key on the keyboard, the letter appears, and if there are any related characters, such as a letter with an umlaut (such as ü), you see a character window above the letter key. Hold and drag your finger to the character you want to insert and then release your finger.

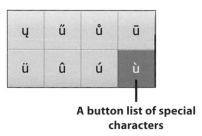

**A button list of special characters**

## What Does the Settings Key Do?

To the left of the spacebar you see a key that has a cogwheel on it. When you tap the key the Samsung Keyboard Settings screen appears so you can change a variety of keyboard settings, such as selecting a new input language and entering text by sliding your finger across the keyboard instead of tapping each key. When you're finished changing and/or reviewing settings, tap the Back touch button to return to the app that uses the keyboard.

# Copy and Paste Data

Android makes it pretty easy to copy and paste text from one app to another. In this example, you learn to copy a term from the Browser app and paste it into the Search app so you can search for the term not only on the Web but also throughout the Galaxy Tab 4.

1. Tap Internet on the Home screen.

2. This example starts on the Google website. Type a search term into the Google search box.

3. Hold down your finger on the search box for a couple of seconds and then release your finger. The search term is highlighted and bracket bars appear below and on each side of the term.

4. Tap Copy in the Edit Text pop-up menu that appears below the selected text.

5. Tap the X at the right side of the Search box to clear the contents of the box.

6.  Hold down your finger on the Google box until the Edit Text pop-up menu appears below the Search box and then release your finger.

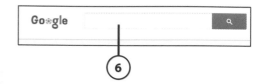

7.  Tap Paste in the Edit Text pop-up menu to insert the copied text.

**Learn how to get details about
the Galaxy Tab 4**

**Learn how to set up your network**

**Learn about synchronizing the Galaxy
Tab 4 with other computers**

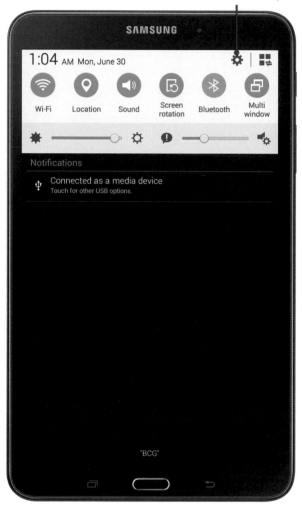

In this chapter, you discover more about your Galaxy Tab 4 and how to connect it with other computers and networks, including:

→ Getting details about the Galaxy Tab 4

→ Setting up your network

→ Syncing the Galaxy Tab 4

# Setting Up the Galaxy Tab 4

You can easily find information about the Galaxy Tab 4 so you can make changes as needed. When you finish making general changes to the Galaxy Tab 4, it's time to set up the network so your Galaxy Tab 4 can connect with the Internet. Finally, you find out how to synchronize your Galaxy Tab 4 with other devices, such as your desktop or laptop PC.

# Getting Details About the Galaxy Tab 4

If you want to get information about the features in your Galaxy Tab 4 from one place, you can use the About Device section within the Settings app.

1. Open the Quick Settings and Notifications screen by tapping and holding your finger on the top edge of the screen and swiping your finger down.

2. Tap the Settings icon.

3. Tap General in the menu bar at the top of the screen.

4. Scroll down the Settings list and then tap About Device.

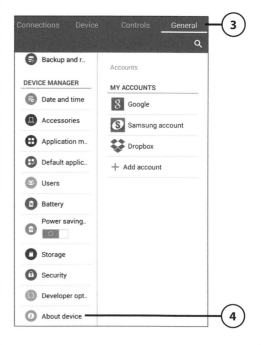

5. See the model number for your Galaxy Tab 4.

6. See the Android and Kernel versions.

7. Scroll down (if necessary) to see the build number for your Galaxy Tab 4.

8. Scroll back up (if necessary) and tap Status.

9. View the status of your Galaxy Tab 4, including battery status and battery charge level, IP address, your Wi-Fi MAC address, Bluetooth address, and the current up time (that is, how long your Galaxy Tab 4 has been on continuously).

About device

Software update

Status
Show status of battery, network, and other information.

Legal information

Device name
Eric Butow (SM-T330NU)

Model number
SM-T330NU

Android version
4.4.2

Kernel version
3.4.0-1337409
dpi@SWDD5909 #1
Mon Apr 21 12:33:36 KST 2014

Build number
KOT49H.T330NUUEU1AND4

SE for Android status
Enforcing
SEPF_SM-T330NU_4.4.2_0011
Mon Apr 21 12:33:09 2014

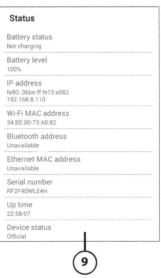

Status

Battery status
Not charging

Battery level
100%

IP address
fe80::36be:ff:fe73:a082
192.168.8.110

Wi-Fi MAC address
34:BE:00:73:A0:82

Bluetooth address
Unavailable

Ethernet MAC address
Unavailable

Serial number
RF2F40WLE4H

Up time
22:58:07

Device status
Official

10. Tap the Back touch button.

11. Tap Legal Information to view a menu that shows Galaxy Tab 4 legal information, privacy information, and license settings.

# Setting Up Your Network

Now that you're familiar with the details about your Galaxy Tab 4 and accessing the Settings app, you need to use the Settings app to do one very important setup task: connect your Galaxy Tab 4 to the Internet. Depending on the phone carrier you use, you can connect with the Internet through a Wi-Fi connection. You also can connect to other devices and networks using a Bluetooth connection or through a Virtual Private Network (VPN).

---

### I Don't Have a Wireless Network…What Do I Do?

If you don't have a Wi-Fi network but you do have a high-speed Internet connection through a telephone (DSL) or cable (broadband) provider, you have several options. First, call your provider and ask for a new network modem that enables wireless connections. Second, ask how much the modem costs—some providers might give you a free upgrade.

Another option is to keep your current box and add a wireless base station of your own, such as ones offered by Apple and Microsoft.

---

## Set Up Wi-Fi

1. On the Home screen, tap the Apps icon.

2. On the Apps screen, tap Settings.

3. Tap Wi-Fi if Wi-Fi is not selected already.

4. If Wi-Fi is turned off, you see a slider button within the Wi-Fi entry in the settings list. Turn Wi-Fi on by sliding the button to the right.

5. Tap Add Wi-Fi Network in the list of Wi-Fi devices on the right side of the screen. You might need to scroll down the list of Wi-Fi devices to view the Add Wi-Fi Network entry in the list.

6. Type the network SSID.

7. Tap the Security field to set the security level.

8. Select the security level; the default is None.

9. Tap Connect.

## It's Not All Good

### Be Secure First!

Your wireless network equipment should have security enabled. You know that security is enabled on the Wi-Fi network when you view the Wi-Fi Settings screen and see a padlock next to the Wi-Fi network in the list. When you select the Wi-Fi network for the first time, you should be asked to supply a password.

If you don't require a password, strongly consider adding one because unsecured networks send unencrypted (plain text) data—such as passwords and credit card numbers—through the air. Anyone else who has a Wi-Fi connection can tap in to your unsecured network and see what you're doing online. If you need more information, consult your network equipment documentation and/or manufacturer's website.

### >>>Go Further

## DISABLE WIRELESS CONNECTIONS ON A PLANE

When you're flying, the flight attendants always remind you to turn off your wireless devices during takeoffs and landings. You can quickly disable your wireless connections until you get to a safe flying altitude and the pilot gives you permission to turn on wireless devices again. Here's how:

1. Tap the Apps icon on the Home screen.
2. In the Apps screen, tap Settings.
3. Tap Airplane Mode.
4. In the slider button within the Airplane Mode entry in the settings list, turn Airplane Mode on by sliding the button to the right.

The slider button turns green to inform you that wireless connections are disabled. Slide the button to the left to turn off Airplane Mode and enable wireless connections.

# Set Up Bluetooth

1. Tap the Apps icon on the Home screen.

2. In the Apps screen, tap Settings.

3. Tap Bluetooth.

4. Turn on Bluetooth by sliding the Bluetooth slider button to the right.

5. Tap the check box to the right of the device name if you want your Galaxy Tab 4 to be discovered by other computers and/or devices that you can connect to using a Bluetooth connection. The Galaxy Tab 4 scans for available devices.

6. If the Galaxy Tab 4 doesn't find one, turn on the Bluetooth device to which you want to connect and then tap Scan in the Settings toolbar.

7. Tap a found device to connect with that device. You can rescan for devices by tapping Scan.

# Set Up a VPN

A VPN enables users in a public network (such as the Internet) to transfer private data by making it appear to the users that they're in a private network of their own. For example, you can set up a VPN between yourself and your boss at the office so you can securely send private company data.

1.  Tap the Apps icon on the Home screen.

2.  In the Apps screen, tap Settings.

3.  Tap More Networks.

4.  Tap VPN. If your Tab 4 is not protected by a password or similar encryption method, you see a dialog box that tells you to set a screen unlock pattern, PIN, or password. Open the Screen Unlock Settings screen and add a password, pattern, or PIN by tapping OK. Refer to Chapter 4, "Customizing Android to Your Liking," for more information about how to add a password, pattern, and PIN.

5.  Tap Add in the Settings menu bar.

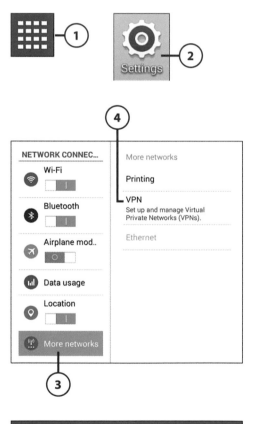

6. Enter the VPN information including the VPN name, type, and server address.

7. Tap Save.

8. Tap the VPN name in the list.

9. Type the VPN username in the Username field and the password in the Password field.

10. Tap Connect.

## How to Disconnect from Your VPN

You can begin the VPN disconnection process by opening the Quick Settings and Notifications screen that is covered earlier in this chapter. On the screen, a notification in the list informs you that you're connected to the VPN. Disconnect from the VPN by tapping the notification in the list and then tapping Disconnect.

**Add VPN**

Name

Name

Type

PPTP

Server address

Server address

☑ PPP encryption (MPPE)

☐ Show advanced options

Cancel          Save

⑥ ⑦

More networks > VPN

**BCG**
PPTP VPN

⑧

**Connect to BCG**

Username

ebutow

Password

•••••••

☐ Save account information

Cancel          Connect

⑨ ⑩

# Syncing the Galaxy Tab 4

Synchronizing your Galaxy Tab 4 with your desktop or laptop computer has a number of advantages.

The Galaxy Tab 4 stores a backup of its contents on your desktop or laptop every time you sync both devices, so if you lose your data on the Galaxy Tab 4—or lose the Galaxy Tab 4 itself—you can restore the data from the backed-up copies on your computer. What's more, if you have music, photos, or video on your computer, you can choose and copy a selection of those files onto your Galaxy Tab 4.

Because Windows is the leading operating system for desktop PCs by far, this chapter describes how to sync music with the Galaxy Tab 4 in Windows. Later chapters cover how to sync other types of data, such as contacts.

## Can I Sync Between the Galaxy Tab 4 and the Mac OS?

Syncing music from iTunes on the Mac OS to the Galaxy Tab 4 requires that you download additional software for your Mac. JRTStudio (www.jrtstudio.com) produces iSyncr, a utility that syncs what you have in iTunes with Android devices. As of this writing, the main app costs $3.99 in the Google Play Store, and that app enables you to sync your Tab 4 with iTunes on your Mac by connecting your Tab 4 to your Mac using the Tab 4 cable.

It's easy to sync music files in Windows Media Player, the default music and multimedia player in Windows, to any model of the Galaxy Tab 4.

1. Connect the Galaxy Tab 4 to your computer with the USB cable that came with your Galaxy Tab 4 if you haven't done so already. After a short while, your Windows PC informs you that it has installed the drivers to connect with your Galaxy Tab 4.

2. Launch Windows Media Player on your Windows PC.

3.  Tap the Sync tab; the Galaxy Tab 4 sync area appears on the right side of the window.

4.  Click the folder in the tree that contains the files you want to sync with the Galaxy Tab 4.

5.  Select the file(s) you want to move and then click and drag the files to the sync area.

6.  Click Start Sync.

7. After Windows Media Player syncs with your Galaxy Tab 4, open the app associated with the type of file(s) you synced on the Galaxy Tab 4. For example, if you synced image files, open the Gallery app; the Pictures tile shows one of the images you synced. You find out how to use the Gallery app in Chapter 11, "Capturing and Managing Photos."

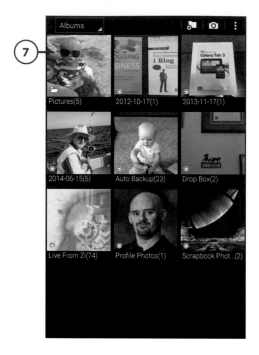

## >>>Go Further
## SYNC WITH iTUNES

It's also easy to sync your Galaxy Tab 4 with iTunes. You can mount the USB drive on the Galaxy Tab 4; then, on your computer, you can drag songs from iTunes and drop them to that drive. You can also sync to iTunes wirelessly by downloading the TuneSync app from the Android Market or from Fireleap Software (www.tunesync.com) for only $5.99. Fireleap also makes a free Lite version if you want to check it out first, but this version limits playlists to 20 songs.

**Learn how to set parental restrictions**

**Learn how to password-protect your Galaxy Tab 4**

**Learn about modifying screen wallpaper**

**Learn about setting alert sounds**

**Learn how to change keyboard settings**

Your Galaxy Tab 4 isn't just a static system that forces you to work with it. It's malleable so you can change many attributes of the system to work the way you prefer. The topics in this chapter include the following:

→ Password-protecting the Galaxy Tab 4
→ Setting parental restrictions
→ Changing the date and time
→ Modifying your wallpaper
→ Setting alert sounds
→ Changing keyboard settings

# Customizing Android to Your Liking

## Password-Protecting the Galaxy Tab 4

One of the first things you should do when you set up your Galaxy Tab 4 is password-protect it so that unauthorized persons can't use it or gain access to the data stored on it.

1. Tap the Apps icon on the Home screen.

2. In the Apps screen, tap Settings.

3. Tap Device in the menu bar at the top of the screen.

4. Tap Security.

5. Tap Encrypt Device.

6. The Encrypt Device page on the screen reminds you that the encryption process takes an hour or more, that the device must be plugged in during the entire encryption process, and that interrupting the process risks the loss of some or all of the data stored on the Tab 4. When you're finished reading these reminders, tap Set Screen Lock Type.

7. Tap Password.

8. Type your password in the Select Password screen. The password must be at least four characters. A couple of seconds after you tap the letter, the letter turns into a dot to hide what you just entered. Tap Continue.

9. Retype the password in the Confirm Password screen and then tap OK.

   The next time you log in to your Galaxy Tab 4, you are prompted to type in your password in the password box. If the keyboard doesn't appear on the screen right away, tap the password box to open the keyboard.

**Type your password in the Enter Password box**

## >>>*Go Further*

### WHAT IF I CAN'T REMEMBER MY PASSWORD?

If you can't remember your password, your only recourse is to reset your Galaxy Tab 4 so that you wipe all the data from it and start from scratch. Unfortunately, this means that all your other data is wiped off the unit as well. Use the following steps to reset your Tab.

1. Turn your Galaxy Tab 4 off if it isn't already. You might need to remove the battery to turn off the unit.

2. Press and hold the Power and Volume Up buttons.

3. When you see the Samsung Galaxy Tab 4 logo, release the Power button but continue to hold the Volume Up button.

4. When the recovery screen appears, tap the Volume Down button until Wipe Data/Factory Reset is highlighted.

5. Press the Power button.

6. In the next screen, press the Volume Down button until Yes—Delete All User Data is highlighted.

7. Press the Power button.

8. After the Galaxy Tab 4 wipes the system data, press the Power button to reboot the system.

# Changing Your Password

It's a good idea to change your password regularly so you have the peace of mind of knowing that you're keeping one step ahead of potential thieves.

1. Tap the Apps icon on the Home screen.

2. In the Apps screen, tap Settings.

3. Tap Device in the menu bar at the top of the screen.

4. Tap Lock Screen.

5. Tap Screen Lock.

6. Type your password in the Confirm Password screen and then tap Continue.

7. Tap Password.

8. Type your password in the Select Password screen. The password must be at least four characters. A couple of seconds after you tap the letter, the letter turns into a dot to hide what you just entered. Tap Continue.

**9.** Retype the password in the
Confirm Password screen and
then tap OK. The next time you
log in to your Galaxy Tab 4 you
are prompted to type in your new
password.

Select password

Confirm password

·····

Cancel                    OK

**⑨**

>>>*Go Further*

## ENTER A PATTERN OR NUMERIC PIN

The Galaxy Tab 4 gives you one of three options for password-protecting
your unit: a text password, a numeric PIN (such as the one you use for an
ATM card), or a pattern that you can draw on the screen. In the Screen Unlock
Settings screen, tap Pattern or PIN to create a new pattern or numeric PIN,
respectively. Then follow the step-by-step instructions to set the PIN.

# Setting Parental Restrictions

Android 4 doesn't include parental restriction settings for specific applications aside from the pattern, PIN, or text password used for full access to the
Galaxy Tab 4.

However, you can find parental control apps in the Google Play Store. Search
for "parental control" or "parental controls," read the user reviews for each app,
and then decide whether you want to download an app to see if it works
for you.

## Change Your Content Filter Settings in the Google Play Store

You can determine what types of apps are shown to anyone who uses your
Galaxy Tab 4 by setting the content filtering settings within the Google Play
Store. You can show all apps or you can show apps by maturity level. You find
out more about how to do this in Chapter 16, "Finding and Managing Apps."

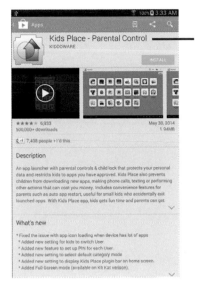

**An example of a parental control app in the Google Play Store**

# Changing the Date and Time

You can set the date and time for your Galaxy Tab 4, change the time zone, change the date format, and display whether you want to display the time as standard 12-hour or 24-hour (military) time.

1. Tap the Apps icon on the Home screen.

2. In the Apps screen, tap Settings.

3. Tap General in the menu bar at the top of the screen.

4. Tap Date and Time.

5. Tap Set Date.

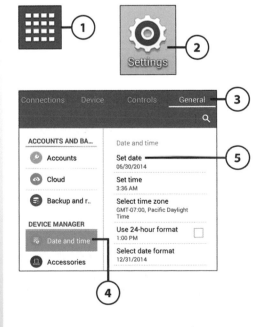

6. Tap the month, date, or year to change the date information. You can also tap the up and down arrow buttons above and below the month, date, or year to move the information up or down one month, one date, or one year, respectively.

7. Tap Set.

8. Tap Set Time.

9. Tap the hour and/or minute to change the time information. You can also tap the up or down arrow buttons above and below the hour or minute to move the hour or minute by one hour or one minute, respectively.

10. Tap the AM or PM box to change the time of day between AM and PM.

11. Tap Set.

12. Tap Use 24-Hour Format to change the format to 24-hour time. Note that the time on the Notification bar reflects the change. You can return to 12-hour time by tapping Use 24-Hour Format again.

13. Tap Select Date Format.

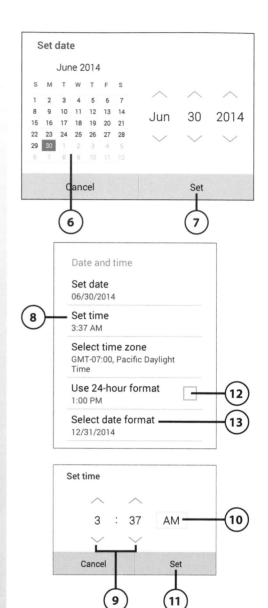

14. Tap one of the three format options to change the date format. If you don't want to change the date format, tap Cancel.

# Modifying Your Wallpaper

The standard wallpaper appears behind both the lock screen and the Home screen. Android makes it easy for you to change the wallpaper to whatever you want.

1. In the Home screen, hold your finger down on a blank area of the screen for a couple of seconds.

2. Tap Set Wallpaper in the Home Screen menu.

3. Tap Home Screen, Lock Screen, or Home and Lock Screens depending on where you want to display your wallpaper. This example uses the Home and Lock Screens option.

4. Select where you want to get the wallpaper by tapping Gallery, Live Wallpapers, or Wallpapers. This example uses the Wallpapers option.

5. Scroll through the thumbnail images of wallpapers. The current thumbnail image appears above the Set Wallpaper button and a larger version of the image appears above the thumbnail images.

6. When you find wallpaper you want, tap Set Wallpaper. The new wallpaper appears on your Home and lock screens.

## The Difference Between Wallpaper and Live Wallpaper

So what makes wallpaper "live" on the Galaxy Tab 4? The difference is animation. For example, if you select the Bubbles live wallpaper then you see the bubbles move around and fade in and out in the background screen. Regular wallpaper doesn't have any animated features.

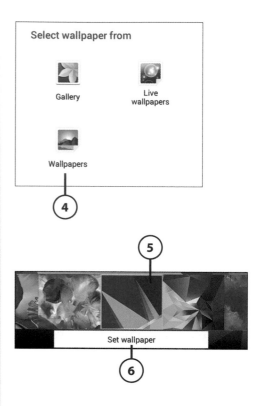

# Setting Alert Sounds

If you want the Galaxy Tab 4 to make noise when you perform different actions, such as when you tap something on the screen, you can change the alert sounds. If you prefer, you can turn them off entirely.

1. Tap the Apps icon on the Home screen.

2. In the Apps screen, tap Settings.

3. Tap Device in the menu bar at the top of the screen. The Sound option is selected by default in the settings list.

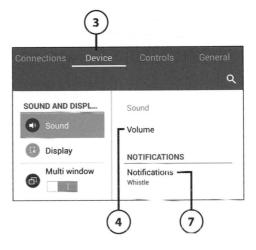

## The One Guaranteed Solution for Silence

The Galaxy Tab 4 makes certain noises by default. For example, the unit plays tones when you use the dial pad on the phone.

If you really want to ensure that the unit doesn't make any noise, the one foolproof solution is to turn off the Galaxy Tab 4 unit.

4. Tap Volume.

5. Change the volume for music, video, games, and other media, notifications, and system sounds by dragging the appropriate slider bar to the left (lower volume) or right (higher volume).

6. Tap OK.

7. Tap Notifications.

8. Set the notification ringtone from the menu. This ringtone plays whenever you receive a notification. If you don't want a ringtone, scroll to the top of the list and tap Silent.

9. Tap OK.

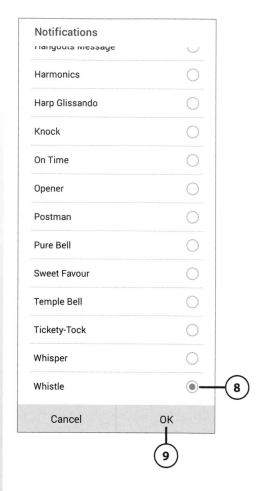

10. Tap Touch Sounds to turn off the feature that plays a sound when you make a screen selection. Turn on this feature again by tapping Touch Sounds.

11. Tap Screen Lock Sound to stop playing sounds when you lock and unlock the screen. Turn on this feature again by tapping Screen Lock Sound.

12. Swipe down the Sound settings list and then tap Adapt Sound to open the Adapt Sound screen and fine-tune the sound output of your earphones. You need to connect your earphones to the headphones/microphone jack on your Galaxy Tab 4 to use Adapt Sound.

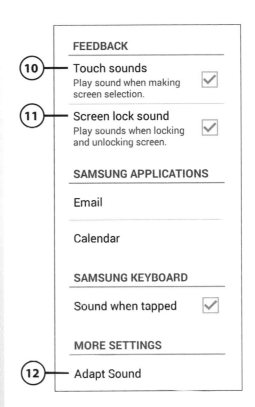

# Changing Keyboard and Voice Settings

The Galaxy Tab 4 7" and 8" come with the Samsung keyboard only. The Galaxy Tab 4 10" gives you two input options: the Samsung keyboard and the Swype keyboard.

The examples in this book use keyboard settings for the Samsung keyboard, which is the default keyboard the Galaxy Tab 4 uses when you type text, as well as built-in keyboard settings that apply to all keyboards.

1. Tap the Apps icon on the Home screen.

2. In the Apps screen, tap Settings.

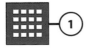

3. Tap Controls in the menu bar at the top of the screen. The Language and Input option is selected by default in the settings list.

4. Because the default is the Samsung keyboard, open the Samsung Keyboard Settings screen by tapping the Settings icon to the right of Samsung Keyboard.

5. Tap Select Input Languages if you want to change the default keyboard input language.

6. Slide the Predictive Text slider to off (the slider turns from a green bar with an I to a gray bar with a O) if you don't want the Galaxy Tab 4 to guess what you're typing and provide suggestions for words so you don't have to keep typing all the time. This is similar to the auto-complete feature in word processors.

7. Slide the Auto-Replacement slider to off (the slider turns from a green bar with an I to a gray bar with a O) so the Tab 4 will guess the word you're typing when you tap the space bar after typing a word.

8. Tap Continuous Input to enter text by sliding the finger across the keyboard to type words. After you release your finger, the word that the Galaxy Tab 4 thinks you're trying to type appears on the screen.

9. By default, you can move a cursor on the screen by sliding your finger across the keyboard. You can turn this feature off and move the cursor only with the keyboard by tapping Cursor Control. Turn the feature back on by tapping Cursor Control.

10. Return to the Samsung Keyboard Settings screen by tapping the left arrow at the left side of the menu bar at the top of the screen.

11. Tap Auto Capitalization to turn off auto-capitalization for words. By default, the Galaxy Tab 4 auto-capitalizes the first word in a sentence. If the Galaxy Tab 4 recognizes a punctuation mark and a space, the next letter is capitalized automatically unless you tap the Shift key to turn it off. (There are exceptions to this rule, such as when you type in the To box when you compose a new email message.) You can turn the feature back on by tapping Auto Capitalization.

**⑩**

**< Samsung keyboard settings**

**INPUT LANGUAGES**

English(US)

＋ Select input languages

**SMART TYPING**

Predictive text

Auto replacement
Complete or replace the word you are typing with the most probable word when you tap the space bar.

Auto capitalization ☑
Automatically capitalize the first letter of each sentence.

Auto spacing ☑
Automatically insert spaces between words.

Auto punctuate ☐
Automatically insert a full stop by tapping the space bar twice.

**KEYBOARD SWIPE**

None ◉

**⑧** Continuous input ○
Enter text by sliding finger across keyboard. This feature is optimized for Qwerty keyboard.

**⑨** Cursor control ○
Slide your finger across the keyboard to move the text cursor

**KEY-TAP FEEDBACK**

**< Samsung keyboard settings**

Complete or replace the word you are typing with the most probable word when you tap the space bar.

**⑪** Auto capitalization ☑
Automatically capitalize the first letter of each sentence.

Auto spacing ☑
Automatically insert spaces between words.

Auto punctuate ☐
Automatically insert a full stop by tapping the space bar twice.

**KEYBOARD SWIPE**

None ◉

Continuous input ○
Enter text by sliding finger across keyboard. This feature is optimized for Qwerty keyboard.

Cursor control ○
Slide your finger across the keyboard to move the text cursor.

**KEY-TAP FEEDBACK**

Sound ☑

Character preview ☐
Show a big character bubble when a key on a Qwerty keyboard is tapped.

**MORE SETTINGS**

Help

Reset settings

**12.** Tap Auto Spacing to turn off the automatic insertion of a space between words. By default, the Galaxy Tab 4 monitors your words as you type and automatically inserts a space between words. Turn the feature back on by tapping Auto Spacing.

**13.** Tap Auto Punctuate to automatically insert a period after a word by double-tapping the space bar.

**14.** Swipe down the Keyboard Settings list to view the remaining settings you can change.

**15.** In the Key-Tap Feedback section, tap Sound to have the Galaxy Tab 4 make no sound each time you press a key. Turn on the key-tap sound feature by tapping Sound.

**16.** Tap Character Preview to display the character you're typing on the keyboard in a box above the key for about a second after you tap the key.

**17.** Tap Help to view quick and easy tutorials about how to use the keyboard in the Help screen.

**18.** If you change your mind after you make settings and decide you want the default settings instead, tap Reset Settings.

**19.** Return to the Samsung Keyboard Settings screen by tapping the arrow at the left side of the menu bar at the top of the screen.

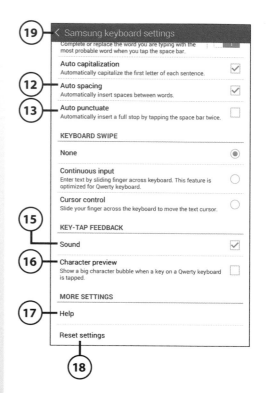

# Modifying More Settings

There are too many settings in Android to cover in this book, but here are some of the more important settings that you should know about.

1. Tap the Apps icon on the Home screen.

2. In the Apps screen, tap Settings.

3. Tap Device in the menu bar at the top of the screen.

4. Tap Display.

5. Set the brightness level by tapping Brightness and then move the slider in the Brightness window to change the brightness level.

6. When you finish changing the brightness level, tap OK.

7. Tap Screen Timeout.

8.  Select the period of inactivity after which the screen times out and goes dark. The default is one minute. If you don't want to change the time interval, tap Cancel.

## Powering Up Your Screen

After the screen goes dark, you can easily start it again by tapping the screen or pressing the Power button. If your Galaxy Tab 4 is password-protected (or PIN or pattern-protected), you must type your password (or PIN or pattern) to start using the Galaxy Tab 4 again.

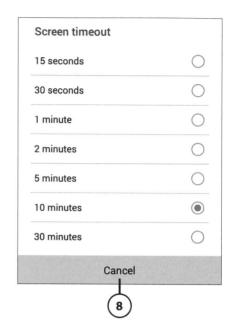

9.  Tap Font in the settings list.

10. Set the font style by tapping Font Style. When you select the font style you can choose from the built-in fonts or you can search for, purchase, and download fonts from the Google Play Store.

11. If you find that the text isn't legible enough, you can enhance clarity of the text by tapping Font Size.

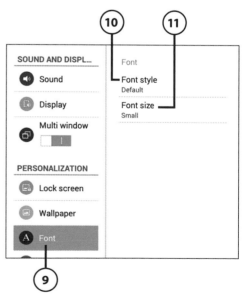

**12.** Tap the font size you want from the Font Size window list.

**13.** After you tap the font size, the new font size appears within the Settings page after a second or two. If you want to change the font size again, tap Font Size in the menu and then tap another font size in the Font Size window list.

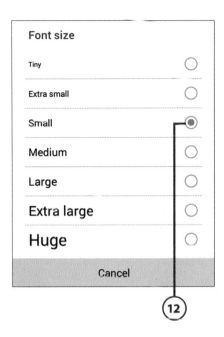

Font size

Tiny ○

Extra small ○

Small ◉

Medium ○

Large ○

Extra large ○

Huge ○

Cancel

⑫

**Learn how to browse widgets and
add a widget to your Home screen**

Widgets are a truly valuable aspect of the Android platform. A widget is a small, portable piece of code that you can interact with like a miniature application. Your Galaxy Tab 4 has quite a few widgets for you to choose from that can make your Tab experience even more convenient. This chapter covers the following:

**5**

→ Accessing the Widgets screen

→ Taking a tour of available widgets

→ Adding a widget to a Home screen

→ Creating a new Home screen

→ Removing a widget

# Adding Widgets to Your Home Screens

## Accessing the Widgets Screen

You can find widgets on the Widgets screen, where 40 preinstalled widgets for different tasks are listed. Tapping a widget can provide you a variety of information such as stock market news or the weather. (By default, you have a weather widget on your Home screen.) A widget can also act as a world clock or initiate functionality from a parent app, such as Maps, when you tap it. Though you can apply widgets to a Home screen, some widgets must be configured.

1. Tap the Apps icon on the Home screen.

2. Tap Widgets.

3. Scroll left and right through the pages of widgets. The number of pages depends on the Galaxy Tab 4 model you have and your screen orientation.

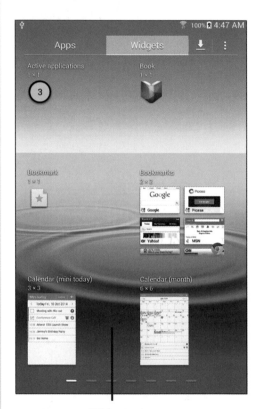

**Widgets**

# Taking a Tour of Available Widgets

Each widget on the page contains the name of the widget, the size of the widget (width by height in number of grid spaces), and a thumbnail-sized graphic that shows you how the widget will appear on the Home screen. Note that if you want to see how big a 1 × 1 icon is, the Book widget icon that belongs with Step 2 in the next task is sized at 1 grid space wide by 1 grid space high.

All the widgets listed in this section are available on all Galaxy Tab 4 models. On the Galaxy Tab 4 8", which is used for the screenshots in this section (and throughout most of this book), six widgets appear on each of the eight pages within the Widgets screen.

## Examine the Page 1 Widgets

1. Active Applications: Opens the Task Manager screen so you can see all active applications, view downloaded apps, and manage memory and storage.

2. Book: Opens the Google Play Books app and shows you a list of all books you've downloaded.

3. Bookmark: Opens the Internet app so you can select a bookmarked website on the Choose a Bookmark screen. After you select the bookmark in the appropriate folder, the bookmarked website appears as an icon on the Home screen. View the website in the Internet app by tapping on the bookmark icon.

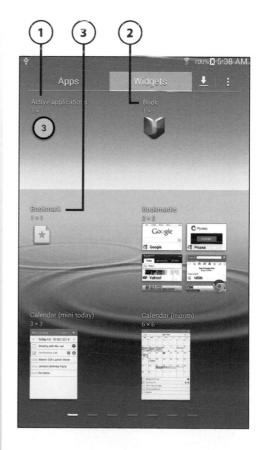

4. **Bookmarks:** Places a larger widget on the screen so you can select a bookmark from directly within the widget. Swipe up and down within the widget to view folders and then tap a folder name; after you find the bookmark you want within the folder you tap it. The website appears in the Internet or Chrome app. When you return to the Home screen, you can navigate to and open a bookmark from within the widget.

5. **Calendar (mini today):** Displays a small calendar for the current day that shows a brief list of your appointments that day.

6. **Calendar (month):** Displays a large calendar for the current month that shows a brief list of your appointments every day during the month as well as a list of your appointments for the current day.

## Choosing Your Browser

After you open a bookmark from the Bookmark or Bookmarks widget, you may see the Complete Action Using window so you can choose between opening the website in the Internet app or in the Google Chrome app. Tap the icon that signifies the app you want to use (Internet or Chrome) and then tap the Always button to open websites using that app in the future or the Just Once button to open the website using your selected app that one time. If you tap the Just Once button then the next time you open the bookmark you will have to choose the browser app in the Complete Action Using window again.

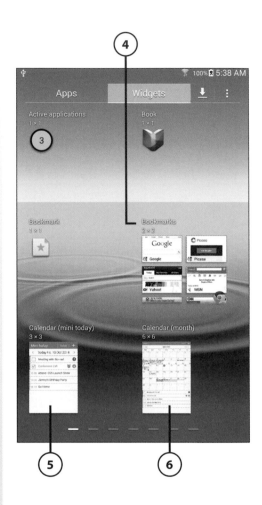

# Examine the Page 2 Widgets

1. **Calendar (month):** Displays a small calendar for the current month that shows a brief list of your appointments every day during the month.

2. **Contact:** Opens the Contacts window app so you can select the contact to display in the widget. After you select the contact, the picture of the contact appears on the Home screen. Tap the contact picture to open the contact window.

3. **Directions:** Opens the Directions app so you can enter your destination address from your current location to get turn-by-turn directions.

4. **Drive:** Displays a small Drive bar so you can open files and folders on your Google Drive online file storage service account.

5. **Drive Scan:** Opens the Upload Scans To window so you can have the Tab 4 upload screenshots to a selected folder on Google Drive.

6. **Drive Shortcut:** Opens the Create Shortcut To window so you can have the shortcut widget on the Home screen take you directly to a file or folder stored on Google Drive.

# Examine the Page 3 Widgets

1. **Dropbox Folder:** Places a Dropbox folder link on your Home screen. You have to open the Dropbox app and log in before you can add this widget. After you log in, you can select the folder to which you want to link in the Create Shortcut window.

2. **Dual Clock (Digital):** Shows times in two different cities as digital clocks. The current date appears below the time for each city.

3. **Email:** Shows the most recent five email messages that are aggregated from all your inboxes. After you add the app to a Home screen, set up the Samsung Email widget app by tapping the widget.

4. **Gmail:** Shows the most recent three messages you received in your Gmail inbox. When you add the app to a Home screen, the Choose Folder window appears so you can select the folder that contains messages you want to read. After you tap the folder name, the most recent messages within that folder appear on the Home screen.

5.  Gmail Label: Adds a Gmail Label, which acts as a shortcut that opens a Gmail folder. When you add the app to your Home screen, the Choose Folder window appears and asks you to select a Gmail folder. The Name Label Shortcut window appears so you can accept the folder name as the shortcut name or type a new name. Tap Done in the window to view the Gmail Label widget on the Home screen.

6.  Google Now: Displays basic Google Now app information such as a brief weather forecast and information about your next appointment. Open the Google Now app and get more information by tapping on the widget on the Home screen.

# Examine the Page 4 Widgets

1. **Google Play Books:** Opens the most recent book you read in the Google Play Books app. The cover of the most recent book you read appears in the widget icon.

2. **Google Play Music:** Plays the next song in your Google Play Music playlist when you tap the Play button in the Google Play Music widget. Open the Play Music app by tapping the thumbnail-sized image on the left side of the widget.

3. **Google Play Music:** Opens the Google Play Music app so you can select a song to play on your Tab 4.

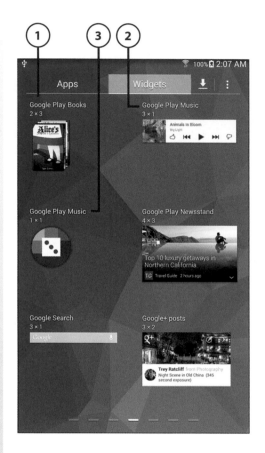

4.  Google Play Newsstand: Displays a slideshow of the latest news stories available in the Google Play Newsstand app. Move to the next slide in the slideshow by tapping the down arrow button in the lower-right corner of the widget. Open the Play Newsstand app by tapping the thumbnail-sized image within the widget.

5.  Google Search: Adds a transparent Google Search box to the home page; this widget box appears on the main Home screen by default.

6.  Google+ Posts: Displays your latest Google+ posts within the widget. Open the Google+ app and view the most recent post by tapping the widget in the Home screen.

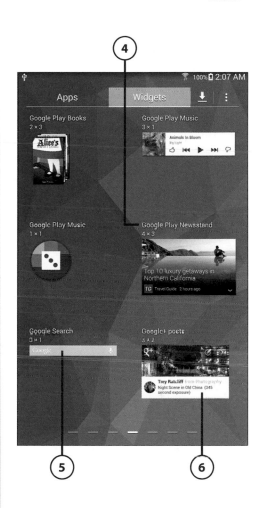

# Examine the Page 5 Widgets

1. Google+ User Locations: Tells you where your Google+ friends are currently when you're signed into Google+.

2. Hancom Office: Shows a list of available files you can open within the Hancom Office app. Tap the file to open the Hancom Office app and view the file contents. You can read more about using Hancom Office in Chapter 15, "Using Apps for Learning, Creating, and Sharing."

3. Hangouts: If you're in a Google Hangout, this widget shows you the conversation within the widget without requiring you to be within the Hangouts app itself. Therefore, you can keep track of the conversation while performing other tasks on your Tab 4.

4. Magazine Here & Now: Installs the My Magazine app on your Tab 4 and then displays a slideshow of the app's latest magazine articles. You can move between slides by tapping the left and right arrow buttons on either side of the widget. Read an article by tapping the thumbnail image within the widget. You can read more about the My Magazine app in Chapter 13, "Reading and Managing Books and Magazines."

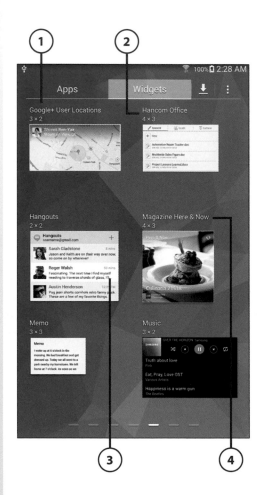

5.  **Memo:** Enables you to write a new memo that will be easily accessible on your Home screen. When you add the memo to the Home screen, the Memo window displays so you can type your memo. After you save the memo, the memo icon appears on the Home screen so you can open it quickly.

6.  **Music:** Displays the Samsung Music Player app that enables you to play songs stored on your Galaxy Tab 4 within the widget itself. For example, you can tap the Play button within the widget to play the song at the top of the list.

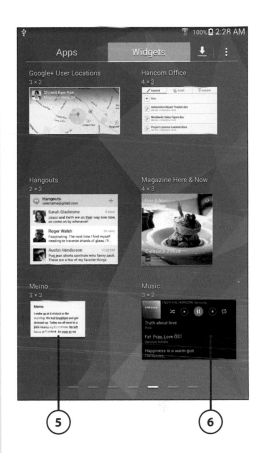

# Examine the Page 6 Widgets

1. **Music Playlist:** Opens the Play Music app window so you can select a playlist that contains the songs you like. After you tap the playlist you want, the playlist icon and name appear on the Home screen. Tap the playlist icon to start playing songs within that playlist.

2. **Picture Frame:** Displays one or more of your selected pictures stored on your Tab 4 within an area on the Home screen.

3. **Play—My Library:** Shows contents of one or all of the Google Play apps. For example, the My Books library shows covers of the most recent books you read. Read the book in the Play Books app by tapping the book cover.

4. **Play Recommendations:** Displays Google Play Store recommendations in one category (for example, Apps) or in all categories. View the recommended app or multimedia file by tapping the widget.

5. **Play Store:** Displays a slideshow of new and interesting apps in the Google Play Store. Open the Play Store app by tapping the widget.

6. **S Bookmarks:** Displays your website bookmark folders. Open the list of bookmarks by tapping the bookmark folder and then tap the bookmark tile to open the website in the Browser app.

# Examine the Page 7 Widgets

1. **Samsung Apps:** Displays suggestions for new apps in the Samsung Apps Store that you can install on your Tab 4. You can read more about installing new apps in Chapter 16, "Finding and Managing Apps."

2. **Video:** Places a link to a selected video on the Home screen; the title appears in the widget. Play the video in the Video app by tapping the widget.

3. **Weather and Briefing:** Displays the current weather for your location and reminders (such as incoming e-mail messages) on the Home screen. This widget appears on the main Home screen by default.

4. **YouTube:** Displays a slideshow of the most recent YouTube videos within various categories such as Most Popular. View the featured video in the slideshow within the YouTube app by tapping the image of the video in the widget.

# Adding a Widget to a Home Screen

It's easy to add a widget from the Widgets screen to an existing Home screen or a new one that you create. When you add a Widget to a Home screen you can specify where that widget—either an icon or the widget area—will reside on the Home screen. If you decide that you want to move the widget to a different location on a same or a different Home screen, you can drag the widget to that new location on the current Home screen, another existing Home screen, or a new Home screen that you create.

Some widgets also enable you to change the size of the widget before you place it on your desired Home screen. If the widget you're trying to add to an existing Home screen won't fit on that Home screen then KitKat adds a new Home screen automatically and places the widget on that new Home screen.

## Place a Widget on a Home Screen

1. Tap the Apps icon on the Home screen.

2. Tap Widgets at the top of the Apps screen.

3. Navigate to the page that contains the Dual Clock (Digital) widget used for this example.

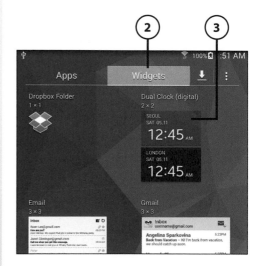

**4.** Press and hold your finger on the Dual Clock (Digital) widget. The Edit Home screen appears; the Home screen appears in a smaller area of the screen and the widget you're moving appears as an outline on the screen.

**5.** Move the outline over the Home screen to which you want to add the widget. The Home screens appear as small thumbnail buttons at the bottom of the screen and each button contains different elements as they appear on the Home screen. The Home screen buttons appear in a row of three and the main Home screen (the one that opens when you start your Galaxy Tab 4) appears second from left in the row.

**6.** Release your finger. The widget appears at the top left of the screen by default. If any other widgets appear on the screen then the Dual Clock (Digital) widget appears to the right of the widget or on the left side of the screen underneath a row of widgets.

**7.** The Dual Clock (Digital) widget lets you configure the information that it displays. Add a new city by tapping the Tap to Add City box.

8. Swipe down the list of cities and tap one. For example, perhaps a friend has traveled to Rome for the summer and you don't want to call her in the middle of the night. Swipe down the list of cities and then tap Rome.

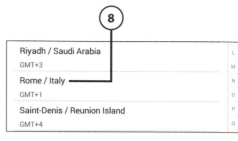

9. Rome is added to the clock, and now you know the current time for the city where your friend is staying.

10. Tap either city to change to a different city. You can search for a city by typing the city name in the Search Cities box.

# Move a Widget on a Home Screen

You can move a widget to a different location on the same Home screen by tapping and holding the widget within the Home screen. This example shows how to reposition the Dual Clock (Digital) widget.

1. Tap and hold the widget you want to move. The widget outline appears on a smaller version of the Home screen so you can see where you can move the widget.

2. Drag the widget to the new location on the Home screen. The Home screen is ordered in a grid format and + signs within the Home screen denote grid corners. As you move the widget to the new location, a lighter copy of the outline appears below and to the right of your widget outline. This lighter outline copy denotes where your widget will reside on the screen. If there's a widget that already resides in the location you want, the widgets reposition themselves on the screen to accommodate your desired location for the widget.

3. Release your finger. The widget appears in your desired location.

## Move the Widget to a Different Home Screen

If you want to move a widget to a different Home screen, drag the widget outline to one of the Home screen thumbnail buttons as described earlier in this chapter. You can also add the widget to a brand-new Home screen by dragging the widget outline over the Home screen thumbnail button at the right side of the button row (it has a + in the button). After you add the widget to the Home screen you want, you can open that Home screen and move the widget to your desired location within that Home screen.

# Resize a Widget

Some widgets come in a preset size. Others allow you to change the size of the widget when you add it to the Home screen. You can also change the size of an adjustable widget after you add the widget to a Home screen. This example describes how to add the Gmail widget.

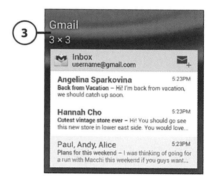

1. Tap the Apps icon on the Home screen.

2. Tap Widgets at the top of the Apps screen.

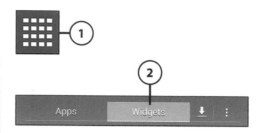

3. Navigate to the page that contains the Gmail widget.

4. Press and hold your finger on the Gmail widget. An overlay of the Home screen that you chose appears and the widget you're moving appears as an outline on the screen.

5. Move the outline over the Home screen to position the widget within the screen. When you're satisfied with the location of the widget on the Home screen, release your finger.

6.  In the Choose Folder window, tap the Gmail folder you want to display in the widget within the list.

7.  The widget appears on the Home screen with an orange box around it. Orange circles, or handles, appear on all four sides of the box.

8.  Resize the widget by tapping and holding on one of the handles and then dragging left and right or up and down depending on the handle you're moving. For example, if you drag the bottom handle up and down then you change the height of the widget. If your widget size is too large for the available area on the Home screen then the box and handles turn red to tell you that the widget is too large for the available space.

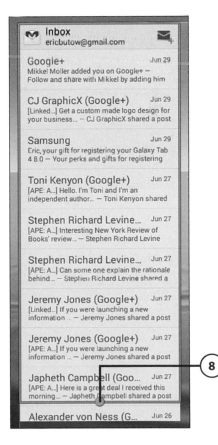

9. Release your finger. The resized widget appears on the Edit Home screen. If the widget is too large for the area you want, KitKat automatically resizes the widget to fill the available width or height.

10. Tap the Back touch button. Your widget appears on the Home screen at your desired size.

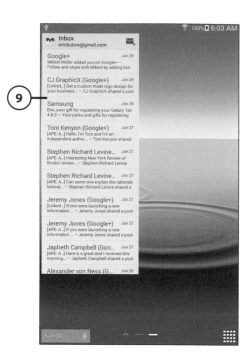

## Resize and/or Move the Widget Again

If you decide that you want to resize the widget, tap and hold on the widget. The Edit Home screen appears so you can resize the widget on the Home screen, move the widget around on the Home screen, or move the widget to a different Home screen.

# Creating a New Home Screen

A task earlier in this chapter describes how to create a new Home screen when you add a new widget. There are two other ways to create a new Home screen: from within an existing Home screen and in the Home screen menu.

1. Tap and hold your finger on a blank area of the Home screen until the Home Screen window appears. A blank area is an area that isn't occupied by another feature such as a widget or icon.

2. Tap Page in the menu.

3. The new Home page appears on the screen and the selected Home page appears to the right of the main Home page. The main home page is denoted by a house icon and the new home page you're viewing is denoted by a white bar.

4. Tap and hold the Recent touch button until the Edit Page screen appears.

5. Tap the Add Page button in the Edit Page screen.

6. The button for the new Home page appears on the screen. Open the new Home page by tapping the button.

5

6

## >>>*Go Further*

### HOW DO I REMOVE A HOME PAGE?

It's easy to remove a Home page if you don't want the Home page and any icons or widgets on that page. Start by pressing and holding the Recent touch button for a couple of seconds. In the Edit Page screen, tap and hold the button with the Home page you want to delete and then drag the button to the Remove icon at the top of the screen. When the button you're dragging turns red, release your finger. The Home page button disappears from the Edit Page screen.

If your Home page has icons or widgets in it when you delete it, the Remove Home Screen Page window appears reminding you that KitKat will remove the Home page and all items within it. Delete the Home page by tapping the OK button.

# Removing a Widget

It's easy to remove a widget from a Home page if you decide that you don't want it any longer.

1. Navigate to the Home page that contains the widget you want to remove. Tap and hold on the widget.

2. Within the Edit Home Page screen, drag the outline of the widget to the Remove icon at the top of the screen. When the Remove icon is highlighted in red, release your finger.

3. The Home screen appears and no longer contains the widget you removed.

**Use widgets designed for KitKat and the Galaxy Tab 4**

Chapter 5 describes how to add a widget to a Home screen. Your Galaxy Tab 4 comes with a number of preinstalled widgets you can use. Some of these widgets are new with the latest version of KitKat and others are unique to the Galaxy Tab 4. The widgets include the Picture Frame widget, the Calendar widget, and more. This chapter covers the following topics:

**6**

→ Finding widgets on the Galaxy Tab 4

→ Getting weather information

→ Adding and viewing videos

→ Viewing photos in the Picture Frame widget

→ Accessing Web bookmarks

→ Using the Calendar widgets

# Finding Widgets

The Galaxy Tab 4 comes with 40 widgets installed on the device. Two of those widgets appear within the Home screen pages. You can also access all the widgets from within the Widgets screen, and in this chapter we focus on several popular widgets for getting current weather conditions, viewing photos and videos, accessing your Web browser bookmarks, and using the Calendar.

# Viewing Default Widgets

By default, two widgets appear on the two default pages on the Home screen:

- The primary Home screen contains the Weather and Briefing widget at the top of the screen. This widget displays the current date and time as well as the current weather conditions for your location. At the bottom-left corner of the screen, the Google Search widget enables you to set up the Google Now app so you can get information you need without having to launch a browser app.

The Weather and Briefing widget

The Google Search widget

- Swipe from right to left on the primary Home screen to view the Samsung Apps widget on the Home screen. This widget doesn't display any information because you haven't set up the widget to display suggested apps from the Samsung App Store yet.

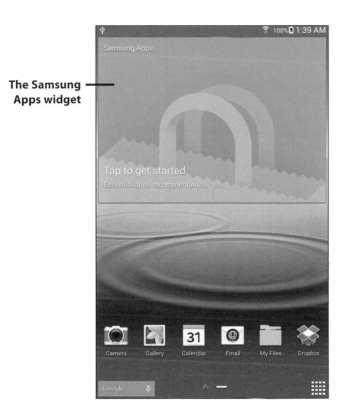

**The Samsung Apps widget**

# Find Widgets on the Widgets Pages

The widgets covered in this chapter are also within the Widgets screen pages. Some of them are already on Home screens by default, but it's useful to know where the widgets are within the Widgets screen in case you remove a widget and want to place it on a Home screen again.

1.  Tap the Apps icon on the Home screen.

2. Tap Widgets.

3. Swipe from right to left to view the Email and Gmail widgets on Page 3 of the Widgets screen.

4. Swipe from right to left to view the Google Search widget on Page 4 of the Widgets screen. This widget is on the primary Home screen by default.

5. Swipe from right to left to view Page 6 in the Widgets screen that contains the Picture Frame widget.

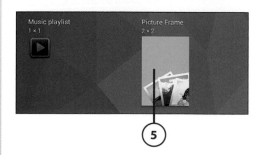

6. Swipe from right to left to view Page 7, the last page in the Widgets screen. The Video and the Weather and Briefing widgets appear on this page.

### Where Should I Put These Widgets?

You can place these widgets anywhere on Home screens (as described in Chapter 5, "Adding Widgets to Your Home Screens"), and it's presumed that you have added the widgets discussed in this chapter to a Home screen. For the purposes of this chapter, widgets that are not on Home screens by default appear on their own Home screens.

# Using the Widgets

All widgets enable you to open the related app on the screen to view more information and make changes to the app. Some widgets have controls contained within the widget to update and/or change information you view in the widget.

Let's begin by viewing the widget that appears on the primary Home screen: the Weather and Briefing widget.

# Learn What It's Like Outside with the Weather and Briefing Widget

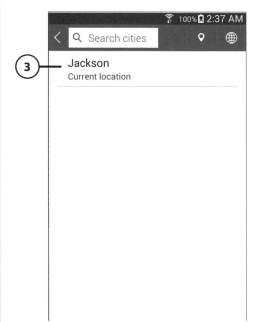

1. On the Home screen, update the current temperature and sky conditions for your area by tapping the Refresh icon. After a few seconds, the sky conditions image and text as well as the current temperature appear on the screen. The time and date of your last refresh appear to the left of the Refresh icon.

2. Open the Weather and Briefing app by tapping a blank area inside the widget.

3. Select the city for which you want to display weather information by tapping the city in the search window.

4. The current weather conditions appear in the lower-left corner of the widget. Open the Weather app by tapping the weather conditions text.

**5.** Four areas comprise the report section at the top of the Weather screen. The top of the screen displays current weather information including the current sky conditions for your area, the current temperature, the forecast high and low temperatures for the day, and information about precipitation, humidity, and the ultraviolet (UV) index.

**6.** The middle of the section includes an extended weather forecast for the next six days.

**7.** Check the bottom of the section to see the date and time the information was last updated. Tap the Refresh icon to get the most current weather information that appears at the top of the screen.

**8.** Below the report section you see a list of all cities you're tracking; tap the city name in the list to view the current weather in the report section.

**9.** Tap More to view more weather information for your area in either the Internet or Chrome app.

**10.** The AccuWeather.com page appears and displays current information for your area. Swipe up and down the screen to view the current wind speed, humidity level, and the amount of cloud cover in the sky.

**11.** Return to the Weather widget screen by tapping the Back touch button.

**12.** View a current weather map by tapping Weather Map.

**13.** A Google map of the larger area around your location appears on the screen. Your current location appears in the center of the map; in this example it's Jackson, California.

**14.** Return to the Weather widget screen by tapping the Back touch button.

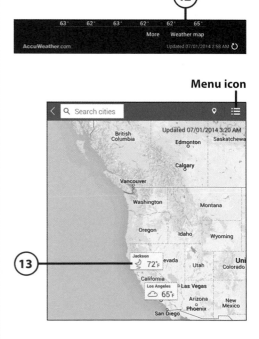

# >>>Go Further

## CAN I GET WEATHER FOR ANOTHER CITY OR AREA?

You can add another city or area to check by tapping the Menu icon at the upper-right corner of the screen. In the Setup screen, add a new city by tapping the plus icon. In the Search screen that appears, type a city to find a city in the AccuWeather database. After you select the city, it appears in the list within the Setup screen. View weather information for that city by tapping the city in the list.

**Plus icon**

**The new city appears below your current city**

# Add Videos to the Video Widget

If you want to view videos without having to open the Video app in the Apps screen, you can view videos directly from within the Video widget on a Home screen. The most recent video you viewed appears within the widget, but if the Video app can't find a video then the widget invites you to tap the widget to add a video.

1. Tap the Apps icon on the Home screen.

2. Tap Widgets.

3. Swipe from right to left to view the Video widget on Page 7 of the Widgets screen.

4. Add the Video widget to the main Home screen under the Weather and Briefing widget. Refer to Chapter 5 if you need more information about how to add widgets to a Home screen.

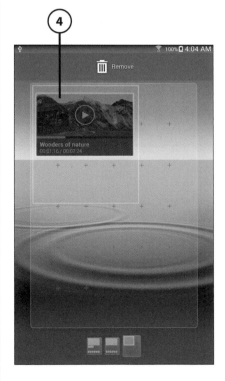

5. Swipe to the Home screen that contains the Video widget.

6. Tap anywhere in the widget.

7. When you start the Video app, the screen tells you that there are no videos. You can drag and drop videos from your computer using Windows Media Player or another media player that you learned about in Chapter 3, "Setting Up the Galaxy Tab 4," or you can record a video with the Camera app. (Find out how to record video in Chapter 12, "Playing Music and Video.")

8. For this example, Eric opened his Dropbox account to view a brief video of his grandfather, a U.S. Navy Commander who was the Commander of a naval base in Kodiak, Alaska, in the early 1950s. When Eric opened the Video widget again, he tapped the thumbnail image in the list to play the video.

9. Tap the List icon in the menu bar to view a list of videos that shows a thumbnail image of the photo as well as file information, view a list of videos along with the folder in which the file is contained, and scan for videos on connected devices such as a smartphone.

10. Tap the Folders icon.

11. The video thumbnail image and file information appear within the Dropbox folder. View the video by tapping the thumbnail image.

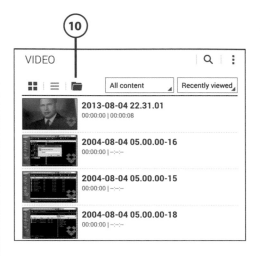

### Can I Search for Files?

If you don't see the video file you're looking for, you can search for it by tapping the Search icon at the right side of the menu bar that appears at the top of the screen. You can then type in your search term(s) and then tap the Search button in the keyboard. Any files the Video Player app finds appear on the Results screen.

# View Pictures in the Picture Frame

The Picture Frame widget enables you to view one or more pictures stored on your Tab 4 within the widget area on a Home screen.

1. Add the Picture Frame widget to your desired Home screen if you haven't done so already. The Select From window opens as soon as you add the widget to the Home screen.

2.  In the window you can select from images stored on your device, an album file that contains images, or shuffled pictures that you view within the widget as a slideshow. For this example, tap Images. In the Gallery window, images in various folders display on the screen.

3.  Tap the folder with the images you want to add to the Picture Frame app. This example uses the Download folder.

4.  The Picture Frame widget appears on the Home screen's Setup screen so you can see how the Picture Frame will look on the screen. If more than one image appears in the widget, you see the slideshow of photos. You can move the widget around on the screen and you can resize the widget by tapping, holding, and dragging one of the four resizing handles on the sides of the widget box.

5.  Tap the Back touch button.

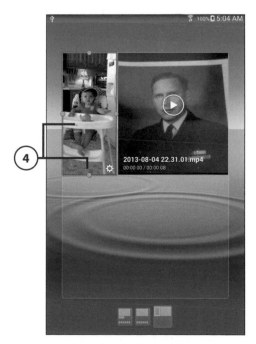

6. The Picture Frame widget appears in your desired location on the Home screen.

## How Do I Change the Picture Frame Settings?

You can change the Picture Frame widget settings by tapping the gear icon at the lower-right corner of the widget. In the Picture Frame screen you can change the pictures you view, the layout of the pictures (for example, you can have one picture appear on top of another within the widget), and change the interval between slides.

**Gear icon**

# Access Chrome Bookmarks Quickly Using Bookmarks

The Bookmarks widget enables you to store bookmarks within the Chrome browser app. After you set up the Bookmarks widget, you can browse for bookmarks directly within the widget and open the bookmarked website in the Internet or Chrome app.

1. Add the Bookmarks widget to your desired Home screen if you haven't done so already.

**2.** The Bookmarks widget appears on the Home screen's Setup screen so you can see how the widget will look on the screen. You can move the widget around on the screen and you can resize the widget by tapping, holding, and dragging one of the four resizing handles on the sides of the widget box. For this example I resized the widget so it takes up the bottom half of the Home screen.

**3.** Tap the Back touch button.

**4.** Swipe your finger up and down within the widget (if necessary) to view all the folders that contain your bookmarks.

**5.** Tap the folder that contains the bookmarked website you want to view.

**6.** Swipe your finger up and down within the widget to view all the bookmarks (and any subfolders) contained with the folder. Go back to the previous folder by tapping the folder name at the top of the folder list.

**7.** Tap the bookmark that contains the website you want to view.

8. If you see the Complete Action Using window, tap the browser app icon to view the website within that browser app. This example uses the Chrome app.

9. Tap the Always button to open websites from the widget using the selected browser app. If you want the app to ask you to select your browser app each time you open a bookmarked website, tap the Just Once button.

10. The website appears in your desired browser app.

11. Tap the Back touch button to return to the Home screen that contains the Bookmarks app.

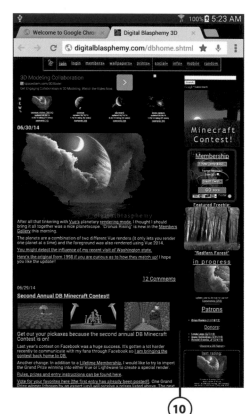

# See Your Calendar at a Glance Using the Calendar Widgets

There are two Calendar widgets: the Mini Today widget that shows you the appointments you have for the current day and the Month widget that shows all your events for the current month.

# Calendar (Mini Today) Widget

You can view events on dates other than the current date and you can also add an event for the current date within the Mini Today widget.

1. After you add the widget to your desired Home screen, the widget appears at your desired location on that Home screen.

2. Tap the left arrow icon to see events on the previous day.

3. Tap the right arrow icon to see events on the following day.

4. If you're viewing events on a day other than the current day, return to appointments on the current day by tapping Today.

5. Tap the plus icon to add a new event.

6. The Event window opens so you can add a new event to your calendar. Read Chapter 14, "Using Productivity Apps to Simplify Your Life," to see how to add an event to your calendar. Tap Save after you've entered the details of your appointment.

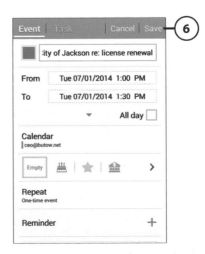

7.  The new appointment appears in the Mini Today widget.

## Calendar (Month) Widget

You can view events for the current month stored in S Planner by adding the Month widget to a Home screen.

1.  After you add the widget to your desired Home screen, the widget appears at your desired location on that Home screen. The current date is highlighted in blue and the date is circled.

2.  Tap the left arrow icon to see events for the previous month. The three-letter abbreviation for the previous month appears to the right of the icon. In this example, June is the previous month and it has the abbreviation Jun.

3.  Tap the right arrow icon to see events for the following month. The three-letter abbreviation for the following month appears to the left of the icon. In this example, August is the next month and it has the abbreviation Aug.

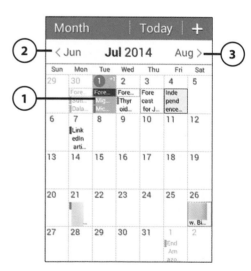

4. Tap another date to highlight that date and also to add an event for that date.

5. If you're viewing events on a day other than the current day, highlight the current day by tapping Today.

6. Add a new event by tapping the plus icon.

7. The Event window opens so you can add a new event to your calendar. Read Chapter 14 for details about how to add an event. Tap Save.

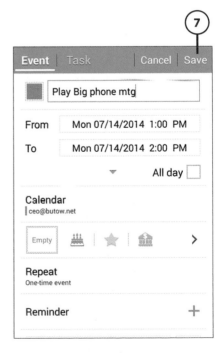

8. The new appointment appears in the Month widget.

**Learn how to browse the Web and view websites using the built-in Internet app**

The Galaxy Tab 4 is a great tool for viewing web pages, whether you're at home or you're on the go. No matter which Galaxy Tab 4 model you use, the screen is much larger than a mobile phone, so you can see more on the Galaxy Tab 4's screen. Because you can touch the screen, you can interact with web content in ways that a computer typically cannot. This chapter covers the following:

→ Browsing to a URL
→ Searching the Web
→ Viewing web pages
→ Bookmarking websites
→ Returning to previously visited websites
→ Deleting bookmarks
→ Filling in web forms
→ Copying text and images from web pages

# Browsing the Web

## Browsing to a URL

It's likely that you already know how to browse to different web pages in your favorite web browser on your computer. The built-in Internet app in Android works much the same as the browser on your computer, but there are some differences.

1. Tap Internet on the Home screen.

① Internet

2. Tap the Address field at the top of the screen. The keyboard opens at the bottom of the screen so you can type a Uniform Resource Locator (URL), which can be a website name or a specific page in a website.

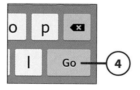

3. Start typing a URL, such as samsung.com or play.google.com. You can also select from one of the search sites in the list that appears below the Address field.

4. Tap Go on the keyboard when you finish typing.

## Smarter Searching

As you type, terms that match the letter(s) you've added appear in the list below the Address field. As you type more letters, Android updates the list to give you what it thinks is a more accurate list of possible terms you're looking for. You can stop typing at any time and scroll down the list to view the terms and then tap the term to open the web page. For example, as you type the first five letters of "android" (without the quotes), you see that you get terms for android and a number of other results.

**Search results when you start typing the word "android" in the Address field**

## Tips for Typing a URL

The Internet app doesn't require you to type the "http://" or the "www." at the beginning of the URL. For example, if you type samsung.com or www.samsung.com, you still go to the Samsung home page. However, there might be some instances when you need to type in "http://" or even "https://" (for a secure web page) at the beginning of the URL. If you do, the Internet app lets you know so you can type in the "http://" or "https://" in the Address field.

# Searching the Web

The Internet app makes it easy for you to search the Web, so you don't need to know every URL of every web page out there (which is good considering there are literally billions of web pages). As you type, the Internet app suggests search terms you've used in the past as well as search terms that you might be looking for.

1. Tap Internet on the Home screen.

2. Tap the Address field at the top of the screen. The keyboard opens at the bottom of the screen so you can type the URL. Start typing your search term. As you type, a list appears underneath the address bar with suggestions. You can stop typing at any time and scroll down the list to find your search term; tap the search term to select it and start the search.

3. If you haven't found what you're looking for, open the Google search page by tapping Go in the keyboard.

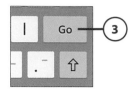

4. The results display in a Google search results page. Tap any link to go to a page; you can also tap one of the links at the bottom of the screen to view more results.

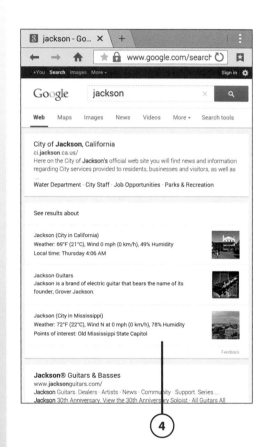

# >>>Go Further

## TIPS FOR SEARCHING THE WEB

You can search deeper within Google itself. For example, if you put a + in front of a search term, you're telling Google that you require the word in the search results. If you put quotes around a search term ("term"), you're telling Google that you want to search for results that contain that term. Scroll to the bottom of the search page and then tap Help to get more information about how you can get the most from your Google searches.

Get a list of search tips
from Google

If you look at the top of Google's search results page, you see links so you can search for more than text terms, including Images and Videos. If you click the More link, a pop-up list displays so you can search a variety of other areas within Google.

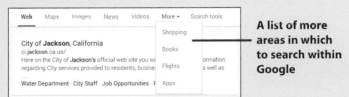

A list of more
areas in which
to search within
Google

# Viewing Web Pages

After you open a website, you can control what you view on the web page in several ways. These techniques enable you to access the entire web page and navigate between web pages in the Internet app.

1. Navigate to a web page using one of the two methods described in the previous tasks in this chapter.

2. As you view a page, you can drag up and down the page with your finger. You can also flick with your finger to scroll quickly. After you flick, the screen scrolls, decelerates, and then comes to a stop.

3. Zoom in by double-tapping an area on the screen. Zoom out by double-tapping again.

4. While you're zoomed in, you can touch and drag left and right to view different parts of the web page.

5. Move to another web page from a link in the current web page by tapping a link. Links are usually an underlined or colored piece of text, but they can also be pictures or images that look like buttons.

## Hunting for Links

Unfortunately, it isn't always easy to figure out which parts of a web page are links and which ones aren't. Back in the early days of the Web, all links were blue and underlined. As web page elements have become more enhanced over time, it's now more common to find links in any color and any text style. What's more, graphics that are links aren't underlined, either.

On a computer's web browser it's easy to find out which element is a link when you move the mouse pointer over the link because the pointer changes shape. In Android, there is no cursor, so you can't find out if a web page element is a link unless you tap it and see what happens.

# Bookmarking Websites

As you browse websites, you might want to save some of the websites in a list of your favorites so you can go back to them later. In browser parlance, this saving process is called bookmarking.

1. Navigate to any page in the Internet app.

2. Tap the Bookmarks button at the top of the page.

3. In the Bookmarks list, tap the Add Bookmark button. The Add Bookmark dialog box opens.

4. Edit the title of the bookmark. The official title of the web page is filled in for you, but you can change the name by tapping the Name field and using the keyboard. To change the folder in which the bookmark is stored, proceed with Step 5. Otherwise, skip to Step 10.

5. To change the folder in which the bookmark is stored, tap the right arrow button to the far right of the folder name, which is Bookmarks in this example.

6. Create a new bookmarks folder by tapping Create Folder.

7. Tap the Enter Name field and then type the name of your new folder.

8. Tap Done.

9. Tap the name of the folder into which you want to place the bookmark.

10. Tap Save.

11. Tap the new folder name in the folder list on the left side of the screen; the new bookmark appears within the folder on the right side of the screen.

## Should I Edit a Bookmark Title?

Because the titles of web pages are usually long and descriptive, it's a good idea to shorten the title to something you can recognize easily in your bookmarks list. Every bookmark also includes a thumbnail picture of what the web page looks like so you can identify the bookmark more easily. If you would rather view your bookmarks by title, press Settings and then tap List View in the menu.

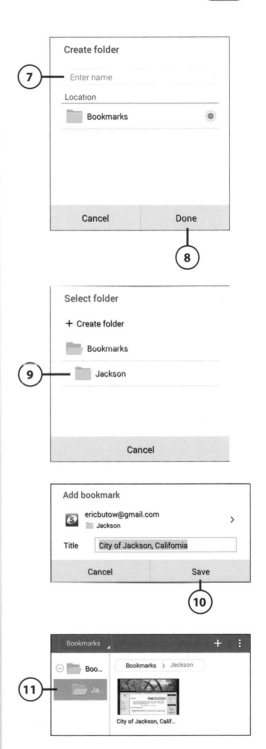

# Returning to Previously Visited Pages

It's easy to return to the last page you visited in the Internet app—just press the Back button. As you keep pressing the Back button, you keep going back to pages you visited. In the History page, the Internet app also keeps a list of all web pages you've visited during your browsing session.

## Browsing Forward

Like any web browser, you can browse more recent pages you've viewed in your current browsing session by tapping the Forward button, which is the right-arrow button immediately to the right of the Back button.

1. Visit several web pages in the Internet app if you haven't done so already.

2. Tap Bookmarks.

3. Tap the Bookmarks button and then tap History in the drop-down list.

4. The list of web pages you visited for the current date appears under the Today heading.

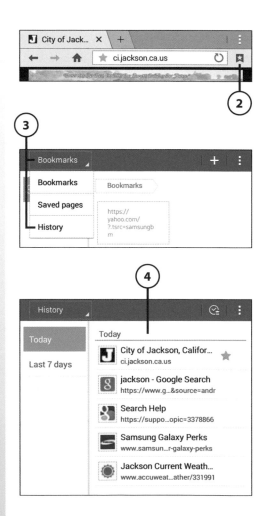

5. You can view web pages you visited on an earlier date by tapping the date range, such as Last 7 Days. You can also view the web pages you've visited most often by tapping Most Visited; the list displays on the right side of the screen. Note that if you don't have any most visited sites then the Most Visited option doesn't appear in the menu.

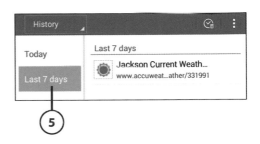

### Tips for Using History

If you want to hide the history for a specific day so you can see history for another day, tap the header for the specific day. For example, if you want to hide all the web pages for today, click the Today header above the first web page in the Today list. The Today header is still visible, but you won't see the web pages. You can view the web pages again by tapping the Today header.

You can also clear the entire history database by tapping the Menu touch button and then tapping Clear History in the pop-up menu.

# Deleting Bookmarks

If you find there are websites that you don't visit anymore or that go to obsolete or missing web pages, you need to cull your bookmark list. You can delete a bookmark from the Bookmarks list or from the History list.

# Delete from the Bookmarks List

The first method uses the Bookmarks list to delete a bookmark.

1. Tap the Bookmarks button at the top of the Internet screen. The thumbnail list of bookmarks appears.

2. Tap and hold your finger on the bookmark you want to delete until you see a green checkmark in the upper-right corner of the bookmark tile.

3. Delete the bookmark by tapping the Trash icon in the menu bar.

4. A dialog box asks if you want to delete the bookmark. Tap OK to delete the bookmark instantly.

# Delete from the History List

The second method uses the History list to delete a bookmark.

1. Tap the Bookmarks button at the top of the Internet screen. The thumbnail list of bookmarks appears.

2. Tap the Bookmarks button and then tap History in the drop-down menu. This brings up a list of web pages you've viewed recently.

3. Tap and hold your finger on the website in the History list until you see a green checkmark to the right of the bookmark name.

4. Tap the Trash icon in the menu bar.

5. Tap OK in the Clear History window. The website no longer appears in the list of web pages.

## Sync Your Bookmarks

You can sync the bookmarks in your favorite web browser on your desktop or laptop computer with the Internet app so you have maximum control over your bookmarks. You can read more about syncing your Galaxy Tab 4 in Chapter 3, "Setting Up the Galaxy Tab 4."

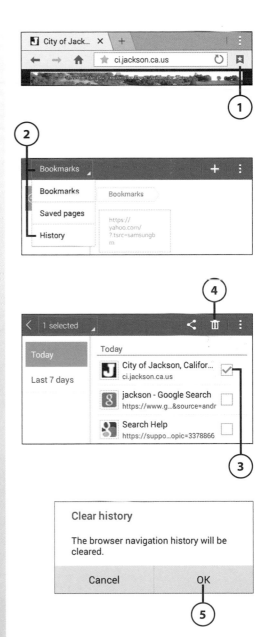

# Filling in Web Forms

On many web pages you are asked to fill in forms, such as for signing up for a company's email newsletter or to get more information about a product. Filling out web forms on your Galaxy Tab 4 is similar to filling out forms on a computer's web browser, but there are differences.

1. Navigate to a page that you know contains a form. (The sample page is at http://code.google.com/p/android/issues/entry.)

2. Tap in a text box.

3. The keyboard appears at the bottom of the screen. Use the keyboard to type text into the box. Tap the Go button when you finish typing.

4. Select an item in a pull-down menu by tapping the box.

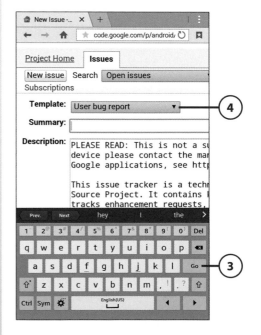

5. Tap an item in the menu to select it. If the menu list is long, touch and drag up and down to view more selections.

6. The selected item appears in the field.

## Special Menus

Some websites use special menus that are built from scratch. In these cases, the menu looks exactly like the one you get when you view the web page on a computer. If the web page is well constructed, it should work fine on the Galaxy Tab 4. However, it might be a little more difficult to make a selection.

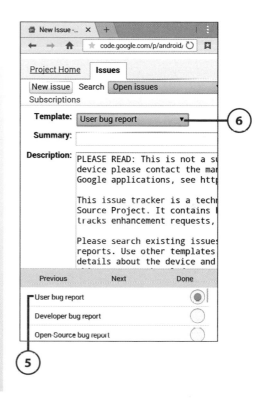

# Copying Text and Images from Web Pages

The Internet app treats web pages like other documents. That is, you can copy text and images from a web page you view in a browser to another app.

## Copy a Block of Text

You can select text from web pages to copy and paste into other documents such as email messages or your own text documents.

1. Navigate to a web page in the Internet app if you haven't done so already.

2. Hold down your finger on the first word in the block of text and then release your finger. The first word is highlighted in blue with "handles" at the beginning and end of the word.

3. Hold down your finger on the bottom handle (the one on the right side of the word) and drag over the text you want to copy. When finished, release your finger. The selected text is highlighted in blue.

4. In the pop-up menu that appears above the selected text, tap Copy.

5. Android informs you that the text has been copied to the clipboard. You can now go to another application, such as Email (or an email form on another web page), and paste the text into a text area.

## Copy an Image

In addition to being able to copy and paste text from the Internet app, you can also copy images from a web page and save them to an email message or a photo collection.

1. Go to a web page that includes an image on the page.

2. Tap and hold your finger on that image for a couple of seconds and then release your finger. A pop-up menu for the image displays.

**3.** Tap Save Image. This saves your image to the Galaxy Tab 4 so you can view and use it in any app where you select images from your photo albums. Note that the menu options may differ depending on the image you select.

**4.** The downloaded file appears as an icon in the Status bar.

**5.** Hold your finger on the Status bar and swipe down to open the Quick Settings and Notifications screen.

**6.** Scroll down the notification area and then tap the image filename to open the file in the Gallery or Photos app.

**Send and receive email from your ISP or an email service**

**Send and receive instant messages**

Your Galaxy Tab 4 makes it easy for you to read and respond to email messages when you're on the go. Before you start, though, you need to configure your email account(s) and then figure out how to use the built-in Email app. Email isn't the only way to communicate. The Galaxy Tab 4 also contains a built-in Messaging app so you can configure your instant message settings to communicate using standard text message (SMS) and multimedia message (MMS) services. This chapter covers the following topics:

→ Configuring and reading email

→ Composing a new message

→ Deleting and moving messages

→ Searching through email

→ Configuring email settings

→ Sending and receiving instant messages

→ Reading email messages with the Email widget

# Sending Email and Instant Messages

## Configuring Email

Following is a complete checklist of the information you need to set up your Galaxy Tab 4 to use a traditional email account. If you have an email service such as Exchange, Google Gmail, or Yahoo! you won't need all this. However, if you don't configure the email settings, you can't use webmail services in other apps (like Gmail) to do things such as email web page links or photos, so you need some of the following information no matter what:

- Email address

- Account type (POP or IMAP)

- Incoming mail server address

- Incoming mail user ID

- Incoming mail password

- Outgoing mail server address

- Outgoing mail user ID

- Outgoing mail password

## >>>*Go Further*

## DO I USE POP OR IMAP?

If you're not sure whether to use POP or IMAP as your account type, keep the following in mind:

*Post Office Protocol*, or *POP*, retrieves and removes email from a server. Therefore, the server acts as a temporary holding place for email. If you receive email using both your Galaxy Tab 4 and your computer, it's more difficult to share your email messages using POP. You need to either set up your email to go to one device and some to another device, or you need to set up one device so it doesn't remove email from the server so another device can retrieve the email as well.

*Internet Message Access Protocol*, or *IMAP*, makes the server the place where all messages are stored. Your Galaxy Tab 4 and computer display all email messages on the server. This is the better situation if you have multiple devices retrieving email from the same account.

1. On the Home screen, swipe from right to left to view the second page of the Home screen.

2. Tap Email.

3. Type the email address in the highlighted Email Address field. When you start typing, the keyboard appears at the bottom of the screen.

4. Tap Next in the keyboard.

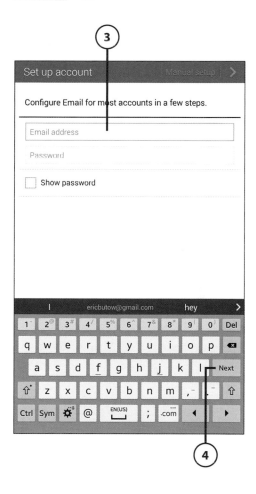

5. Tap the password for your email account in the Password field. As you type in the password characters, they become dots so the password is hidden right away.

6. Tap Done in the keyboard.

7. Tap the button that corresponds to the account type you have.

8. Type the incoming server settings into the appropriate fields.

9. Tap the right arrow icon in the menu bar.

10. After the Galaxy Tab 4 checks your incoming server settings, type the outgoing server settings into the appropriate fields.

11. Tap the right arrow icon in the menu bar.

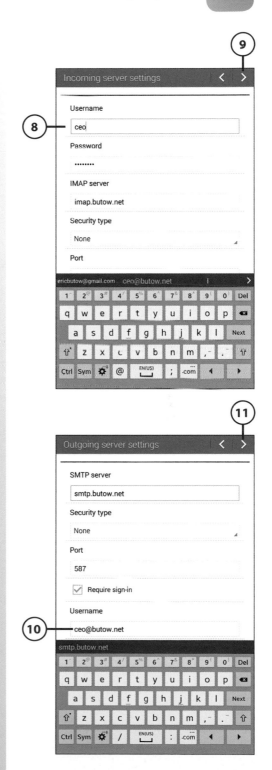

12. Tap the check box to automatically download files attached to email messages. You can also uncheck the Notify Me When Email Arrives box if you don't want to be notified when you have new messages.

13. Tap the Period to Sync Email field to change the amount of time the Email app keeps messages on your Tab 4. The default time is 2 weeks, but you can have the Tab keep messages on the Tab 4 for 1 day, 3 days, 1 week, or 1 month. You can keep all messages on your Tab 4 by tapping All. Note that if you have more than one email account and you keep messages from all the accounts for a long period of time (1 to 2 weeks or longer) then you will take up more memory on your Tab 4 and that might affect your ability to store data and run apps on your device.

14. Tap the Sync Schedule field to change the checking frequency at which your Tab 4 checks for new messages. The default frequency is to check your inbox every 15 minutes. You can have the Tab check for new email as often as every 5 minutes. If that's too often, you can have the Tab check every 10 minutes, 15 minutes, 30 minutes, every hour, every 4 hours, or once per day. You can set the time yourself by tapping Manual.

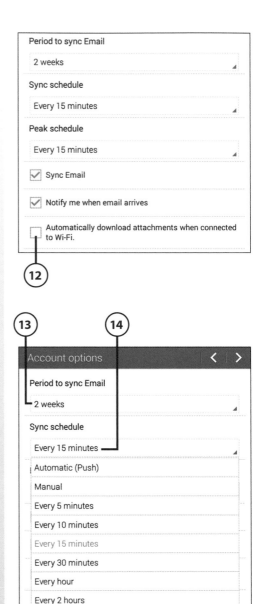

15. Tap the checking frequency in the list.

## What's the Peak Schedule?

The Peak Schedule field reflects how often the Email app checks for new messages. The default frequency is 15 minutes during working hours, which are from 8:00 a.m. to 5:00 p.m. The "Configuring Email Options" section later in this chapter explains how to change the working hour start and stop times.

16. Tap the right arrow icon in the menu bar.

17. Type an optional name into the Give This Account a Name field.

18. Type your name as you want it to be displayed in outgoing messages.

19. Tap Done. A list of your email messages appears in your Inbox screen.

## What Happens if the Settings Won't Verify?

If your settings don't verify, a dialog box displays, asking you to tap the Edit Details button to return to the previous screen and double-check all the information you entered. When something is wrong, it often comes down to misspelled information, such as a misspelled word or a letter that needs to be capitalized, or other incorrect information, such as a different outgoing server port number.

## Can I Still Check My Mail Even if the App Never Checks Mail Automatically?

You can still check your mail list by tapping the Refresh icon in the Inbox screen as shown in the figure. After you tap the Refresh icon, the app checks for new messages. Any new messages appear at the top of the Inbox.

**The Refresh icon**

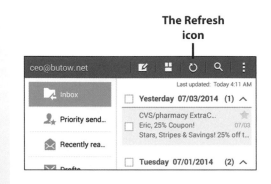

## Can I Add a Gmail Account to the Email App?

The Gmail app is preinstalled on your Tab 4, but you can still add one or more Gmail accounts in the Email app if you prefer to check all your accounts from one app. Before you add a Gmail account, be sure to set up your Gmail password within your Google account at http://security.google.com/settings/security/apppasswords. Note that you won't see some of the steps listed in this section when you configure a Gmail account, such as incoming and outgoing server settings.

# Reading Email

You use the Email app to navigate, read, and type your email messages.

1.  On the Home screen, swipe from right to left to view the second page of the Home screen.

2. Tap Email. Your list of Inbox folder messages displays with a list of folders on the left side of the screen. New, unread messages appear in the list with a white background; read messages have a gray background. A folder you're currently in is highlighted in blue in the folder list and the number of new messages appears to the right of the Inbox folder name.

3. Tap a message in the list to view the entire message on the screen.

## How Do I Get Back to the Message List?

Tap the left arrow icon at the top-left corner of the screen to return to your list of messages and folders.

**Unread message**

**Read message**

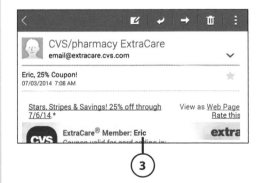

4. Tap the sender's name at the top of the page.

5. Tap Create Contact to add the sender to your list of contacts.

6. Tap Device and then select the account to which you want to add the contact.

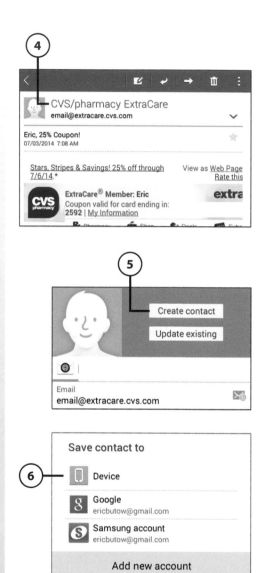

7. Type information into the Create Contact window fields if you want. (You learn more about adding a contact in Chapter 14, "Using Productivity Apps to Simplify Your Life.") Tap Save to save the new contact and return to the message list.

8. Tap the left arrow icon at the top-left corner of the screen to return to your list of messages and folders.

9. View another account (if you have more than one account in the Email app) by tapping the email account name in the upper-left corner of the screen and then tapping the account name in the list.

10. Scroll down the folder list to view folders within the Inbox and tap a folder to view messages within that folder. If necessary, tap the Load More Messages button at the top of the list to view messages in the folder.

11. The number of messages in the folder appears to the right of the folder name; if the folder name isn't long then the list of messages within that folder appears to the right of the folder list.

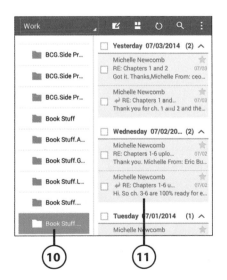

12. Scroll up the folder list until you see the Inbox folder. Tap it.

13. Tap the Refresh icon to refresh the message list on the right side of the screen. Any new messages that have come in appear at the top of the list and the Last Updated text at the top of the message list reflects the new time the Email app checked for messages.

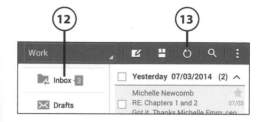

# >>>Go Further

## HOW DO YOU CREATE FOLDERS?

You can't create folders inside the five default email folders at the top of the folder list—that is, the Inbox, Drafts, Sent, Trash, or Junk folders. You can create subfolders within existing folders in the Folders for This Account section in the list, like so:

1. Tap the menu icon at the right side of the blue menu bar at the top of the screen.

2. Tap Create Folder in the drop-down list.

3. Within the Create Folder window, scroll down in the Folders for This Account section and then tap the folder in which you want to add the subfolder.

4. Type the new folder name in the New Folder field.

5. Tap OK.

### How Do I Combat Spam?

The Galaxy Tab 4 has no spam filter built in. However, most email servers filter spam at the server level. If you use a basic POP or IMAP account from an ISP, unfortunately you might not have any server-side spam filtering. If you use an account at a service such as Gmail, you get spam filtering on the server, and spam mail goes to the Junk folder, not your Inbox.

# Composing a New Message

The process for composing a new message and composing a reply to a message is similar. This section covers composing a message from scratch.

1.  Tap the New Mail icon in the Email app.

2.  Enter the recipient's address in the To field.

3.  Tap the Contacts button to select the recipient(s) from your list of contacts.

4.  Tap the +Me button if you'd like to send a copy of the message to your own email address so that you have a record of what you sent.

5.  Tap in the Subject field and then type a subject for the email.

6.  Tap below the Subject field in the body of the email and then type your message.

7.  Tap Send.

Attach icon

---

## Add Attachments

If you've copied text or images to your clipboard, you can add that text or image as an attachment, just as you can with any email program on your computer. Just tap the Attach button, which has a paper clip icon and is located underneath the subject line near the far right of the window. Then you can pick your text, image(s), contacts, or location from the Attach window.

---

## >>>Go Further

### HOW DO I REPLY OR FORWARD A MESSAGE?

When you're reading a message, you can choose to reply to the sender or forward the message to another recipient.

At the right side of the menu bar that appears above the message, you see a series of five icons. The Reply icon appears as an arrow pointing left. After you tap the icon you see the reply message screen so you can type your response to the message. The Subject field contains the RE: prefix that denotes you're replying to the original message. View the original message by swiping down the screen. Send the message by tapping Send in the menu bar.

The Forward icon appears as an arrow pointing right. After you tap the icon you see the forward message screen. You can type the recipient in the To field as well as any recipients you want to copy or blind copy in the Cc/Bcc field. You can also type a message to the recipient within the body of the email. Any attachments that came with the original message are also attached to the forwarded message. You can view the original message by swiping down the screen. When you finish composing your forwarded message, tap Send in the menu bar.

**The Forward icon**

**The Reply icon**

## Creating Your Own Signature

You can create a signature that automatically appears at the end of your messages. You create your signature in the Email app.

1. On the Home screen, swipe from right to left to view the second page of the Home screen.

2. Tap Email.

3. Tap the Menu icon in the menu bar.

4. Tap Settings.

5. Tap your account name in the list.

6. Tap Signature. You can disable the signature field in your email messages by moving the slider from right to left. The slider button turns gray and displays an O (for Off), but you can turn it back on by sliding the bar to the right so the button turns green and displays an I (for On).

7. Type what you want the signature to say (such as your full name) in the Edit Signature screen.

8. Tap Done.

9. The signature as it will appear in your Message Composition field appears under the Signature heading.

### Can I Have Multiple Signatures?

You can have only one signature per email account on your Galaxy Tab 4, so technically you can't have multiple signatures. However, the signature is placed in the editable area of the Message Composition field, so you can edit it like the rest of your message and create multiple signatures that way.

# Deleting Messages

When you view a message, you can tap the Delete icon and move the message to the trash.

1. In the Email app, go to any mailbox and any subfolder, such as your Trash folder.

2. Tap a check box at the left side of the message entry that you want to delete. You can select multiple check boxes if you want to delete multiple messages.

3. Delete the messages by tapping the Trash icon.

4. Tap Delete in the confirmation box.

## Can I Move Messages to Other Folders?

Unfortunately, you can't move messages in the Email app from one folder to another. If you use an IMAP server, you can log in to the web interface for that server and move messages around there. The next time you log in to the Email app, the app reflects the changes you made in the IMAP server. If you're using a POP server, though, the only way you can move messages is to do so in another email program like one on your desktop or laptop computer.

# Searching Through Email

By default, the Galaxy Tab 4 doesn't let you search through your email messages. You can change this quickly and then search text in your email messages.

1. On the Home screen, swipe from right to left to view the second page of the Home screen.

2. Tap Email.

3. Open a folder or subfolder and then tap the Search icon.

4. Type the search term into the Search field.

5. As you type, updated results display below the field. In my example, I opened the Chambers. Folsom subfolder and typed **fols** into the field.

6. If you don't find the search results you want, continue searching for messages that match your search term(s) on all connected devices by tapping Search All Devices.

7. The message list displays all recent email messages in this folder that match your search term. If the messages in the folder aren't recent, as in this example, tap Continue Searching to search for older messages in the folder.

8. Messages appear in the list so you can read a message by tapping it. Note that it may take a few seconds for all folder messages to appear in the list.

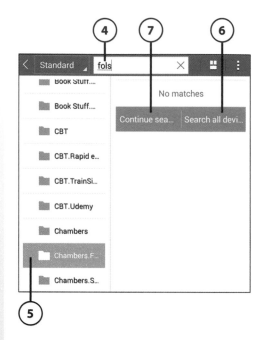

## What's the Continue Searching on Server Link?

If you use an IMAP server, you can search other locations on your server (such as other email accounts) for the search term you entered by tapping the Continue Searching on Server link. After you tap this link, more results (if any) appear underneath your original search results. If you use another type of email service, such as POP, you won't see this link.

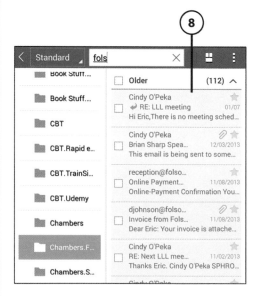

# Configuring Email Settings

The Galaxy Tab 4 enables you to update your email account settings as needed.

1. Follow the steps from earlier tasks in this chapter to open the Email app if you aren't there already. Then tap the Menu icon in the menu bar.

2. Tap Settings.

3. Tap your account in the Account Manager list if there is more than one. If not, your account appears on the screen automatically.

4. Tap Email Notifications to specify whether the Galaxy Tab 4 should notify you when email arrives. This feature is activated by default. Deactivate it by tapping the check box.

5. Tap Select Ringtone to select a ringtone or to designate that there should be no ringtone at all. Select the ringtone from the Select Ringtone pop-up window. The default ringtone is Postman.

6. Tap Sync Settings; in the Sync Settings list that appears, tap Sync Schedule.

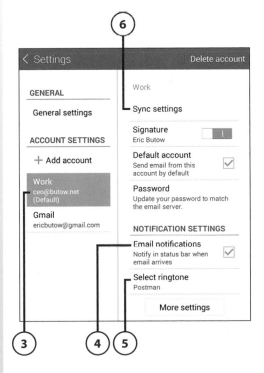

7. Tap Set Sync Schedule and then select the time interval in the Sync Schedule window as described in the "Configuring Email" section earlier in the chapter.

8. Tap the Peak Schedule check box if you don't want to set a separate email syncing schedule. When you clear the check box, the app disables all the options in the Peak Schedule section underneath the checkbox.

9. Tap Set Peak Schedule to change the peak schedule syncing interval in the Set Peak Schedule window. Tap the appropriate interval for syncing during the peak schedule. (Each interval is the same as in the Sync Schedule field.)

10. By default the peak days are Monday through Friday, and the peak days are highlighted in green. Tap a day to select or deselect it to add or delete it from the peak schedule, respectively.

11. Change the peak start time by tapping Peak Start Time.

12. Change the time by tapping on the up and down arrows above (from left to right) the hour, minute, and AM/PM settings.

13. When you finish setting the time, tap Set.

14. Your new peak start time appears. Change the peak end time by tapping Peak End Time.

**15.** Change the peak end time in the window as you did with the peak start time. The new peak end time appears.

**16.** Go back to the main Settings screen by tapping the left arrow icon in the menu bar.

**17.** Tap Size to Retrieve Emails to open the Size to Retrieve Emails list and change the default amount of data you can receive in an email message. When you receive messages, the Email app only downloads the first 50KB of data in a message by default. If the message has more than 50KB of data then at the bottom of the message the app asks if you want to download the rest of the message. You can choose from 2KB to 100KB.

**18.** Go back to the main Settings screen by tapping the left arrow icon in the menu bar.

19. Tap the Signature field to change your signature. Read the "Creating Your Own Signature" task earlier in this chapter for more information about signatures.

20. The Default account check box is checked when the Email app sends and receives email automatically from the account you're viewing. If you don't want to send email from that account, clear the check box by tapping Default Account.

21. Tap More Settings.

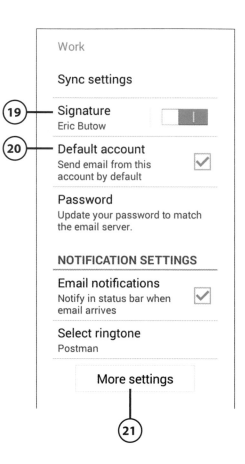

Work

Sync settings

Signature
Eric Butow

Default account
Send email from this
account by default

Password
Update your password to match
the email server.

**NOTIFICATION SETTINGS**

Email notifications
Notify in status bar when
email arrives

Select ringtone
Postman

More settings

**22.** Tap Account Name to change your account name.

**23.** Tap Your Name to add or change your name.

**24.** Tap Always Cc/Bcc Myself and then select Cc or Bcc in the pop-up window if you always want to add your email address in the Cc or Bcc box.

**25.** Tap Show Images to automatically show images in a message when you view it.

**26.** Tap Auto Download Attachments to download file attachments in a message to the app automatically.

**27.** Tap Auto Resend Times to change the number of times you automatically resend a message if it doesn't go through the first time. Then tap the number of times (1, 3, 5, 10, or 20) you want the Email app to resend the unsent message before giving up. The default is No Limit.

**28.** Set advanced security options by tapping Security Options. In the Security Options screen that appears, you can encrypt all outgoing email, sign all outgoing email, and create and manage encryption keys for keeping your email messages private.

**29.** Change your incoming settings (as you did with a new account earlier in this chapter) by tapping Incoming Settings.

**30.** Change your outgoing settings (as you did with a new account earlier in this chapter) by tapping Outgoing Settings.

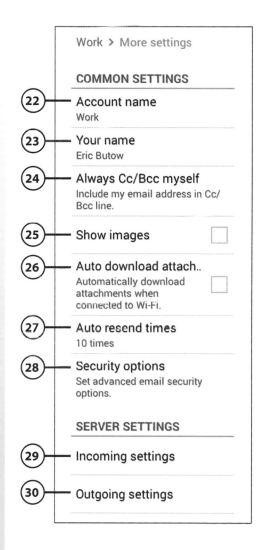

Work > More settings

**COMMON SETTINGS**

(22) Account name
Work

(23) Your name
Eric Butow

(24) Always Cc/Bcc myself
Include my email address in Cc/Bcc line.

(25) Show images ☐

(26) Auto download attach..
Automatically download attachments when connected to Wi-Fi. ☐

(27) Auto resend times
10 times

(28) Security options
Set advanced email security options.

**SERVER SETTINGS**

(29) Incoming settings

(30) Outgoing settings

# Sending and Receiving Instant Messages

You can send and receive instant messages using the built-in Hangouts app from Google.

## You Need a Google+ Account

You need to have an existing Google+ account that is tied to your primary Gmail account. If you don't have a Google+ account, Google Hangouts has you set up your Google+ account before you continue setting up Google Hangouts.

1. Open the Apps screen and then swipe from left to right to view the second page in the Apps screen.

2. Tap Hangouts.

3. Tap the plus icon to select the circles or names with which you want to connect in the Contacts window.

4. Tap the recipient field and then type the name of the person with whom you want to chat.

5. As you type, matches appear in the drop-down list underneath the field. Tap the name of the person with whom you want to chat.

6. Add more people you want to include in the conversation by tapping Anyone Else?, scroll down the list of users or Google+ groups in the window, and then add the user or group to recipient field by tapping the user or group name.

7. Type your message in the Send Hangouts Message field.

8. Add an emoticon to better convey the meaning of your message by tapping the emoticon icon to the right of the Send Hangouts Message field.

9. Swipe down the section of emoticons and then tap the emoticon you want. The emoticon appears at the end of your message.

10. Return to the keyboard by tapping the ABC key.

11. Tap the Send icon to send your message.

12. Your message appears above the Send Hangouts Message field. If you receive a message from the recipient, your message will be moved up and you will see the recipient's response above the Send Hangouts Message field.

## What if I Don't Use Either Google+ or Google Hangouts for Instant Messaging?

If you use a different instant messaging service then visit the Google Play Store by tapping Play Store on the Home screen. Then search for the instant messaging app you're looking for. If you use Skype, for example, there is a Skype app for Android available that you can download free of charge. You discover more about downloading apps in Chapter 16, "Finding and Managing Apps."

# Configuring Google Hangouts Settings

You can change your Google Hangouts settings so you can manage your messages to your liking, determine how you want to be notified of new messages that come into your message Inbox, and change your Google+ profile.

1. Open the Apps screen and then swipe from left to right to view the second page in the Apps screen.

2. Tap Hangouts.

3. Tap the Menu icon in the menu bar.

4. Tap Settings.

5. Tap your Google account email address in the list.

**6.** Tap Profile Photo to change your Google+ profile photo. You can take a photo using the Camera app or you can choose a photo within the Gallery app.

**7.** Tap Share Your Status if you want to let everyone in your Google+ circles who use Hangouts know what you're doing. You can display an emoticon showing how you're feeling currently, what device you're currently using (that is, smartphone, tablet, or computer), and if you're currently busy with a video or phone call on one of your devices.

**8.** Tap Hangouts Messages & Invites to change what happens when you get messages and Invites, and tap Video Calls to change what happens when you get video calls. The options in subsequent steps in this section are the same when you tap Hangouts Messages & Invites or Video Calls.

**9.** The Notifications and Vibrate check boxes are checked by default so you receive notifications about new Google Hangouts (which are live video chats) started by one of your contacts and when you receive a request to join a Google Hangout. If you don't want to be notified about any Hangouts, tap Notifications to clear the check box.

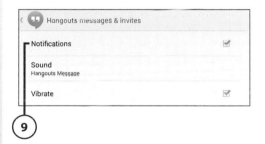

10. Tap Sound to open the Sound window and set a tone that notifies you when someone has joined your Hangout or you have received a request for someone to join your Hangout. By default you will feel the Tab 4 vibrate and see a message on the screen.

11. Select from the preselected silent mode, the default ringtone, or a number of other ringtones. Scroll up and down the list to view the entire list and tap the button to the right of the tone so you can listen to the sound.

12. Tap OK when you've selected a sound. The name of the selected sound appears within the Sound entry in the Hangout Notifications section.

13. Tap Vibrate if you don't want the Tab 4 to vibrate when you receive a message or invite, or if you receive a video call, depending on the screen you're in. You can turn on vibrations by tapping Vibrate again.

14. Return to the main Hangout Settings screen by tapping the Google Hangouts logo at the left side of the menu bar.

15. Tap Customize Invites to determine who can join your Hangouts.

16. In the Customize Invites screen, you can determine the circles that can join a Hangout with you or request that you accept them as a Hangout participant. Circles include ones that you created in Google+ as well as the default Public circle that includes all Google+ users. Change how users in each circle can request Hangout participation by tapping the circle name in the list. In the window that appears, you can tap Hangout with You or Invite Only.

17. After you change the request type, the type appears underneath the circle name.

18. Return to the main Hangout Settings screen by tapping the Google Hangouts logo at the left side of the menu bar.

19. Tap Google+ Profile to change your Google+ profile settings within the Internet browser app.

20. Tap Blocked People to view a list of blocked users. In the Blocked People screen that appears, you see a list of users (if any) that you blocked in Google+.

21. Tap Hidden Contacts to view a list of Google+ contacts you're connected with but who aren't visible on your Google+ profile page.

22. Tap Sign Out to sign out of Google Hangouts and close the Hangouts app.

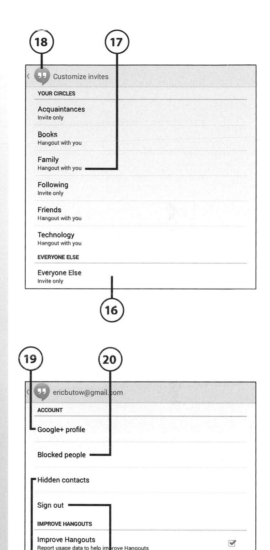

23. Tap Improve Hangouts if you don't want to report your usage data to Google to help improve the Hangouts app.

24. Return to the Hangouts screen by tapping the Google Hangouts icon at the left side of the menu bar.

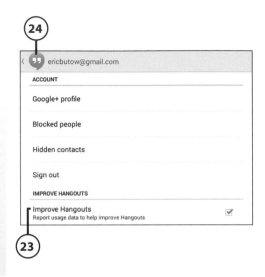

# Reading Email Messages Using the Email Widget

Chapter 5, "Adding Widgets to Your Home Screens," explains how to add widgets to your Home screens to perform certain tasks. In this task you see how to add the Email widget to a Home screen so you can view your latest email messages without having to open the Email app.

1. Tap the Apps icon on the Home screen.

2. Tap Widgets.

3. Swipe on the Widgets screen from right to left until you see the Email widget.

4.  Tap and hold on the widget and then add the widget to the Home screen you want as described in Chapter 5.

5.  The number of messages you see in the widget depends on the size of the widget on your Home screen. In this example, the five most recent messages in my Inbox folder appear in the widget. By default you see all messages from all email accounts that you set up in the Email app.

6.  View a message in the Email app by tapping the message within the widget. If you want to view email in a specific account, tap the arrow button at the left side of the menu bar

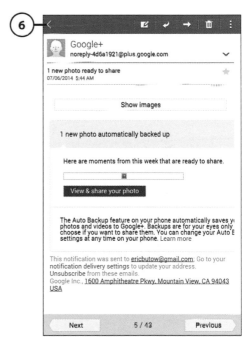

7.  View messages in an individual account by tapping the Combined View button and then selecting the account in the list. The button label changes to reflect one of your accounts and the list of messages changes to display the most recent messages in that account's Inbox folder. Tap the button again to view Inbox folder messages in another account.

8.  Return to the Email widget by pressing the Home button.

9.  Tap the New Mail icon to write a new message in the Email app as described in this chapter.

10. Tap the Refresh icon to have the widget check for new messages in the Inbox folder.

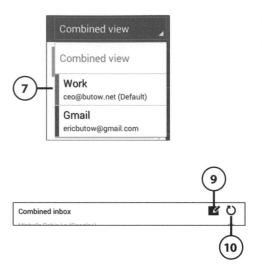

**Connect to other devices using Wi-Fi Connect**

**Connect to the cloud with the Dropbox app**

The Galaxy Tab 4 is a great tool for viewing web pages, whether you're at home or you're on the go. No matter which Galaxy Tab 4 model you use, the screen is much larger than a mobile phone so you can see more on the Galaxy Tab 4's screen. Because you can touch the screen, you can interact with web content in ways that a computer typically cannot. This chapter covers the following:

9

→ Connecting using Wi-Fi Connect

→ Printing wirelessly

→ Using the Dropbox app

→ Finding other cloud services

→ Sharing music and video

# Connecting to the Cloud

## Connecting Using Wi-Fi Direct

If you need to wirelessly transfer data to or connect with another device such as your smartphone, you don't need to buy a cable or even a wireless router to connect your Galaxy Tab 4 to another device. You can use the Tab 4 Wi-Fi Direct feature to connect to another device that also has Wi-Fi Direct enabled.

## Set Up Wi-Fi Direct

1. Tap the Apps icon on the Home screen.

2. Tap Settings.

3. Tap the Wi-Fi option in the menu on the left side of the screen if the option isn't selected already.

4. Tap Wi-Fi Direct.

5. The name of your Galaxy Tab 4 appears in the My Device Name section of the Wi-Fi Direct setting options area.

6. The Tab 4 searches for available devices available near you and displays those devices in the Available Devices section.

7. Tap Multi Connect if you want to show only those devices that can connect to multiple devices through a Wi-Fi Direct connection, such as a wireless printer.

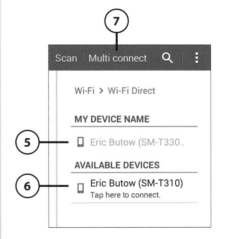

8. Tap the device name to which you want to connect.

9. The list shows the device is connected.

10. Disconnect from the device by tapping End Connection.

### How Do I Know I'm Connected to a Device Through Wi-Fi Connect?

If you're not sure you're connected to another device through Wi-Fi Connect, look in the Status Bar at the top of the screen. The Wi-Fi Connect icon appears to the left of the Wi-Fi icon at the right side of the bar.

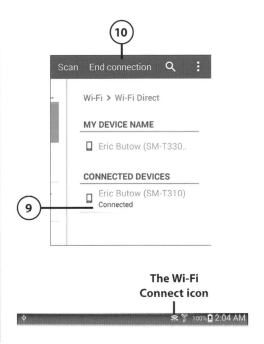

The Wi-Fi Connect icon

# >>>Go Further
## TROUBLESHOOTING CONNECTION ISSUES

If the Galaxy Tab 4 can't find your Wi-Fi Direct device, check the other device's Wi-Fi connection and ensure the other device offers Wi-Fi Direct. In the Tab 4 Settings screen, try connecting to your Wi-Fi Direct device again by tapping Scan at the right side of the menu bar.

You should also check the Wi-Fi Alliance website to learn if your device is Wi-Fi Direct enabled. The Wi-Fi Alliance is a nonprofit group founded in 1999 that was formed to grow Wi-Fi acceptance in the marketplace, support industry standards, and provide a forum so Wi-Fi companies can collaborate and improve Wi-Fi technologies. You can begin searching for products that include Wi-Fi Direct functionality by opening the Internet app and then accessing the Certified Products page at https://www.wi-fi.org/certified-products-search.

# Printing Wirelessly

It's easy to print a file such as a word processing document or spreadsheet from your Galaxy Tab 4. You don't need any cables, and you don't need to transfer your files to another computer, either. However, there are some limitations to the printing functionality built into the Tab 4, but you can download apps and use web-based services to get around those limits.

## Connect a Wi-Fi Printer

Your Tab 4 automatically scans for wireless printers that are available through a Wi-Fi connection. Note that you might have to enable a Wi-Fi connection on the printer as well. For this example, I use my Hewlett-Packard (HP) Officejet Pro X576dw printer, which I refer to from here on out as the Officejet Pro. The Officejet Pro requires the user to enable HP Wireless Direct functionality on the printer before any device can see the printer.

1. Tap the Apps icon on the Home screen.

2. Tap Settings.

3. Connect to the printer by tapping the printer name in the Wi-Fi Networks list.

4. If you need to enter a password, type it in the window and then tap Connect.

5. The Tab 4 might take a few seconds to find the printer's IP address; after it does, the printer appears at the top of the Wi-Fi Networks list and displays the Connected status.

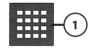

## What If the Tab 4 Can't Find My Wireless Printer?

If the Galaxy Tab 4 doesn't recognize your wireless printer, you might need to bring your Tab 4 closer to the printer. You can scan for the printer again by tapping Scan in the Settings menu bar that appears at the top of the screen. When the wireless printer appears in the Wi-Fi list, connect to the printer by tapping the printer name.

# Connect a Bluetooth Printer

If you have a Bluetooth printer, you can also connect that printer to your Galaxy Tab 4 so you can print wirelessly.

1. Tap the Apps icon on the Home screen.

2. Tap Settings.

**3.** Tap Bluetooth.

**4.** Swipe the slider button from left to right to turn on Bluetooth connectivity. The Tab 4 finds your printer.

**5.** Tap the printer name.

**6.** Type the printer PIN in the Bluetooth Pairing Request window using the keypad at the bottom of the screen. You will need to consult your printer documentation and/or the printer manufacturer's website to find the PIN. When you're finished, tap Done.

**7.** Tap OK.

**8.** The paired Bluetooth printer appears in the Paired Devices section.

**9.** Tap the Settings icon to the right of the printer name to change the printer name and unpair, or disconnect, the printer from the Tab 4.

# >>>Go Further

## DOWNLOAD A PRINT APP

Samsung boasts that you can print directly from within an app on your Galaxy Tab 4 to any compatible printer without having to connect to a Wi-Fi or Bluetooth printer. Unfortunately, what Samsung doesn't tell you is that you can only print to Samsung's printers. You find this out when you try to print from an app for the first time and see a "You can only print to a Samsung printer" message. Fortunately, there are apps available from the Google Play Store so you can print to other printers.

For example, if you have a Hewlett-Packard printer as I'm using in this example, you can download the HP ePrint app. You can also search for your printer manufacturer in the Google Play Store to see if a printing app is available. There are also apps available from the Play Store for printing to a variety of devices such as PrinterShare Mobile Print, which is free.

If you find a printing app in the Google Play Store that doesn't work for you (or doesn't work at all), another option is to use Google's Cloud Print service. This service connects your printers to the Web so any web-enabled device, including the Tab 4, can access a printer connected to Cloud Print. As of this writing, Google Cloud Print is still in beta test status, so be aware that the service's performance might not match your expectations.

You can access the Google Cloud Print website in the Internet app at www.google.com/cloudprint/learn. After you open the site, you're invited to log in using your Gmail account. After you log in, you can add a printer that's connected to a laptop or PC, or you can add a Cloud Ready printer that is a printer that connects directly to the Web.

**The Google Cloud Print website**

# Sharing Files

A "cloud storage" service enables you to upload files onto its server computers. Cloud storage services make it easy for you to share large files with others, especially because the maximum file attachment sizes in email messages can vary depending on the email service you use. And downloading email messages with large file attachments can take a long time, anyway.

## Use the Dropbox App

The Dropbox app came installed on your Galaxy Tab 4, and you might have set up your Dropbox account when you set up your Tab 4. You can give another Dropbox user access to one or more folders in your account so that other users can upload files to and download files from that folder. The Dropbox icon is available on the main Home screen and/or within the Apps screen.

## Add Galaxy Tab 4 Images to Dropbox and Create an Album

1. Swipe to the second Home screen and then tap Dropbox.

2. Tap Sign In in the Welcome to Dropbox screen.

3. Type your Dropbox email and password in the Email and Password fields.

4. Tap Sign In.

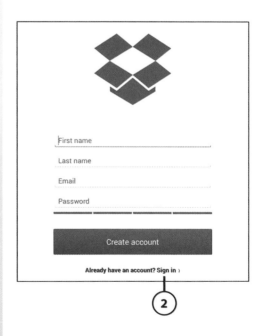

## What If I Don't Have a Dropbox Account?

If you need a Dropbox account, tap New to Dropbox? and create a free account at the bottom of the Dropbox login page. The app takes you step by step through setting up your account.

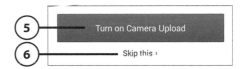

5. Tap Turn On Camera Upload (which is what this example does) to automatically upload all the images stored on your Galaxy Tab 4 to Dropbox.

6. Tap Skip This if you don't want to upload your images to Dropbox.

7. Swipe up and down in the Photos page to view all the photos that were uploaded to Dropbox.

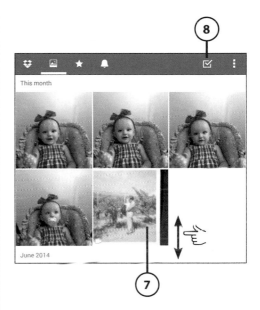

8. Tap the Select icon to add photos to an album.

9. Tap the photo(s) you want to add to the album. Selected photos contain a blue checkbox in the upper-right corner of the photo.

10. Tap Add to Album.

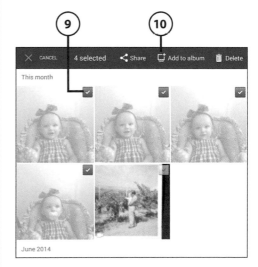

**11.** In the Add to Album window, tap Create New Album.

**12.** Type the name of your album in the Name Your Album field.

**13.** Tap Done in the keyboard. The completed album displays on the screen.

**14.** Tap Share Album to share a link to the album on your Dropbox account.

**15.** Tap the service or app you want to use to share the link. Tap See All at the bottom of the window to view all the services and apps.

**16.** For now, return to the album page by tapping on the screen outside the window and then tapping the Back touch button.

**17.** View your list of albums by tapping Albums.

**18.** View photos in the album within the album page by tapping the album name in the list.

**19.** Go to the Dropbox home screen by tapping the Dropbox icon in the menu bar.

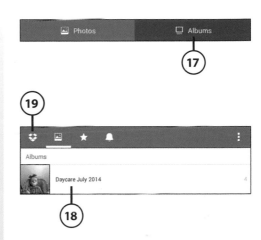

# View and Share Files in Dropbox

The Dropbox home screen contains all files and subfolders within the Dropbox folder.

**1.** View files within a folder by tapping the folder name in the list.

**2.** Swipe up and down in the screen to view all the files within the folder. When you find a file that you want to view, tap the file to view it. If the file is a photo or image file as in this example then the file opens within the built-in Dropbox image viewer.

3. After a couple of seconds, the menu bar at the top of the image disappears so you can view the image in its entirety. Open the menu again by tapping on the image.

4. Tap the Trash icon to delete the image from Dropbox.

5. Tap the Share icon to share a link to the file.

6. Tap the service or app you want to use to share the link in the Share a Link to This File message. For now, return to the image viewer screen by tapping the Back touch button.

7. Tap the Favorites icon to add the image file you're viewing to your Favorites folder and save the image file to your Tab 4 so you can access it when you don't have a Wi-Fi connection to your Dropbox account.

8. Tap the Menu icon so you can either open the file in another app (such as the image file) or export the file. You can export the file to an SD card, to a photo app, through a direct connection such as Bluetooth or Wi-Fi, in an email message, or on Google+.

9. Return to the folder page by tapping the Back touch button.

10. You can return to the main Dropbox folder by tapping Up to Dropbox at the top of the list or by tapping the Back touch button.

## Access Menu Options

1. The Dropbox home screen icon appears by default and the icon contains a white line under it, which indicates that the home page is active.

2. Tap the Photos icon to view, add, and delete photos and albums in your Dropbox account.

3. Tap the Favorites icon to view all the files you marked as favorites in the Favorites screen.

4. Tap the Alerts icon to view recent alerts from Dropbox, such as a new file added to one of your Dropbox folders.

5. Tap the Menu icon and then tap Search to search for files in Dropbox.

6. Type your search term(s) in the Search My Dropbox field.

7. Tap the Search button in the keyboard. Results display in the Search Dropbox screen.

8. Swipe up and down the screen to view all the files in the list. Tap on a file to view the contents on the screen.

9. Return to the Dropbox home screen by tapping the Back touch button.

10. Open a menu with more options by tapping the Menu icon in the menu bar.

11. Tap Upload Here so you can upload files to the current folder you're viewing.

12. Tap New Folder to add a new sub-folder within the current folder.

13. Tap New Text File so you can type a new text file within the New Text File screen. This new text file will appear in the folder and is useful if you want another Dropbox user who has access to the folder to read important information.

14. Tap Sort to change the sort order. The default is alphabetical order, but you can change the order to list files from newest at the top of the list to oldest at the bottom.

15. Tap Refresh to refresh the list of files and/or subfolders.

16. Tap Help to get answers to your most common questions about Dropbox.

17. Tap Upgrade Account to pay for an upgrade your Dropbox account, such as to the Dropbox Pro plan with 100GB of space.

18. Tap Settings to get information about your account, change your account settings, and learn more about Dropbox.

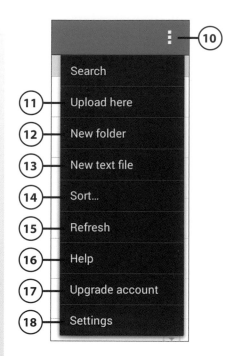

19. Tap Sign Out of Dropbox if you don't want to use Dropbox with your Tab 4 any longer but you still want to keep the Dropbox app.

20. Tap Turn Off Camera Upload to tell Dropbox not to upload anymore photos from the Tab 4.

21. Return to the Dropbox home screen by tapping the Dropbox icon in the menu bar.

## >>>Go Further
## GET MORE DROPBOX SPACE

The most important feature on the Settings screen is the amount of space used in the Space Used area. The default amount of space you receive is 3GB. When you run the Dropbox app for the first time you receive an email message inviting you to add 48GB to your total space so you have more than 51GB of space available for the next 12 months. After the 12-month period is over, you're asked to renew use of that space for a fee.

When you visit the Dropbox website (www.dropbox.com), you see different ways to add more space to your account—many of them free. For example, if you refer someone to Dropbox and that person signs up, you get 500MB of extra space per friend up to 16GB (that is, 32 friends). You can also purchase monthly plans starting at $9.99 per month for 100GB of space.

# Find Other Cloud Services

If you prefer to use another cloud storage app other than Dropbox, you can shop the Google Play Store for other cloud storage apps that are optimized for the Android operating system.

1. Tap Play Store on the Home screen.

2. Tap Apps.

3. Tap the Search icon in the menu bar.

4. Type **cloud storage** in the Search Google Play field.

5. Tap the search button in the keyboard.

6. Swipe up and down within the list of apps in the search results screen. Tap a tile to view more information about the app. You learn more about shopping for apps in the Play Store in Chapter 16, "Finding and Managing Apps."

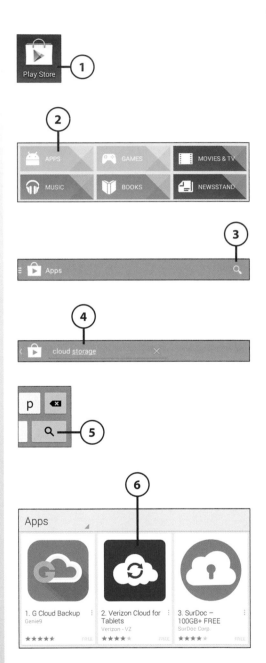

# Sharing Music and Video

There are a number of ways you can share your music and video between different devices or between your computer and your Galaxy Tab 4. If you have a computer that runs Windows, you can connect the Tab 4 to your computer and copy files with Windows Media Player. You can also connect your Tab 4 to your Windows computer and tell Windows that your Tab 4 is a storage device. One other alternative is to connect your PC or Mac to your Tab 4 using Samsung's free Kies application.

## Copy Files with Windows Media Player

When you connect your Galaxy Tab 4 to your PC with the data cable, you can choose how you want to connect and/or synchronize media files with your Tab 4. One option is to sync your computer and your Tab 4 with Windows Media Player. This example connects the Tab 4 to a PC running Windows 8.1.

1. Connect the data cable from the Tab 4 to the USB port on your computer. An AutoPlay window opens.

2. Click the window and then click Sync Digital Media Files to this Device: Windows Media Player in the list.

**3.** Tap the Sync tab within the Windows Media Player window.

**4.** Click and drag the song title(s) you want to copy to the Sync list.

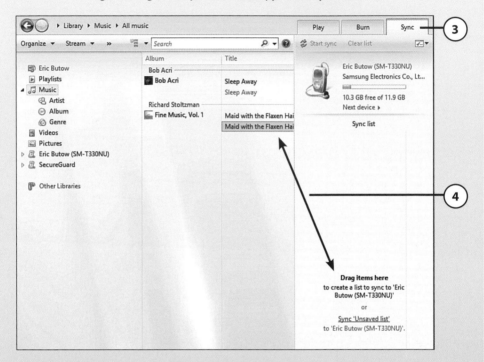

**5.** The list of music you select appears in the Sync list. All tracks in the albums are selected by default. You can deselect any songs that you do not want to copy by right-clicking the song and clicking Remove from List.

**6.** Tap Start Sync to begin copying the files from your PC to your Galaxy Tab.

7.  After sync is complete, the music is available for playback when you tap the Music app on your Tab 4.

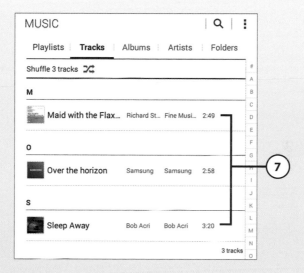

## Connect as a Mass Storage Device

You can drag and drop files from a PC to your Galaxy Tab 4 by connecting as a removable disk. Follow these steps to transfer music from your PC to your Tab 4.

1.  Connect the data cable to the Tab 4 and the USB connector to the USB port on your computer. An AutoPlay window opens.

2.  Click the window and then click Open Device to View Files: File Explorer in the list.

3. Your Tab 4 appears as a removable disk in the Computer section within the File Explorer window.

4. Display the home Tablet directory by clicking the folder name in the tree.

5. Locate the files that you want to transfer from your computer and then drag them to the Music folder on your Tab 4. The files are copied to your device.

6. After you have finished copying files to your Tab from your computer, remove the USB cable from the PC.

7. When you open the Music app on your Tab, the music you have transferred is available for playback.

## >>>Go Further
### CONNECTING TO A MAC

You need extra software to connect your Tab to a Mac. Android File Transfer is an application for Macs running OS X 10.5 or later that enables you to view and transfer files between your Mac and Galaxy Tab 4. This application works with Android devices running Android 3.0 or later. You can download Android File Transfer from www.android.com/filetransfer/.

## Samsung Kies for PCs and Macs

The Samsung Kies application makes it easy for you to manage your music, movies, and photos between your computer and your Galaxy Tab 4. When you connect your Tab to your PC or Mac, Samsung Kies acts much like iTunes and Windows Media Player, enabling you to sync your content libraries.

### PC and Mac Interfaces
The Multimedia Sync interface is slightly different in PC and Mac versions. You can perform these first few steps on either version, regardless of a few interface differences. The following steps are demonstrated on a PC running Windows 8.1.

1. After you have installed Samsung Kies onto your computer, connect your Tab to your PC or Mac.

2. Launch Samsung Kies on your computer. Your Tab 4 opens under the Connected devices list in the sidebar on the left side of the window.

## Kies Says It Needs an Update

When you start Kies, the app automatically checks the Samsung website to see if there are any updates available. The Galaxy Tab 4 requires Kies version 3, and if you have an older version of Kies installed, then the app displays a window asking you to upgrade. Begin the installation process by clicking the OK button and then go through the steps in the installation wizard app to install Kies 3. After the app is installed, you have the option of starting Kies 3 from the installation wizard.

3. If this is your first time using Samsung Kies, you need to populate the library with music located on your computer. Click Music under Library.

4. Click the Add Music File button.

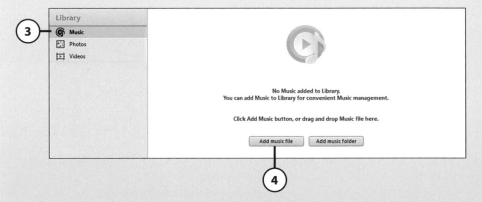

5. Go to the Music folder on your PC and select one or more files; when you're done, click the Open button.

**5**

6.   View the album titles without the covers by clicking on the Titles button.

7.   Select files by clicking the check boxes to the left of the titles.

8.   Click the Transfer to Device button.

9. After Kies copies the file(s) to your Tab 4 successfully, a message appears in the status bar.

10. Click the Music folder under Connected Devices.

11. The copied files appear in your Music directory within Kies and on your Tab 4.

12. Click the Tab 4 name in the Connected Devices list.

13. Click the Sync tab.

14. Select the content that you want to sync to your Tab 4. As soon as you click the check box for a category, you are able to select all content for that category or select only specific content.

15. Click Sync. The content is synced to your Tab 4.

## It's Not All Good

**Usage Restrictions**

Some of the music in your Library is Digital Rights Management (DRM) protected, which means use of those files has been restricted. These music files are from a time when music was not DRM free on iTunes. You won't be able to transfer these songs without upgrading them for a fee. Visit the iTunes Store for more information.

**Search for locations and get directions**

**Receive turn-by-turn GPS navigation and
voice-command directions**

**Locate businesses and quickly receive
more information about them**

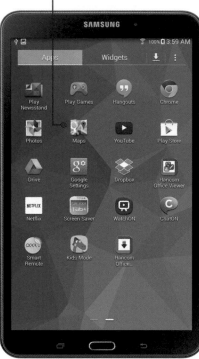

**Share locations
with friends**

In this chapter, you find out how to use the Maps app to find locations, get directions, and connect with friends. Topics include:

→ Enabling GPS
→ Getting around with maps
→ Getting voice-command directions
→ Finding local information
→ Enabling wireless networks
→ Sharing locations with Google+ friends

# Using Maps

Your Galaxy Tab 4 is equipped with the Maps app that can help you get where you need to go. In Android 4.4 (or KitKat, if you prefer), the Maps app is one comprehensive app that combines several apps that were previously separate in earlier versions of Android:

- The app can supply detailed destination directions for a specific address.

- The app can provide voice-guided turn-by-turn directions to a location.

- You can also use Maps to quickly locate local businesses and access contact information, coupons, and customer reviews.

What's more, the Google+ app enables you to share your location with Google+ friends and view their locations on a map.

# Enabling GPS

Before you can begin to use the many features of your Galaxy Tab 4 that utilize GPS, you must first enable your Tab's GPS capabilities.

1. Open the Quick Settings and Notifications page by tapping and holding on the Status Bar at the top of the page and then swiping down the screen.

2. Tap Location into the on position if it isn't on already. The icon turns green and a green bar appears beneath the setting to indicate that GPS is on.

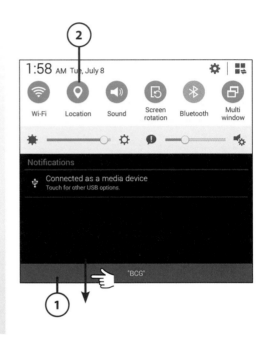

# Getting Around with Maps

Maps is great when you're planning a trip across town or the nation. You can change your map view by adding layers that include traffic, terrain, satellite imagery, transit lines, and more. You do not even have to have an address for Maps to help you get where you need to go. Just specify the general area on a map and let the Maps app generate directions.

# Find a Location with Maps

The Maps app on your Galaxy Tab 4 gives you the capability to find locations, get directions, and pinpoint locations. It also gives you access to features in other apps, such as Navigation, Local, and Location Sharing. The Maps app can help you pinpoint your exact location if you ever find yourself in an unfamiliar place. As soon as you launch Maps, your Tab uses GPS to pinpoint your current location.

1. Tap the Apps icon on the Home screen.

2. Swipe to the second page in the Apps screen and then tap Maps.

3. Tap the Accept & Continue button.

4. Tap Yes, I'm In if you want Google to improve your search suggestions. A map displaying your current location opens.

5. Tap the Search field at the top of the screen to find a location. If you see a message asking you to store your personal data on the Tab 4, tap OK.

6. Type the address of the location you want to find. As you type, a list of possible locations displays.

7. Tap the correct address in the list. Your Tab 4 displays the location on the map. If you cannot find the address you need in the list, Maps might not have complete data for that area or the information Google Maps has might be outdated.

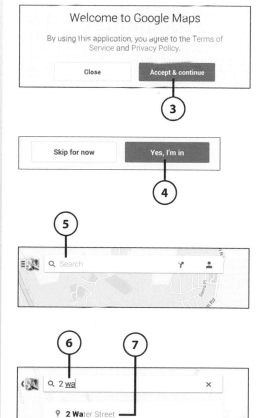

## It's Not All Good

### Inaccurate or Incomplete Data

The Maps application is not always correct. Some of the directions and navigation data that it presents might be inaccurate or incomplete due to change over time. Complete information might not be available for some locations. Always use your best personal judgment and pay attention to road signs, landmarks, traffic conditions, and closures when following directions generated on your Tab 4.

8. Tap the location overlay.

9. Tap Save to save this location for future searches. There are many options you can access from this window including Share, Directions, and Street View.

10. Tap the Google Maps icon to close the window.

11. Tap the Google Maps icon to add additional layers of information to the current map.

12. Tap the layer of information that you want to add to the map in the menu. The information is added to the map, changing the map view.

### Switching Map Views

You can view a location map as a satellite image by tapping Satellite in the menu. You can also overlay a traffic, public transit, or bicycling layer on top of the map or satellite image.

13. Pinch outward to enlarge the
    map. You can also double-tap
    your finger in a specific location
    on the map to enlarge the area.
    As you move in closer on the
    map, you start to notice that new
    information appears in the map,
    such as the names of banks and
    restaurants.

14. Use your finger to physically move
    the map and pinpoint locations.

# Get Directions
# with Maps

Maps can help you get from point
A to point B by providing detailed
directions. You can get step-by-step
driving, public transportation, biking,
and walking directions to a specified
destination by designating addresses
for a starting location and a desired
destination.

1. Tap the Apps icon on the Home
   screen, swipe to the second page
   on the Apps screen, and then
   tap the Maps icon. A street map
   opens and displays your current
   location as a blue dot.

2. Tap the Directions icon.

3. By default, your Tab 4 is able to pinpoint your current location, which appears as My Location in the top field. You can also type a different starting address in the top field. As you type, suggested addresses appear in a list below the box; you can tap an address in the list to place that address in the box.

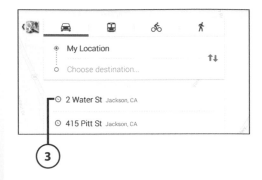

4. By default, the address you searched for appears in the End Point box. You can change the address by tapping in the box and typing a new address. As you type, suggested addresses appear in a list below the box; tap an address in the list to place that address in the box.

5. By default, the car button is selected so you can determine how long your trip will take by car. You can also select how long the trip will take by bus, bicycle, or walking.

**Tap to get route options**

6. Tap the estimated travel time to receive directions. A screen of detailed directions appears as a list. The estimated travel time appears above the list.

## Bookmarking Locations

Each time you generate directions within maps, they are bookmarked and appear underneath the My Location field with a pencil icon to the left of the address or contact name. To use these bookmarked directions, tap the location for which you want to generate directions.

7.  Swipe up and down the Directions list to move through each step in the directions.

8.  Tap any step in the directions to review it on the map.

## >>>Go Further

## UPDATING/MODIFYING DIRECTIONS

After Maps generates the directions, you can instruct Maps to generate new directions that avoid highways and toll roads. Tap Route Options that appears underneath the destination location to designate which options you want. Tap OK for updated directions.

# Specify Locations with Maps

Maps can help you find locations for which you do not have an address. For example, you might know that a café that you would like to visit is located downtown, but you do not know how to get downtown from your hotel. Maps enables you to specify a vicinity on a map where you want to go and generates directions from your current location.

1. Tap the Apps icon on the Home screen, swipe to the second page in the Apps screen, and then tap the Maps icon.

2. Use your finger to move the map to your desired location and then tap and hold on the location until the pin appears on the location.

3. Tap the location address.

## It's Not All Good

### Current Location Unavailable

Occasionally, your Tab might not be able to pinpoint your current location because of lack of area coverage or a temporary disruption in the system. If for some reason Maps gives you the "Your Current Location Is Temporarily Unavailable" warning, you might have to enter your location by hand.

**4.** The location appears on the map so you can save the location, share it with someone else, or get driving directions. Tap the car icon to get driving directions.

**5.** Get driving directions by tapping the estimated travel time.

**6.** Swipe up and down the Directions list to move through each step in the directions.

**7.** Tap any step in the directions to review it on the map.

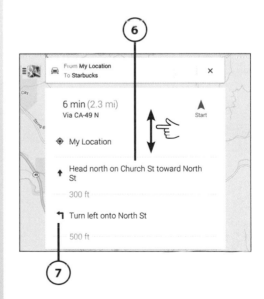

# Getting Voice-Command Directions

After you get driving directions, you can turn your Galaxy Tab into a turn-by-turn voice-command GPS device using the Maps app.

1. Tap the Apps icon on the Home screen.

2. Swipe to the second page in the Apps screen and then tap Maps.

3. Tap the Directions icon.

4. Type the name of the destination for which you need directions in the Choose Destination field or select your destination from the list below the field.

5. If you type the destination, a list of possible destinations appears in the list; tap the correct destination.

6. A street map appears with a high-lighted route; tap the estimated travel time to your destination.

7. If you have a vehicle mount in your car, attach the Tab 4 to the vehicle mount. Appendix A, "Finding Galaxy Tab 4 Accessories," has more information about vehicle mounts.

8. Tap Start in the directions list.

9. Drive the route. Much like a dedicated GPS, your Tab senses where you are on the route and proceeds to give you instructions, verbally and graphically.

10. Tap the Menu button to view more options.

11. Tap Alternate Routes to view information about the route and alternative routes, respectively.

12. Tap Step-by-Step List to view directions as a step-by-step list.

13. Return to the map by tapping the Back touch button.

14. Return to the step-by-step directions list and map by tapping the Close button in the menu bar.

## Exploring Route Options

You can access alternative routes by tapping Alternate Routes. You can compare different route options by reviewing their distances in miles as well as overall travel times and highlighted map routes. View more information about the alternative route by tapping the route travel time on the screen.

# >>>*Go Further*
## VIEWING THE MAP

You can find the current step in the directions in the green bar at the top of the screen. Within each direction entry in the list you can view the direction you are supposed to travel in the current step by tapping the right arrow button at the right side of the green bar. Then you see the distance on the black bar at the top of the screen that gives you the estimated traveling distance for completing the step and the direction to take when you complete the step. Directions take the form of a left turn arrow, straight arrow, right arrow, or a U turn. Tap the left arrow icon to move to the previous step or the right arrow icon to move to the next step.

**The direction you will turn upon completion of the step**

**The miles to travel to complete the step**

**The direction to turn on the map**

**Your route on the map**

**15.** Tap to view the options menu list.

**16.** Tap to overlay a traffic status layer on the map.

**17.** Tap to overlay a public transit route layer on the map.

**18.** Tap to overlay a bicycling route layer on the map.

**19.** Tap to view a location map as a satellite image.

**20.** Tap to overlay a 3D geographic terrain and altitude information layer on the map.

**21.** Tap to download the Google Earth app and then view your map within the app.

**22.** Tap Settings to view your account information; edit your home or work address; change location information; view your maps history; change distance units; send feedback; get tutorials and help; and to read the terms, privacy policy, and notice information.

**23.** Tap to launch tutorials and help for the app.

**24.** Tap to send feedback about the app to Google.

**25.** Tap to play a map trivia game on the Google Maps Smarty Pins website within the Internet or Chrome browser.

**26.** Tap to get quick tips and tricks about using the Maps app.

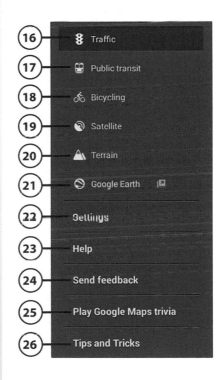

# Finding Local Information

The Maps app enables you to locate places of interest and retrieve information, such as addresses, hours of operation, and phone numbers for those places. You can use Local to pinpoint the exact locations of restaurants, bars, ATMs, gas stations, and more, or you can create a new location, such as a pharmacy or hospital. The Maps app offers a great way to explore nearby areas with which you might not be familiar.

1. Tap the Apps icon on the Home screen.

2. Swipe to the second page in the Apps screen and then tap Maps.

3. Tap the Directions icon.

4. Type the name of the destination for which you need directions in the Choose Destination field or select your destination from the list below the field.

5. A street map appears with a highlighted route; close the route information by tapping the Close icon.

6. Tap the Search field.

7. The most recent place you searched appears at the top of the list underneath the Search field. You can display a list of related establishments in and around that place by tapping the category name in the Explore Nearby window. For this example I tapped Eat to find restaurants.

8. Swipe up and down to view all the results in various categories. At the bottom of each category tile, view all the results in the category by tapping View More from This List.

9. Swipe up and down the list to view all the results. When you want to find more information about an establishment, tap the appropriate tile.

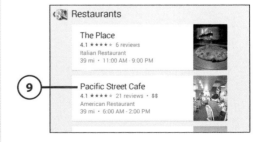

10. The business type, address, and hours of operation appear underneath the business name.

11. Tap Save to save this location for future searches.

12. Tap Share to share information about this business to other users on Dropbox, ChatON, email or Gmail, via a Bluetooth or Wi-Fi Direct connection, Flipboard, Google+, Google Hangout, to your Google Drive account, to the clipboard, or in a memo.

13. Tap to get driving directions to the business location.

14. The aggregated review ranking based on the number of written reviews appears in the Review Summary tile. Ratings vary from 1 star (bad) to 5 stars (great).

15. Tap to view a map of the location on the entire screen.

16. Swipe down the screen to view more options.

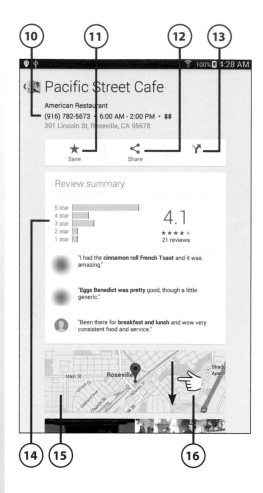

**17.** Tap to open the business website in the Internet or Chrome browser app.

**18.** If you're viewing a restaurant and a menu is available, tap to view the menu in the Internet or Chrome browser app.

**19.** Tap to get more information about the business.

**20.** Tap to report a problem with the business so Google can update the business entry in Google Maps. For example, if the business listing has the wrong contact details you can send the correct details to Google. You can also ask Google to notify you when the problem has been resolved so you can check the revised listing for accuracy.

**21.** Tap to rate and review the business. Your review will be read by other Google Maps users who are interested in visiting the business. Swipe down the screen to read other user reviews.

**22.** Return to the map by tapping the Google Maps icon.

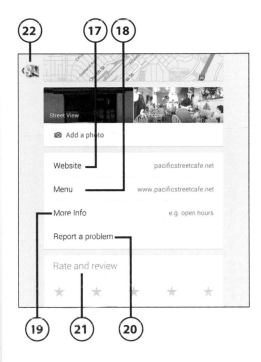

# Sharing Locations with Friends

The Google Maps app enables you to see the location of your Google+ friends on a map or as a list. You can set up Google+ to share your location with individual friends or circles of friends.

## Where Can I Learn More About Google+?

If you want to learn how to use the Google+ social networking site beyond the specific application discussed in this section, refer to Chapter 15, "Using Apps for Learning, Creating, and Sharing."

1. Tap the Apps icon on the Home screen.

2. Tap Google+.

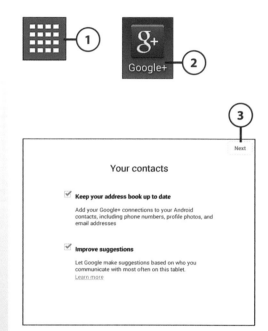

3. By default the Google+ app adds your Google+ contacts to your Contacts database on the Tab 4, and the app also makes suggestions about using Google+ more effectively based on who you communicate with using the Tab 4. Tap Next.

4. Tap Done to back up the photos stored on your Galaxy Tab 4 onto Google+.

### I Don't See the Screens in Steps 3 and 4

If you don't see the screens shown in Steps 3 and 4, that means you've already set up Google+. In this case, after you tap the Google+ icon you will see your news feed on the Google+ screen.

5. Tap the Google+ icon.

6. Tap Locations.

7. Tap the Menu button in the menu bar and then tap Location Settings.

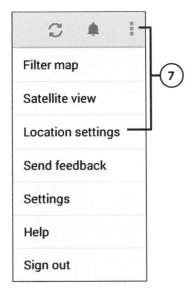

8.  Tap Choose People to Share With in the Pinpoint Location tile if you want to share your exact location with others.

9.  Alternatively, tap Edit in the City Location tile if you only want to share your city. This example uses the city location.

10. Swipe up and down in the screen to view the circles and individual friends with whom you want to share your location information.

11. Select a circle or friend by tapping the check box to the right of the circle or friend name.

12. The circles and friends you added appear above the circles list.

13. Tap Done when you've made all your selections.

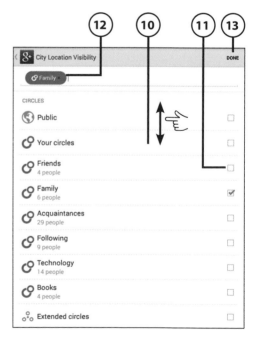

**14.** The City Location tile reflects the sharing changes you made.

**15.** Return to the map page in Google+ by tapping the Google+ icon in the menu bar.

**16.** The name and photo of the person who appears nearest you and is sharing his contact information appears at the bottom of the screen. The information includes the person's current location and how long ago the person checked in at that location.

**17.** The person's photo appears above the person's current location in the map.

**18.** See a list of more contacts who are sharing their locations by tapping the Contact icon.

City Location ⓘ

Sharing with:
Family and Friends

Edit

⑭

⑮

| 8+ | Location Sharing |

⑰

⑱

Eric Butow
Jackson, CA, USA
51m ago

⑯

19. Tap the name of a person in the list.

20. The person's current location appears on the map and more information about the person appears at the bottom of the screen.

>>>*Go Further*

## INVITING MORE PEOPLE TO SHARE THEIR LOCATIONS

If you want to find out where someone is currently but that person isn't sharing their location, you can ask that person to share her location by tapping Invite More People in the Sharing Location with You window. In the message composition screen is a default message so you can select the circle(s) or friend(s) to whom you want to send the invitation. Your message will be sent to all your recipient(s) on Google+.

**Browse, manage, and share photos**

**Capture photos**

**Edit and share photos**

In this chapter, you find out how to capture photos and screenshots, share photos via email and slideshows, and view and manage photos with Gallery:

→ Using the camera

→ Navigating Image Viewer

→ Tips for capturing photos

→ Working with Gallery

→ Editing and sharing images

→ Performing screen captures

# Capturing and Managing Photos

Along with transferring images from other sources, such as your computer or microSD card, to your Galaxy Tab 4, you can also take high-quality photos with your Tab 4, which can house thousands of photos organized in categories. You also have the capability to take screenshots of the Tab's interface.

Your Tab's high-resolution screen offers a great way to showcase photos to friends and family, but you don't have to stop there. You can also use Photo Editor and Photo Studio, which are accessible from Gallery, to perform basic photo edits. You can even share pictures via AllShare, Bluetooth, Gmail, Picasa, and more.

# Using the Camera

All Galaxy Tab 4 models use a 3.0 megapixel rear-facing camera located on the back of the device to take photos along with a 1.3 megapixel front-facing camera that you can use for self-portraits.

Taking a photo can be as simple as choosing a subject, composing your shot, and pressing a button. The Galaxy Tab 4 is also equipped with some helpful features commonly found on dedicated photo cameras, including shooting modes, scene modes, manual exposure, white balance, flash, manual exposure, and ISO settings.

1. On the Home screen, swipe from right to left to open the second page on the Home screen, and then tap Camera.

2. If you have a microSD card inserted, you can either tap OK to change the storage settings to the SD Card or tap Cancel to use your Tab's storage to store photos and videos.

3. Tap the right arrow icon to customize camera quick settings.

---

### Order of Menu Options Differs

If you are using the Tab 4 7.0, it is important to note that the order within the Settings menu is slightly different than what is described here.

---

4. Five icons appear underneath the Settings icon so you can customize the first five camera setting shortcuts in the menu: Timer, Brightness Control, Recording, Share, and Viewfinder Ratio. The Viewfinder Ratio features changes the display proportion of the photo on the screen between 16:9 (the default) and 4:3, but does not change the size or proportion of the photo itself.

5. You can swap out these settings with others that appear when you tap and hold a shortcut icon for a second or two. After you release your finger, the list of settings appears in the window underneath the five setting shortcut icons. Just drag a new setting on top of an old one to replace it.

6. Tap the Back touch button after you've finished replacing your quick setting icons.

7. Change the scene mode by tapping the Mode button.

8. Swipe back and forth between the tiles; the selected tile appears at the top of the tile stack and a description of the mode appears above the tile for a few seconds. The default mode is Auto.

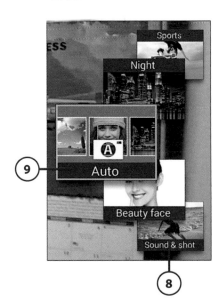

9. Tap the mode tile you want to use.

## >>>Go Further
## EXPLORING SCENE MODES

The scene mode options optimize your camera for special shooting situations. For example, Panorama mode enables you to take a picture and then use the onscreen guide to move the viewfinder and take seven more shots. This is a great mode for capturing wide vistas, such as landscapes and cityscapes.

Night mode uses a flash in combination with a slow shutter speed to brighten dark backgrounds. Sports mode uses a fast shutter speed to capture moving subjects without blurring.

**10.** Tap the Settings icon.

**11.** Tap the Settings icon in the window.

**12.** Tap Location Tag to enable or disable GPS tagging of the photos you capture. Embedded GPS information can come in handy if you use a photo-editing and managing application such as iPhoto 9 and later, which enables you to use the location information to manage and showcase photos.

**13.** Tap Review to turn the review screen off or on. If Review is turned on, then you see a preview of the photo or video you just shot in the Review screen.

**14.** Tap Volume Key to determine if the volume key acts as the zoom key or the Camera/Recording key. The default is the zoom key.

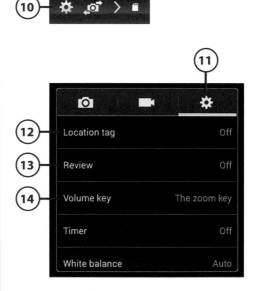

15. Tap Timer to designate how long the Tab should wait before the camera takes a picture. This is great when you want to set up the shot and then place yourself in the frame.

16. Tap to adjust the white balance for the camera. The white balance features help accurately reproduce colors when you are shooting in various lighting situations so that neutral colors, such as white and gray, are truly neutral and all colors are rendered without undesired color casts.

17. Swipe down the list to view more options.

18. Tap Guidelines to enable or disable an onscreen grid that can help you with composition.

19. Tap Contextual Filename to enable or disable the ability to include your Tab 4 GPS information in the photo or video filename.

20. Tap Save as Flipped to horizontally flip a photo taken with the front camera, which eliminates the "mirror" effect.

21. An image that is too light or too dark degrades the appearance of your photos. To take full advantage of the camera feature of the Tab 4, you must adjust the brightness level for various bright or dark lighting conditions. Tap Brightness.

**22.** Drag the brightness level up to achieve a proper level in a low-light shooting environment, or drag it down for a very bright shooting environment.

**23.** When you're finished changing the exposure level, the brightness slider bar disappears after a couple of seconds. Return to the Settings menu by tapping the Settings icon as you did in Step 9.

**24.** Swipe down the list until you can tap Storage to determine whether the photos you capture are stored on an optional memory card or on your Tab.

**25.** Tap to reset the Camera settings to the default settings.

**26.** Tap to get some quick onscreen help for the Camera app.

**27.** Tap the Camera icon.

**28.** Tap to set how the camera measures or meters the light source. This setting determines how the camera factors light in a scene to achieve the proper exposure.

**29.** Return to the Viewer by tapping the Back touch button.

**30.** Tap to switch between the rear-facing and front-facing cameras.

**31.** Compose the subject in the Viewer. By default, Camera automatically focuses on what is in the center of the Viewer.

**32.** Hold your finger on the Camera button, level the shot, and then remove your finger from the button to capture the image. A thumbnail of the image appears in the Image Viewer.

**33.** Tap the Image Viewer to review the image you just captured. You can also access your photos by tapping the Gallery icon under Applications from any Home screen.

**33**

>>>*Go Further*

## TALKING ABOUT CENTER-WEIGHTED AND SPOT METERING

The default Metering setting is Center Weighted. Your other choices are Matrix, which measures light intensity in several points to achieve the best exposure, and Spot, where only a small area in the scene is measured. Matrix metering is usually considered the most accurate form of metering because it measures the entire scene and then sets the exposure according to an average. Spot measuring is generally used to capture very high contrast scenes, such as when a subject's back is to the sun.

# Navigating Image Viewer

Image Viewer provides a quick-and-easy way to review the photos that you have just taken. It also enables you to quickly share your pictures as soon as you capture them or set them as wallpaper. You can also edit and delete unwanted photos in Image Viewer.

As soon as you take a picture, a thumbnail of that photo appears next to the camera button. You can tap that thumbnail to review the picture you have taken and browse other photos.

1. Tap the Image Viewer to review the image.

2. The image opens full screen, the controls appear, and then they fade away. Tap the middle of the screen to access the controls again.

3. Tap the AllShare Play icon to share your photo with another device that has an AllShare Play account.

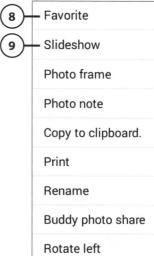

4. Tap the Share Via icon to access many options for sharing your photos through services such as Group Play, ChatON, Dropbox, Wi-Fi Direct, Picasa, Google+, Flipboard, Hangouts, Bluetooth, Gmail, and email. The button next to the Share Via icon displays the last option you used to share photos.

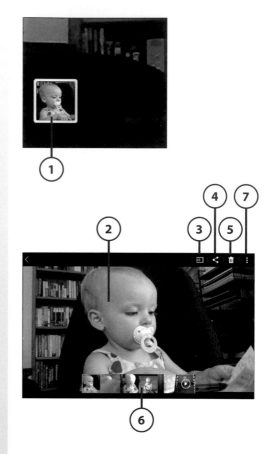

5. Tap to delete the currently displayed photo.

6. Flick the image from left to right or tap the thumbnail representations of photos at the bottom of the screen to navigate through all the photos you have captured.

7. Tap the Menu icon to access more options.

8. Tap Favorite to add the photo to your Favorites album. If the photo is already one of your favorites then tap Unfavorite to remove the photo from your Favorites album.

9. Tap to begin a slideshow of your photos. After the slideshow begins, you can tap anywhere onscreen to end the slideshow.

| 8 — | Favorite |
| 9 — | Slideshow |
| | Photo frame |
| | Photo note |
| | Copy to clipboard. |
| | Print |
| | Rename |
| | Buddy photo share |
| | Rotate left |

**10.** Tap to edit your photo and place it within a frame image.

**11.** Tap to edit your photo to make it look like the back of a printed photo.

**12.** Tap to copy the current image to the clipboard.

**13.** Tap to print the photo, such as to a Bluetooth printer.

**14.** Tap to give the currently displayed image a new name.

**15.** Tap to share the photo using face detection.

**16.** Swipe down the list to view more options.

**17.** Tap to rotate the photo to the left.

**18.** Tap to rotate the photo to the right.

**19.** Tap to crop the currently displayed photo.

**20.** Tap Set As to set the current picture as a contact photo, Home and lock screens, lock screen, or wallpaper.

**21.** Tap to view details about the photo including the time it was taken, aperture, and exposure settings upon capture.

**22.** Tap to view and change more Camera app settings.

**23.** Close the menu by tapping the Back touch button.

**24.** With the menu closed, double-tap the image to enlarge it. You can double-tap it again to return it to its normal size. You can also touch the screen with two fingers and then move them apart to enlarge an image.

**25.** Tap the Back touch button to return to the Camera app and take more pictures.

(24)

# Tips for Capturing Photos

Shutter lag is the amount of time that elapses between your press of the shutter release button and the moment the picture is captured. A longer shutter lag is common among most compact cameras and also the Galaxy Tab 4. What this means for you is that is that you have to be particularly mindful of timing your shots when recording moving subjects. Shutter lag can cause you to miss out on a key action if you do not anticipate the shot.

One important thing to know about your Tab is that the shutter does not fire as you place your finger down on the Camera button; the shutter fires when you lift your finger off the button. Use this knowledge to your advantage by pressing your finger on the shutter button and holding while you frame the shot and focus on an object about the same distance as where the subject will pass, to anticipate the shot, and then lift your finger. This means you need to hold your Tab completely still for a little bit longer. Anticipating moving subjects to capture dynamic, moving shots can take some practice.

The Galaxy Tab's slow shutter makes it prone to producing blurry photos if you do not remain perfectly still during capture. Even the smallest movement can have an adverse effect on your photographs; this is especially true in low-light situations. A photo might appear to be fine when you review it on the Tab display, but when you download it and view it on a larger display, you can see the problem.

# Working with Gallery

Gallery offers a more robust photo and video management system than Image Viewer, but it has similar options for viewing, sharing, and editing photos.

## Manage Photos with Gallery

By default, you can access the Gallery icon by flicking the main Home screen from left to right, or you can access it from the Apps menu.

1.  Tap Gallery on the Home screen.

2.  Content is arranged in categories/albums. If you have downloaded videos, such as video podcasts or recorded videos, with your Tab and transferred images from your computer, they are in here, too. Tap the Camera icon to access the Camera feature from Gallery.

3.  Tap the Albums menu to group your photos and videos in other ways. The name of this particular menu changes depending on which grouping method you have selected.

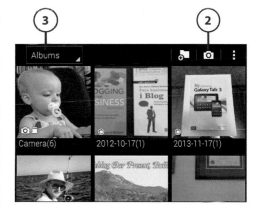

4. Tap the Albums option to arrange photos based on the folder in which they are stored.

5. Tap All to arrange all photos on the Galaxy Tab 4 based on the time they were captured from newest to oldest; the newest photos appear at the top of the screen.

6. Tap Time to arrange photos based on the time they were captured. The most recent photos appear in the row at the bottom of the screen.

7. Tap Locations to arrange photos based on their GPS location.

8. Tap People to arrange photos based on pictures where a face was detected.

9. Tap Favorites to arrange photos in your Favorites album.

10. Close the menu by tapping the Back touch button.

11. Tap the Menu icon.

12. Tap to select one or more complete albums to stream to another device, share, or delete. On the Gallery home screen, you can also hold your finger on an album cover photo for a few seconds to select it.

13. Tap to view a slideshow of photos. The first frame of any video that you have shot also plays in the slideshow. You can tap the screen again to stop the slideshow.

14. Tap to view all albums by All Content, Content in Device, Content in Dropbox, Content in Facebook, or Content in Picasa.

15. Tap to share photos with nearby devices, such as a friend's smartphone.

16. Close the menu by tapping the Back touch button.

17. Tap an album to view all photos in it.

18. After you have captured many photos and videos, the thumbnail representation of images in this category becomes long. Flick the screen up and down to view all thumbnails in the album.

19. Tap the Camera icon to capture another photo.

20. Tap the Menu icon to reveal the options Select Item and Slideshow. Select Item enables you to select one or more items that you want to stream to another device, share, or delete. The Slideshow option enables you to view a slideshow of pictures within the album.

21. Touch and hold your finger to a photo to reveal more Gallery options.

22. To delete images within an album, touch each image you want to delete (the check box in the upper-right corner of the image is checked) and then tap the Trash icon.

**Select all photos within the album**

23. You can touch the number of selected images to reveal the option to Select All photos in the album.

24. Tap the Menu icon and then tap Slideshow to show your selected photos as a slideshow.

25. Tap to copy or move your photos to a different album or to your external SD card.

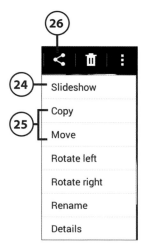

26. Tap the Share icon to view options for sharing the displayed image with friends and family via ChatON, Dropbox, to another device using a Bluetooth connection, your Google Drive account, email, or post the photo or video on your Flipboard account. Swipe down the window to view more sharing options including Gmail, Google+, Hangouts, placing the photo or video in a memo, sharing in the Picasa and Photos apps, or sharing with another device using a Wi-Fi Direct connection.

**27.** Turn off the image selection feature by tapping the Back touch button, and then tap a photo in the album to open it full screen.

## Viewing the Tag Buddy Window

You might see the Tag Buddy window that tells you if you tag someone in a picture then some information, such as the location, person's name, and the picture date, will appear briefly when you view the picture. Close this window for good by tapping the Do Not Show Again check box and then tapping the OK button.

**28.** Touch the middle of the screen to reveal the controls and then tap the left arrow icon in the menu bar to return to the previous screen.

# Email Photos from Gallery

Emailing your photos to friends and family can be accomplished in just a few taps on your Galaxy Tab 4.

1. Open the album that has the photo you want to email, and then touch and hold your finger to that photo to access more Gallery options.

2. Touch more photos that you want to share. A green check mark appears within the check box that appears in the upper-right corner of each photo, letting you know that it is selected. Email providers have varying file size limitations, so make sure you are aware of your provider's limitations before emailing photographs.

3. Tap the Share icon to access the options in the Share Via menu. You can access these same Share options even if you are viewing a single photo in full screen mode.

## Additional Sharing Options

Keep in mind that as you add an email account or Facebook account on your Tab 4, those options also display in the Share Via menu.

4. Tap the Gmail app icon or Email. This example uses Gmail. The Gmail application opens with the images you selected attached. Note that you don't see the actual images but an image icon with the image filename and size.

5. Tap the X located at the bottom-right corner of a photo to remove the attachment. Keep in mind that you do not have the option to attach a new image at this stage, if you choose to remove an attachment.

6. Type the recipient's email address into the To field. If you see the name of the recipient in the drop down list as you type, tap the name of the recipient. After you add a recipient to the list, you can add another one by typing the recipient name; you don't need any separator characters, such as a semicolon.

7. Tap in the Subject field and then type a subject for the email.

8. Tap in the Compose Email field to compose a message.

9. Tap Send to send the message.

## >>>Go Further
### EMAILING FROM CAMERA

You can also email a photo from Camera within Image View. After you tap the Camera button to capture the image, a thumbnail of the image appears in the Image Viewer. Tap the Image Viewer to review the image, and then tap the Share icon to access your email. Email providers have varying file size limitations, so make sure you are aware of your provider's limitations before emailing photographs.

# Creating Screen Captures

You Galaxy Tab 4 has a very helpful feature that enables you to take screen captures of its interface. The ability to take screenshots can come in handy for educational purposes, especially if you want to post a few Galaxy Tab tips online.

1. Open the screen that you want to take the screen shot of and position the Tab into the orientation in which you want to grab the screen capture: vertical or horizontal.

2. Press and hold the Power button and Home button at the same time. You hear the shutter sound effect as it takes the screen capture.

3. The screenshot is saved to the Screenshots folder in the Gallery app, and the image is also saved to the clipboard.

## *It's Not All Good*

**Difficulties Taking Screen Captures**

It might not be possible to capture some of your Tab's menus using the Screen Capture function. For example, if you access the Quick Settings menu by tapping the notification icons at the bottom right of the screen and then tap the Screen Capture button, the Quick Settings close and the screenshot is not captured.

**Record video**

**Play and manage your videos**

**Purchase and download music from your Tab 4**

**Play and manage music from the Google Play Store**

**Download and manage podcasts**

In this chapter, you find out how to get the most out of the media and entertainment capabilities of the Galaxy Tab 4. Topics in this chapter include the following:

→ Purchasing music, movies, and TV shows

→ Playing videos

→ Recording video

→ Adding a podcast app

→ Playing songs

→ Creating your own playlists

→ Viewing YouTube videos

# Playing Music and Video

Your Galaxy Tab 4 is a digital media player packed with entertainment possibilities as well as a camcorder capable of recording 1080p HD video. You can play music, movies, TV shows, podcasts, audiobooks, and videos; read eBooks; view photos; and access YouTube. Your Tab 4 is preloaded with a variety of apps for purchasing and downloading media.

## Downloading Movies and TV Shows

The Google Play Store makes it easy for you to browse, purchase, and download the latest music, movies, and popular TV shows to your Galaxy Tab 4. If you want to find movies and television shows within the Google Play Store more quickly than shopping in the Play Store itself, try using the preinstalled Play Movies & TV app.

The Play Movies & TV app enables you to shop for movies and television shows, pay for a movie or show if necessary, download the movie or show, and then watch the movie or show within the app. In this example, you find out how to download a free television featurette.

# Download a TV Show

1. Tap the Apps icon on the Home screen.

2. Tap Play Movies & TV.

3. Tap Shop in the menu. The Movies page displays.

4. Tap TV to view TV shows. In this example, I download one of the free TV show featurettes.

5. Swipe down the TV page until you see the Free Featurettes section. Tap More.

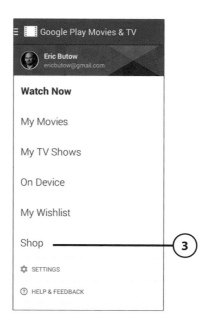

6. Swipe down the page until you see the tile that contains the featurette you want to download and then tap the tile.

7. In the middle of the page, information about the selected featurette appears below the title including an image, summary, and reviews from other Play Store users who have watched the video. Swipe down the page to read more reviews.

8. Tap Free to the right of the featurette title.

9. The video begins to play in horizontal screen orientation.

10. When you finish viewing the featurette, tap the Back touch button. View the featurette again by tapping the tile.

11. Return to the My TV Shows screen by tapping the Movies & TV icon in the menu bar.

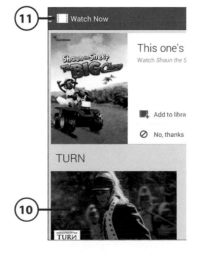

# Play the TV Show

The TV show you downloaded appears within the My TV Shows section so you can play it whenever you want.

1. On the Movies & TV app home screen, open the menu by tapping the Movies & TV icon in the menu bar. (Skip this step if the menu is open already.)

2. Tap My TV Shows. The shows you downloaded appear in each category; the most recent videos you downloaded appear at the top of the screen.

3. Tap a tile to view more information about each video within the section.

4. Tap a tile to begin playing the video in horizontal screen orientation.

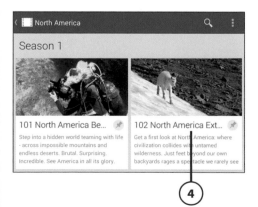

# Shop for a Movie

It's easy to shop for movies that you can buy and keep on your Tab 4 so you can watch movies anytime you want.

1. On the Movies & TV app home screen, open the menu by tapping the Movies & TV icon in the menu bar. (Skip this step if the menu is open already.)

2. Tap Shop.

3. Tap Movies.

4. Tap Categories.

5. Tap the category you're interested in.

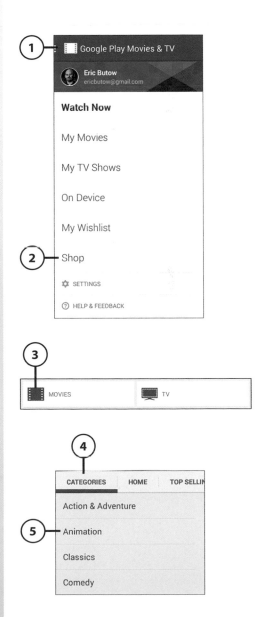

**6.** Swipe up and down in the page to view all the Top Selling movies in the category you selected. You can view new releases in the category by tapping New Releases.

**7.** Tap the tile with the movie you want more information about.

**8.** The name of the movie, the category, and buttons to either rent or buy the movie at the stated price appear at the top of the screen.

**9.** Swipe up and down the information area to view the video trailer, rate and review the movie, view user reviews, read the synopsis, cast, and credits, and get rental period information.

**10.** Tap the Buy From button to purchase the movie and download it to your Galaxy Tab 4 so that you can watch it whenever.

## HD Format Movies

If your Tab 4 supports HD format, you can buy the HD version of the movie for a higher price. The Galaxy Tab 4 7.0 does not support HD playback, but you can purchase HD format movies to play on the Tab 4 8.0 and 10.1 models.

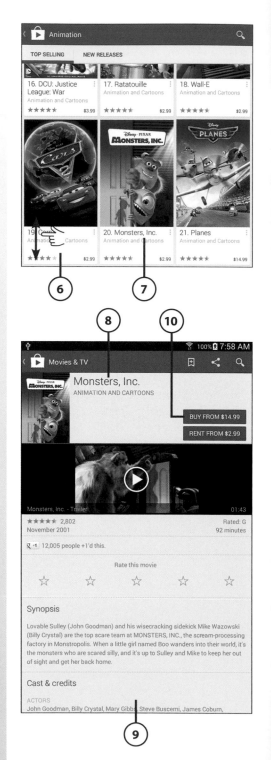

11. Tap one of the Buy options.

12. The Buy window shows you the credit card that you have on file with Google Play, which you need in order to buy a movie or TV show (even free ones) from the Play Store. If you don't have a card on file, Google Play takes you through the steps to register your credit card.

13. Buy the movie by tapping Buy. Google Play charges the card you have on file and downloads the movie to your Tab 4 so you can view the movie.

# Playing Videos

There are two ways to view movies, TV shows, and other videos on your Galaxy Tab 4. One is to watch in the Play Movies & TV app. The other is the Video app that makes it easy for you to browse and play your downloaded and recorded videos.

## Play Movies and TV Shows in the Play Movies & TV App

1. Tap the Apps icon on the Home screen.

2. Tap Play Movies & TV.

3. Swipe up and down in the Watch Now screen to view movies and TV shows you downloaded as well as get recommendations for movies and TV shows from Google Play.

4. Open and watch the video by tapping the movie or TV episode tile.

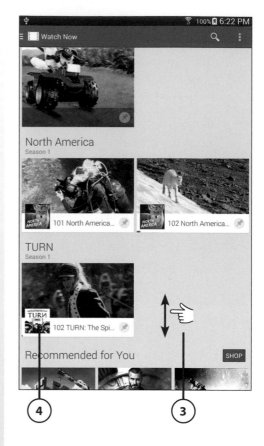

# Play Videos in the Video Player App

1. Tap the Apps icon on the Home screen.

2. Tap Video.

3. By default the Video Player screen displays videos in Thumbnails view. That is, the video plays in a small area of the screen.

4. Change the screen view by tapping the List icon, which shows a list of video files on your Tab 4.

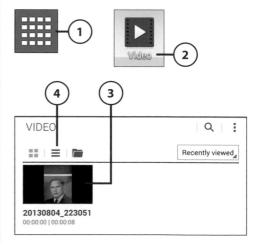

5. View your video files and the folder that contains those files by tapping the Folders icon.

6. Tap a video in the list to begin playing it.

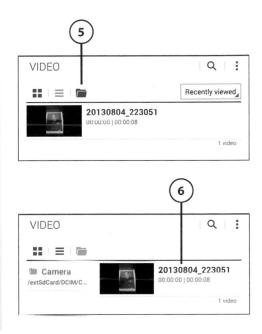

## >>>Go Further
## OTHER VIDEO OPTIONS

Tap the Menu icon at the top-right corner of the screen to choose how videos are shared and deleted or to customize playback options. The Scan for Nearby Devices option enables you to scan for other devices near you, such as a smartphone, so you can view the video on the other device. The Share Via option enables you to upload videos to YouTube, ChatON, Google+, Google Drive, the Photos or Picasa apps, Bluetooth, Wi-Fi Direct, Dropbox, email, and even Gmail. You use the Delete option to select one or more videos and then delete them. The Auto Play Next feature is set to Off by default, but you can configure your Tab 4 to automatically begin playing the next video in the list after the current video ends. You also can touch and hold your finger on a video in the list to reveal contextual menu options including Share Via, Rename, Delete, and Details.

7.  After the video has started, tap in the middle of the screen to bring up the playback controls.

8.  Adjust the volume of the video by tapping your finger on the Volume icon and then sliding your finger on the Volume slider.

9.  Tap the AllShare icon to select the device with which you want to share the video through the AllShare Play service.

10. Tap the Screen View icon to change the display mode to full screen or to return to the normal view.

11. Tap the List icon to view a list of other videos in a window at a bottom of the screen while the video you're currently viewing continues to play at the top of the screen.

12. Tap the Viewfinder icon to change the size of the video between normal and full screen views.

13. Drag your finger across the Movie Timeline to advance through the video or jump to a new location. You can also tap the timeline in a new location to jump to that location.

14. The Play button, located in the Playback controls, turns into a Pause button as the video plays. Tap the Pause button to pause the video.

15. Tap the Rewind or Fast Forward buttons to move to the beginning or end of the video, respectively.

16. Tap the Menu icon.

17. Tap to edit the beginning and end of a video by performing a trim.

18. Tap Share Via to share the video using ChatON, Dropbox, Google+, Google Drive, Bluetooth, Wi-Fi Direct, YouTube, Picasa, Photos, Gmail, or Email.

19. Tap to view each slide within the video.

20. Tap to share the video with other devices via Bluetooth.

21. Tap to set the app to view closed-captioned subtitles on the screen as you view the video.

22. Tap to configure video settings such as play speed, subtitles, and brightness levels.

23. Tap to view details of the video such as Name, Size, Resolution, Format, and Last Modified.

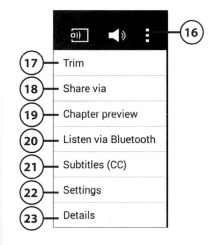

# Viewing YouTube Videos

The high-resolution screen of the Galaxy Tab 4, along with its portability and built-in video camera, makes it great for viewing and sharing videos online. The preinstalled YouTube widget gives you the capability to browse and view videos posted by users from around the world. You can also upload videos as soon as you shoot them with your Tab 4.

1. Tap the Apps icon on the Home screen.

2. Move to the second page in the Apps screen by swiping from right to left on the screen.

3. Tap YouTube.

4. A list of your channels appears on the left side of the screen that overlaps a list of videos on the screen. In this example, the list of videos is within the selected What to Watch channel.

5. Swipe down the list and then tap Browse Channels to view channels YouTube recommends for you.

6. View channels by swiping up and down the screen. You can see videos and more information about the artist channel by tapping the channel tile.

7. Return to the YouTube home screen by tapping the YouTube icon in the menu bar.

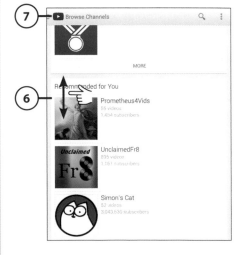

8. Tap the Search icon to search for a YouTube video.

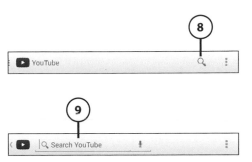

9. Type the search terms in the Search YouTube field.

10. When you're finished typing, tap the Search button in the keyboard. The results appear on a separate Search page.

11. Hold your finger on the right side of the screen and swipe to the left to view all videos in your selected subscription channel.

12. View videos within a subscription channel by tapping the channel name in the Subscriptions list.

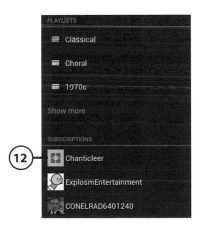

13. Tap a video tile to play the video on the screen.

**14.** Tap the Bookmark icon to book-mark a video, add to Favorites, and create a new playlist.

**15.** Tap the Share icon to share a link to the current video via Wi-Fi Direct, ChatON, Google+, Google Hangouts, Google Drive, Bluetooth, Dropbox, Flipboard, to the clipboard, a memo, Gmail, or email.

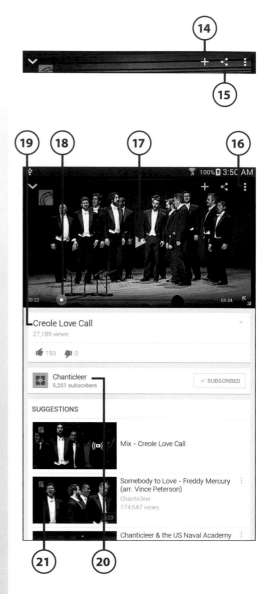

## Other Sharing Options

Other sharing options might appear in this list if you have downloaded apps that allow for additional sharing features, such as BeyondPod.

**16.** Tap the Menu icon so you can turn closed captioning on and off, change the video quality, and flag the video for inappropriate con-tent so Google can review it.

**17.** Tap to pause and play the current video.

**18.** Drag the button in the timeline slider to move through the cur-rent video.

**19.** The video description appears below the video.

**20.** Tap to visit the channel of the user who posted this video.

**21.** Swipe up and down in the page to read more about the artists, view similar videos and artists, read comments about this video from other users, and create a response of your own.

**22.** Return to the channel screen by tapping the Back touch button.

**23.** The video continues to play in the window in the lower-right corner of the screen. View the video screen by tapping and holding in the window and then flicking upward. Close the video screen by tapping and holding in the window and then flicking to the right.

**24.** Return to the main YouTube screen by tapping the YouTube icon in the menu bar.

# Recording Video

Your Galaxy Tab 4 is capable of recording 1080p HD video with its main 3-megapixel camera located on the rear of the device. The Galaxy Tab 4 is also equipped with some very helpful features commonly found on dedicated camcorders, including white balance, a video light, manual exposure, and effects.

1. On the Home screen, swipe from right to left and then tap Camera on the second page of the Home screen. The Camera app opens in horizontal screen orientation. If you see a window asking you to change the storage location to the SD card, tap the OK button.

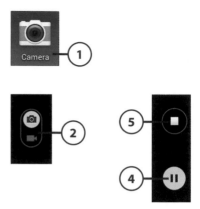

2. Switch to video mode by swiping the button from the photo icon to the video icon.

3. Start recording by tapping the Record button, which has a red circle in the center.

4. Pause recording by tapping the Pause button. After you tap the Pause button, the button changes and shows a red circle in the center. Resume recording by tapping the button with the red circle in the center.

5. Stop recording by tapping the Stop button.

## Quick Settings Options

Some of the quick settings available when you tap the right arrow icon in the Quick Settings list are the same settings represented as separate icons in the Camera interface. For example, the Brightness option in the Quick Settings menu includes the same controls as when you change brightness settings in the Camera. The next few steps cover settings options that are unique to the Settings menu. Anything omitted in the Settings menu is covered under its respective icon on the interface.

## Order of Menu Options Differs

If you are using the Tab 4 7.0, it is important to note that the order within the Settings menu is slightly different.

6. Tap the right arrow icon in the Quick Settings list to customize Video settings.

7. Tap Edit Quick Settings to customize the first five short-cuts to camera settings in the Settings menu: Timer, Brightness, Recording Mode, Share, and Viewfinder Ratio. The Viewfinder Ratio feature changes the display proportion of the video on the screen between 16:9 (the default) and 4:3, but does not change the size or proportion of the video itself.

8. You can swap out these settings with others that appear when you tap and hold a shortcut icon for a second or two. After you release your finger, the list of settings appears in the window underneath the five setting shortcut icons. Just drag a new setting on top of an old one to replace it.

9. Tap the Back touch button after you've finished replacing your Quick Settings icons.

10. Tap the Settings icon.

11. Tap the Video icon.

12. Tap Video Size to set a size for the images you capture.

13. Tap the Settings icon.

14. Tap to choose an automatic white balance for the camera. The white balance features help accurately reproduce colors when you are recording in various lighting situations so that neutral colors, such as white and gray, are truly neutral and all colors are rendered without undesired color casts. Scroll further down the menu to reveal more options.

15. Tap to enable or disable an onscreen grid that can help you with composition of the video. Scroll down to the bottom of the list of options.

16. Tap Storage to determine whether the videos you capture are stored on an optional memory card or on your Tab.

17. Tap Reset to return the Video settings to the default settings.

18. An image that is too light or too dark degrades the appearance of your videos. To take full advantage of the camera feature of the Galaxy Tab, you must adjust the brightness for various bright or dark lighting conditions. Swipe up in the list and then tap Brightness.

19. Drag the brightness level up to achieve a proper brightness level in a low-light shooting environment, or drag it down for a very bright shooting environment. After you set the brightness level, the slider bar disappears after a few seconds.

20. Tap the up arrow icon at the bottom of the screen to add camera effects to your videos as you capture them. Your choices are Grayscale, Sepia, and Negative.

21. Tap the down arrow icon to close the Effects area.

## Adding Video Effects

Keep in mind that when you use any of the video effects, such as Grayscale, Sepia, and Negative, they become a permanent part of your videos. To give yourself more choices in the future as to how you use your images, consider purchasing a video-editing app that enables you to perform such effects but still maintain your original video.

22. Tap the right arrow icon.

23. Tap the Timer icon to designate how long the Tab should wait before the camera starts to record. This is great for allowing time for you to set up the shot and then place yourself in the frame.

24. Tap the Recording mode icon to optimize your video for being sent as an email attachment and limit the size of the video you record to 50 megabytes.

25. Tap the left arrow icon.

26. Tap to switch between the rear-facing and front-facing cameras.

27. Tap the Video button to begin recording. When you finish, tap the Stop button.

28. The video you just recorded appears in the Image Viewer in the lower left of the window. Tap the Image Viewer to review the recorded video in the Gallery app.

# Purchasing Music

The Galaxy Tab 4 includes the preinstalled Google Play Music app for finding, previewing, purchasing, downloading, and playing music to your Tab 4. This app isn't the only one you can use, however—there are plenty of other music apps available for download in the Google Play Store.

1. Tap the Apps icon on the Home screen.

2. Tap Play Music.

3. Tap Try All Access to play any song in the Google Play music catalog free for 30 days. After the 30-day trial period, you can choose to purchase a membership for $9.99 per month.

4. For now, tap Use Standard to continue.

5. Tap Learn More to discover more about adding songs and copying music to your phone.

6. Tap Shop if you want to shop for tracks.

7. For now, tap Done.

8. Tap the Google Play Music icon in the menu bar.

9. Tap Shop in the list.

10. The Music screen shows the latest free music and exclusive videos. Swipe up and down the screen to view more featured songs and albums in a variety of categories.

## How Do I Know If a Song Has Explicit Lyrics?

If you don't want to listen to songs with explicit lyrics (and/or don't want your kids to listen to them), you can easily see which songs and albums have explicit lyrics by looking for the Explicit warning within the song or album tile.

**The Explicit warning label in the album tile**

**11.** Tap More to view more songs and albums in the category.

**12.** Tap Top Albums to view the best-selling albums in Google Play.

**13.** Tap New Releases to view the newest albums in Google Play.

**14.** Tap Top Songs to view the best-selling songs in Google Play.

**15.** Tap Genres to view categories of music you can choose from.

**16.** View all the genres by swiping up and down in the list. When you find a genre you want, tap the genre name in the list.

**17.** Swipe up and down the screen to view different sections of the genre page.

**18.** Tap a category to view new releases and recommendations in the genre.

19. Tap Genres to view a list of sub-genres within the main genre.

20. Tap a subgenre in the list.

21. Top-selling albums in that sub-genre appears on the screen. Scroll up and down the screen to view all the top albums.

22. Tap Top Songs to view the best-selling songs in the subgenre.

23. Tap New Releases to view newly released songs and albums within that subgenre.

24. Tap the Back touch button to return to the genre page.

25. Tap the album or song tile on the screen to view more information.

**26.** The title and album cover appear at the top of the screen. You can purchase the entire album by tapping the purchase button that contains the album price.

**27.** Tap a song name to play a 90-second snippet of that song.

**28.** Tap Play All to play all the snippets in the album.

**29.** Purchase a song on the album by tapping the purchase button that contains the price of that specific song.

**30.** Swipe from bottom to top on the page to view the remaining songs and reviews from other Google Play users who downloaded the songs or album, see more albums by the artist, and also view similar artists.

**31.** Purchase the album by tapping the purchase button at the top of the screen.

**32.** The Google Play window appears with the price of the album and the credit card Google Play will use to process the transaction.

**33.** Tap Buy to purchase the album.

**34.** After you purchase a song, a Shopping bag with a check mark tells you that you have downloaded the song to your Tab 4 successfully.

**35.** Tap the Listen button to the right of the song you've purchased to listen to the song.

# Playing Songs

In the Music app, you can play songs you added to your play queue within the app. You can also listen to music you downloaded from the Google Play Store within the Music app.

The Music app on your Galaxy Tab 4 was designed to make it easy for you to browse and play your music collection downloaded onto your Tab 4. A great set of headphones can enhance the enjoyment of your favorite music. The ability to browse your music library and understanding your playback options are a big step toward getting the most out of your many entertainment possibilities on the Tab 4.

## Play Music in the Music App

1. Tap the Apps icon on the Home screen.

2. Tap Music.

3. Tap Recently Added in the list.

4. The most recent song you listened to appears at the top of the Recently Added list. Swipe up and down in the screen to see other songs in the list.

5. Tap a song in the list to listen to that song in the Music app.

6. The song plays automatically and the playback controls appear in a window at the bottom of the screen.

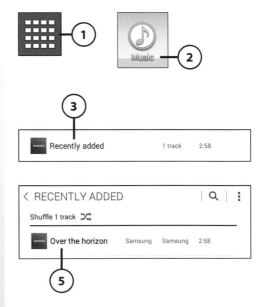

7. Tap the Pause button to pause playback.

8. Tap the Rewind icon to begin playing at the beginning of the song.

9. Tap the Fast Forward icon to move to the end of the song.

10. Tap and hold your finger on the button in the timeline to move to different points in the song.

11. Tap Shuffle to have the Music Hub player play songs in your Play Queue at random.

12. Tap the Back touch button to go back to the Player screen.

## Play a Song Even When the Music App Is Closed

After you start playing a song in Music Hub, you see the play icon in the Status Bar at the top of the screen. Pause the song by opening the Quick Settings and Notifications screen and then tapping the Pause button. When you close the Quick Settings and Notifications screen, you see the pause icon in the Status Bar. You can read more about opening the Quick Settings and Notifications screen in Chapter 3, "Setting Up the Galaxy Tab 4."

**The Play icon in the Status Bar**

13. Tap Tracks to view all the tracks you can play in the Music app.

14. Tap and hold your finger on the selected track in the list to view more options in the song options window.

15. Tap to set the song as your alarm tone when you receive a notification.

16. Tap to add the song to a playlist, which you'll learn more about later in this chapter.

17. Tap to add the song to your Favorites list.

18. Tap to delete the song from the Music app.

19. Tap to get details about the song including the song length, genre, and format.

20. Close the song options window by tapping the Back touch button.

| Over the horizon | |
|---|---|
| ⑮ — | Set as alarm tone |
| ⑯ — | Add to playlist |
| ⑰ — | Add to Favorites |
| ⑱ — | Delete |
| ⑲ — | Details |

# Playing Music in the Google Play Music App

1. Tap the Apps icon on the Home screen.

2. Tap Play Music.

3. Tap the Use Standard button in the introductory screen as you did earlier in this chapter.

4. Tap the Done button in the Other Ways to Play screen as you did earlier in this chapter.

5. Tap the Google Play Music icon in the menu bar as discussed earlier in this chapter.

6. Tap My Library.

7. Tap Songs.

8. Swipe up and down the list of songs in the album (if necessary) and then tap on the song title in the list.

9. Tap the Pause button while you're playing the song to pause playback.

10. Tap the Play button to resume playing the song.

11. Tap the Rewind icon to begin playing at the beginning of the song.

12. Tap the Fast Forward icon to move to the end of the song.

13. Rate the song so other Google Play users can view it by tapping the thumbs up (good) or thumbs down (bad) icons.

14. View more song options by tapping the Menu icon to the right of the song title in the list.

15. Have the Play Music app play all songs in the list randomly by tapping Start Instant Mix.

16. Play the next song in the list by tapping Play Next.

17. Download the song to your Galaxy Tab 4 by tapping Add to Queue.

18. Add the song to a new playlist by tapping Add to Playlist.

19. Within the Add to Playlist window, tap a playlist to add the song to a playlist.

20. Tap New Playlist to add the song to a new playlist.

21. Type the playlist name in the New Playlist window.

22. Tap Create Playlist. A pop-up box appears at the bottom of the screen that informs you that Play Music added the song to your playlist. Open the song options menu again by tapping the Menu icon to the right of the song title.

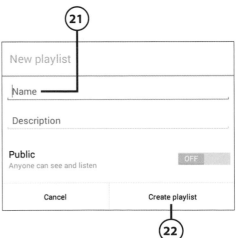

23. View all the artist's albums that you've added to your library by tapping Go to Artist.

24. View the album you've added to your library by tapping Go to Album.

25. Tap Delete to delete the song from your Galaxy Tab 4 and from your playlist within the Play Music app.

26. Tap Share to share the music file with other Google+ users in a Google+ post.

27. Tap Shop This Artist to shop for more music from the artist in the Google Play Store.

28. Tap the Back touch button to return to the main Play Music screen.

23 — Go to artist
24 — Go to album
25 — Delete
26 — Share
27 — Shop this artist

# Creating Your Own Playlists

Playlists are a great way to create a compilation of your favorite songs for playback in the Music app. Use playlists as an opportunity to organize the best songs from your favorite artists, acoustic selections, party music, classic rock, orchestral masterpieces, relaxation tracks, and more.

1. Tap the Apps icon on the Home screen.

2. Tap Music.

3. Tap Create Playlist.

My playlists

+ Create playlist

No playlists

4.  Type the name for your new playlist.

5.  Tap OK.

6.  Tap Add Tracks.

7.  Tap the songs that you want to appear in the playlist. After you tap a song, a green check mark appears in the check box to the left of the song name. Tap the song title again to clear the check box and delete the song from the playlist.

8.  Tap Done when you are finished creating the playlist. Alternatively, tap Cancel to cancel the new playlist.

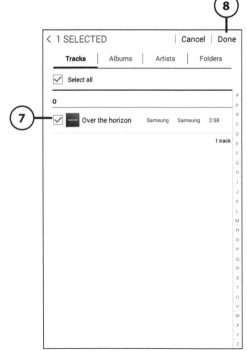

>>>*Go Further*

## REMOVING AND ADDING SONGS IN A PLAYLIST

You can remove songs from a playlist by selecting the playlist, tapping the Menu icon in the upper-right corner of the screen, and then tapping Remove in the application menu at the top of the screen. In the removal selection screen, select the track(s) you want to remove by tapping the check box next to each item and then tapping Done. You can add a song to a playlist by opening the playlist to which you want to add the song and then tapping the Add icon in the menu bar at the top of the screen. You can then select additional music from the library.

# Adding a Podcast App

One popular podcast manager is BeyondPod for Tablets, and the lite version of it is free. The lite version has all of the features of the Pro version except scheduling of updates is disabled, you can update only one feed at a time, and you can download only one podcast at a time.

During the first 7 days after installation you can use the full version of BeyondPod at no charge. If you decide you want all the bells and whistles BeyondPod has to offer, you can purchase an unlock key for $6.99. If not, you can continue to use the free lite version indefinitely.

1. Find the BeyondPod for Tablets app in the Google Play Store and install it. (Read Chapter 16, "Finding and Managing Apps," for more information on getting apps from the Google Play Store.) After you have installed the app, tap Open to launch the app.

2. Tap Continue in the Welcome screen.

3. Scroll up and down the feeds list on the left side of the BeyondPod home screen; tap a podcast to view the episodes.

4. Slide up and down the list of episodes on the right side of the screen. View episode notes in the episode screen by tapping on the episode title or summary description.

5. Tap and hold on the episode title to open the menu bar at the top of the screen so you can perform more tasks.

6. Tap Add to Playlist to add the episode to your playlist.

7. The number of episodes in your playlist appears in the upper-right corner of the podcast tile in the feeds list. View all episodes in your playlist for that feed by tapping on the playlist number.

8. Tap the Play icon to play the episode.

9. Tap to browse popular feeds and add a new feed in the Add Feed page.

10. Tap to refresh all feeds on the page.

11. Tap to refresh the current feed on the page.

12. Tap the pushpin icon to download the episode to your Tab 4.

13. Use the playback controls to pause or jump forward or backward in the video.

14. Use the slider to shuttle through the video. When the video ends, BeyondPod begins to play the next episode in the playlist, if any.

15. View more podcast information and controls by tapping the up arrow icon.

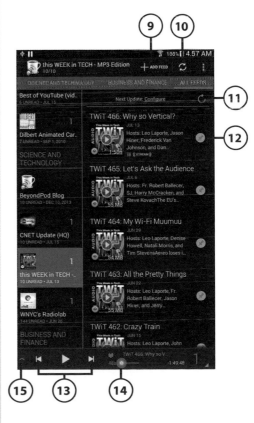

16. Change the playback speed by tapping 1x to change the speed. Note that you can't change the speed of streamed podcasts, which are podcasts that play while the podcast app receives the rest of the podcast.

17. Turn on sleep mode to pause the playback automatically after a certain period of time by tapping Sleep and then tapping the amount of time you want to play the podcast before it stops playing.

18. View a menu with more options by tapping the Menu icon.

19. Tap Mark All Read to mark all episodes in the feed as read.

20. Tap Feed to update the feed, edit feed settings, or delete the feed.

21. Tap Purchase Unlock Key to get the unlock key for the full version of BeyondPod for Tablets.

22. Tap Search to search for a feed in the BeyondPod database.

23. Tap Help to find answers to your questions and get more support from BeyondPod.

24. Tap More to change BeyondPod settings, manage feed categories, view the app update log, export feeds to a file, suggest a new feature to the BeyondPod team, and get information about BeyondPod.

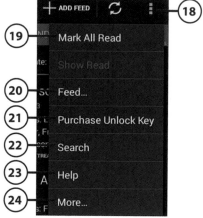

## Automatically Updating Feeds

By default, feeds are set to automatically update on a configurable interval. You can change the interval by tapping the Menu icon, tapping More, tapping Settings, and then tapping Feed Update Settings to change the interval.

## Deleting Feeds and Episodes

If you want to delete a downloaded episode, tap the orange pushpin icon to the right of the episode description and then tap Yes in the window that appears. If you want to delete a feed, tap and hold your finger on a feed on the left side of the screen. A pop-up menu displays that includes a Delete Feed option.

Purchase and read
magazines with Play
Newsstand

Purchase and read
books with Play
Books

Find out how to purchase books and magazines using the preinstalled Play Books and Play Newsstand apps and how to read them on your Galaxy Tab 4. Topics in this chapter include:

→ Purchasing books

→ Using reading aids

→ Adding bookmarks, highlights, and notes

→ Organizing your books and magazines

→ Finding other book and magazine readers in the Play Store

# Reading and Managing Books and Magazines

Your Galaxy Tab 4 offers a great outlet for you to enjoy books and magazines. The Play Books app that is installed on your Tab 4 offers a stylish e-reader that enables you to browse, purchase, download, and read e-books on your device. The Tab 4 also includes the preinstalled Play Newsstand app so you can read the latest magazines on your device.

Both the Play Books and Play Newsstand apps enable you to enhance your reading experience by offering reading aids such as the ability to increase font size and change background color. If you prefer a different e-reader, you can shop Google Play for other apps and then download and add books from other sources. Consider trying out a few of the available readers to see which one you like the best.

# Using Google Play Books

When you open the Play Books app, you can start shopping for books in the Google Play Store right away. Books are available for purchase or available for free, and after you download (and purchase, if necessary) a book you can read it within the Play Books app. You can also use built-in reading aids such as changing how the page appears on the screen.

## Browse the Catalog

1. Tap the Apps icon on the Home page.

2. Tap Play Books.

3. Tap Shop to begin shopping for books.

4. Swipe up and down the screen to view recommendations and books in various categories. View more books in a category by tapping More.

5. Tap New Releases in Fiction to view the newest fiction books.

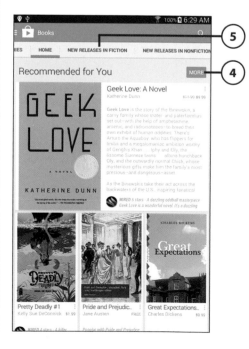

6. Swipe from right to left within the menu bar to view books in the New Arrivals in Nonfiction, Top Selling, and Top Free sections.

7. View a list of book categories by swiping from left to right on the menu bar and then tapping Categories.

8. Swipe up and down in the list to view all categories; tap a category in the list to view featured books within the category.

9. View the entire list of featured books by swiping up and down the screen.

10. Tap New Releases to view all the latest books Google has added in the category you're viewing.

11. Open a book in a subcategory by tapping Categories, swiping up and down the category list, and then tapping a category name in the list.

**12.** Tap a book cover to open the book description page.

## Purchase a Book

From a book's description page, you can purchase books that are currently available as well as pre-order books that will be released soon so you will receive the book on your Galaxy Tab 4 as soon as possible.

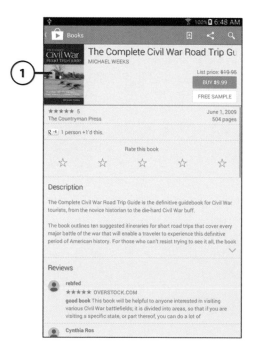

**1.** The title of the book, the book cover, and the Buy button appear at the top of the page.

### What If the Book Isn't Available Yet?

If the book hasn't been published yet, the estimated publication date appears above the purchase button. When the book is available, a notification icon displays in the Status Bar. You can read your delivered book in the Play Books app by opening the Quick Settings and Notification screen and then tapping the notification on the screen.

2. Ratings, the publication date, and the number of pages appears at the top of the description area.

3. In the Rate This Book section, tap a rating star on a scale from one to five. For example, if you tap the second star from the right then the first four stars from left to right are highlighted in blue, which signifies that you give the app four stars on a five-star scale. Then you can type your review in the Review window.

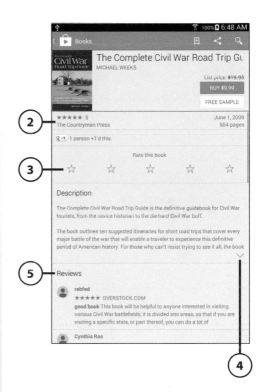

## When I Tap the Rating Star, I See an Information Window Instead

The first time you tap a rating star in Play Books, you see a window telling you that reviews in Google Play are also linked to your Google+ profile and are public, so anyone on Google+ can read your book review. Close the window by tapping OK, and then repeat Step 3 to type your review in the Review window.

4. View the entire description by tapping the down arrow in the Description area.

5. Read the entire review by tapping the review summary entry in the Reviews section.

6. Swipe upward on the screen to view more books by the author, related books, and an author biography.

7. View more information within a section, such as related books, by tapping the More button.

8. Tap the Buy button to begin the purchase process.

9. Tap the price to access more payment options.

10. Tap Payment Options to change or add a credit or debit card, redeem Google Play credits, or buy Google Play credits.

11. Tap Redeem to redeem Google Play credits to purchase this book in whole or in part.

12. Tap Buy to purchase the book. After you purchase the book, you will see the book in the Play Books app so you can read it as described in the next section.

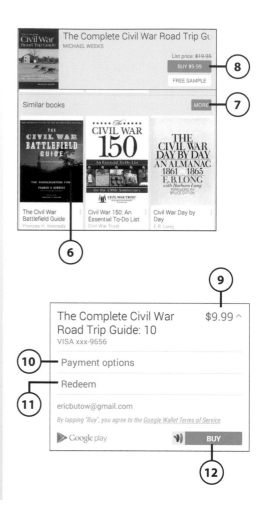

# >>>Go Further

## DOWNLOADING A FREE BOOK SAMPLE

Some books give you the opportunity to download a free sample of the book so you can read some of what the book is about before you decide to buy it. If a free sample is available, the Free Sample button appears below the Buy button. You can then read the free sample in Play Books as you would with any other book.

# Download and Read a Book

There are plenty of free books you can download from the Google Play Store so you can start reading classics and favorites right away.

1. Open the Play Books app as you did earlier in this chapter.

2. Swipe from right to left in the menu bar and then tap Top Free.

3. View all books in the list by swiping down. Tap the tile of the book you want to download.

4. Get information about the book, read reviews, add your own rating and review, and see related books as described in the previous section.

5. Tap the Add to Library button to add the book to your Play Books library.

**6.** The first page of the book appears in the Play Books app. Move to the next page by tapping the right side of the screen.

## Changing Settings

If you need to change settings before you start reading the book, such as if you want the screen to rotate when you rotate the Galaxy Tab 4, tap the Menu touch button and then tap Settings in the menu. You can then view or add a Google account to use with Play Books, change the auto-rotation setting for the Play Books app only, determine how you download book files, change how you turn pages, and tell Play Books to automatically read the book aloud if the correct accessibility setting is on. Return to the book page by tapping the Back touch button.

I

**THE ADVENTURE OF THE EMPTY HOUSE**

IT was in the spring of the year 1894 that all London was interested, and the fashionable world dismayed, by the murder of the Honourable Ronald Adair under most unusual and inexplicable circumstances. The public has already learned those particulars of the crime which came out in the police investigation, but a good deal was suppressed upon that occasion, since the case for the prosecution was so overwhelmingly strong that it was not necessary to bring forward all the facts. Only now, at the end of nearly ten years, am I allowed to supply those missing links which make up the whole of that remarkable chain. The crime was of interest in itself, but that interest was as nothing to me compared to the inconceivable sequel, which afforded me the greatest shock and surprise of any event in my adventurous life. Even now, after this long interval, I find myself thrilling as I think of it, and feeling once more that sudden flood of joy, amazement, and incredulity which utterly submerged my mind. Let me say to that public, which has shown some interest in those glimpses which I have occasionally given them of the thoughts and actions of a very remarkable man. that they are not to blame me if I have not shared my knowledge with them, for I should have considered it my first duty to have done so, had I not been barred by a positive prohibition from his own lips, which was only withdrawn upon the third of last month.

It can be imagined that my close intimacy with Sherlock

## Use Reading Aids

The Play Books app contains many options for enhancing your e-book experience, including changing background color, font size, jumping to locations within the book, and organizing your book titles.

**1.** Open the Play Books app as described earlier in this chapter.

**2.** Tap the Google Play Books icon in the menu bar.

**3.** Tap My Library.

Google Play Books

**Read Now**

My Library

Shop

4. Swipe down the My Library page if necessary and then open the book by tapping the book cover image.

5. Tap the right side of the book page to progress to the next page. Tap the left side of the page to revisit the previous page. You can also flick left or right to turn pages.

6. Go to a page with text and then tap the middle of the screen to access reading aid controls.

7. Tap the Contents icon to access the table of contents for the book. You can jump to a chapter by tapping its title in the contents.

8. Tap About This Book to read an overview of the book.

9. Close the Chapters list by tapping the Back touch button.

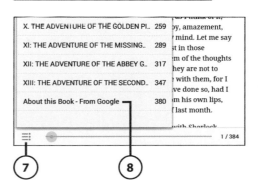

10. Tap the Search icon to search for text in the book.

11. Type the search term(s) in the Search in Book field.

12. Tap the Search button in the keyboard.

13. View all the results and the page number on which each result appears by swiping up and down in the list.

14. View the page that contains your desired passage by tapping the entry in the list.

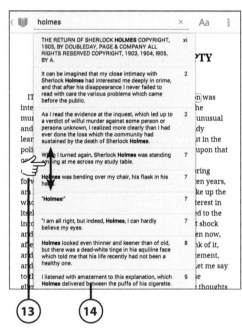

**15.** The search term(s) appear high-lighted on the screen.

**16.** Return to the previous page in the book that contains the search term(s) on that page by tapping the left arrow icon.

**17.** Go to the next page that contains the search term(s) by tapping the right arrow icon.

**18.** Return to the search results list by tapping the Play Books icon in the menu bar. Close the search results list by tapping the Play Books icon again.

**19.** View reading aid controls by tapping the Back touch button.

**20.** Drag the slider to jump to different pages in the book.

**21.** After you drag the slider to jump to a different location, you can tap the arrow to jump back to where you were last reading.

**22.** Tap the Style icon at the right side of the menu bar to access more options.

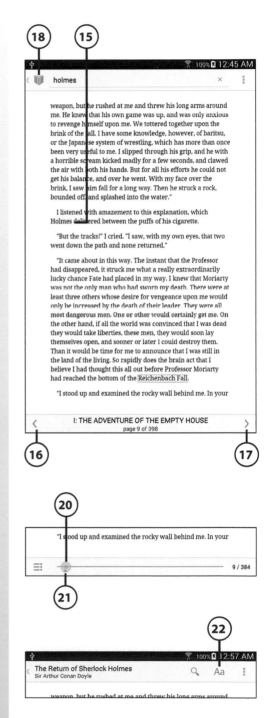

23. Tap to change the text and background color theme for the page. Your choices are Day (black text on a white background), Night (white text on a black background), and Sepia (black text on a beige background).

24. Tap to change the overall font style for the book. Your choices are Default, Sans, Serif, Merriweather, Sorts Mill Goudy, and Vollkorn.

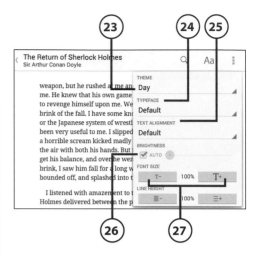

25. Tap to change the overall text alignment for the book. Your choices are Default, Left, and Justify.

26. Change the screen brightness in the Brightness slider. Set the brightness level to its default level by tapping the Auto checkbox.

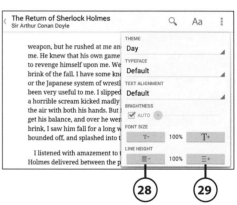

27. Tap the T- and T+ buttons to decrease and increase, respectively, the size of the book font on the screen.

28. Tap the decrease button to decrease the size of the height between lines in the book.

29. Tap the increase button to increase the size of the height between lines in the book.

# Add Bookmarks, Highlights, and Notes

Play Books provides the convenience of placing a bookmark where you stopped reading so you can begin at the right location later. You also have the capability to highlight text in a book and to leave notes.

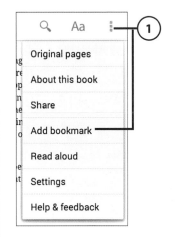

## Add a Bookmark and Go To a Bookmarked Page

1. Bookmark the page you're currently reading by tapping the Menu icon and then tapping Add Bookmark.

2. A bookmark icon appears below the right side of the menu bar.

3. Close the book by tapping the book title in the menu bar.

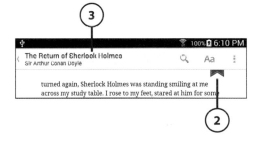

4. Open the book in the My Library page by tapping the book cover image as described earlier in this chapter.

5. Tap the Contents icon.

6. Tap Bookmarks.

7. Tap the bookmark in the list.

8. The bookmarked page appears on the screen. Tap the middle of the screen to close the reading aid control and view the bookmark in the upper-right corner of the screen.

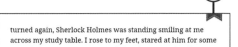

# Highlight Text

1. You might want to specify a block of text in a block as a point of interest by highlighting it. Press your finger on the screen and hold. Blue handles appear on either side of the word.

2. A dictionary definition appears at the bottom of the screen.

3. Drag the handles of the arrows to specify the text you want to highlight.

4. Tap the Highlight icon in the menu bar.

5. The highlighted text appears on the page.

## Removing Highlights from Text

You can remove the highlight from text by pressing your finger to the highlighted text, selecting the text that includes the highlight you want to remove, and then tapping the Delete Highlight icon (it has a box with an X inside).

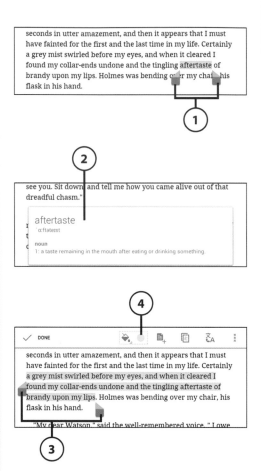

# Add a Note

1. You can insert a note for an excerpt of text. Press your finger on the screen and hold. The highlighted word appears with handles on either side of the word.

2. Tap the Add Note icon.

3. Type the note in the Add Note field.

4. Tap the book page when you're finished typing.

5. The passage of text is highlighted and an icon of a note sheet appears at the right side of the screen.

## Deleting a Note

To modify or delete a note, you can tap the icon of a note sheet that appears at the right side of the screen to reveal the notes on that page. You can then edit your notes or select the text in the note that you want to cut, tap the Menu icon in the upper-right corner of the Note field, and then tap Delete in the menu bar.

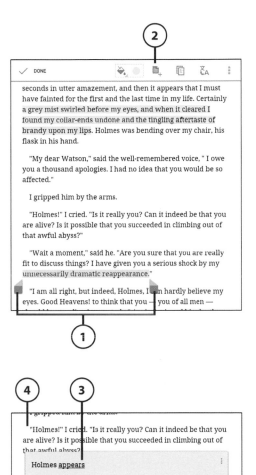

2

✓ DONE

seconds in utter amazement, and then it appears that I must have fainted for the first and the last time in my life. Certainly a grey mist swirled before my eyes, and when it cleared I found my collar-ends undone and the tingling aftertaste of brandy upon my lips. Holmes was bending over my chair, his flask in his hand.

"My dear Watson," said the well-remembered voice, " I owe you a thousand apologies. I had no idea that you would be so affected."

I gripped him by the arms.

"Holmes!" I cried. "Is it really you? Can it indeed be that you are alive? Is it possible that you succeeded in climbing out of that awful abyss?"

"Wait a moment," said he. "Are you sure that you are really fit to discuss things? I have given you a serious shock by my unnecessarily dramatic reappearance."

"I am all right, but indeed, Holmes, I can hardly believe my eyes. Good Heavens! to think that you — you of all men —

1

4   3

"Holmes!" I cried. "Is it really you? Can it indeed be that you are alive? Is it possible that you succeeded in climbing out of that awful abyss?"

Holmes **appears**

"Wait a moment," said he. "Are you sure that you are really fit to discuss things? I have given you a serious shock by my unnecessarily dramatic reappearance."

"I am all right, but indeed, Holmes, I can hardly believe my

5

## >>>Go Further

### VIEWING ALL NOTES AND MARKS

Your Galaxy Tab 4 offers a quick and convenient way to view and jump to all notes and highlights you have made in a book. Tap the middle of the screen to reveal the book options. You can then tap the Contents icon. Within the Chapters window on the left side of the screen, tap Notes to view all of your highlights and notes.

## Organize Your Books

After you have accumulated many titles in your Play Books library, you need a method to the madness of organizing your books. By default, your books are ordered by the most recently downloaded on the Play Books home page. You have a couple other sorting options to choose from.

1. Tap the Play Books icon in the menu bar.

2. Tap My Library to view all the books in your library.

3. Tap the Menu icon in the menu bar.

4. Tap Sort to choose from the sorting options. Your choices are Recently Read, Title, and Author.

5. Tap Refresh to update your library with all of your latest, purchased content.

## >>>Go Further

## REMOVING AND ARCHIVING BOOKS

You can access the option to remove books from your device by tapping the Menu icon that appears to the right of the book title. A menu opens from which you can choose the Delete from Library option. The book is removed from the library page, but remains archived in your Play Books account.

**The Delete from Library menu option**

**The Menu icon**

# Using Google Play Newsstand

If you want to read magazines without wasting paper then the preinstalled Play Newsstand app on the Galaxy Tab 4 is for you. This app enables you to shop for magazines in the Google Play Store, purchase one or more issues of the magazine, and then read the magazine within the app.

## Shop for Magazines

1. Tap the Apps icon on the Home page.

2. Swipe to the second page in the Apps screen.

3. Tap Play Newsstand.

4. Tap the Play Newsstand icon in the menu bar.

5. Tap Explore.

6. Swipe up and down the screen to view magazine topics in various categories. View more magazines in a category by tapping the category tile.

7. Tap Store to shop for magazines in the Play Store or tap Featured to view featured magazines in Play Newsstand.

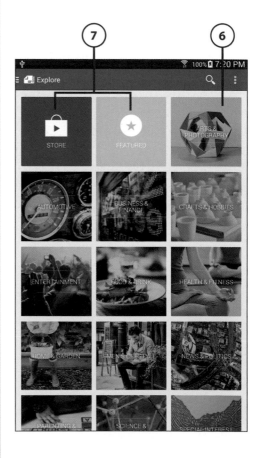

8. Shop for all magazines within the category by tapping Shop.

9. View the entire list of top magazines by swiping up and down the screen.

10. Tap New Magazines to view all the latest magazines Google has added in that category.

11. Tap a magazine cover to open the magazine description page.

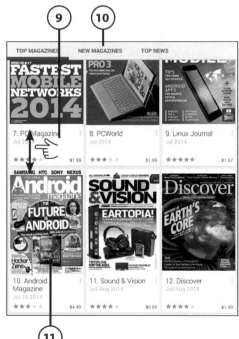

# Purchase a Magazine

1. The title and issue of the magazine, the cover of the current issue, the Subscribe button, and the Buy button appear at the top of the page.

2. Ratings and the number of issues published in a specific timeframe (such as 13 issues per year) appear at the top of the description area.

3. In the Rate This Publication section, tap a rating star on a scale from one to five. For example, if you tap the second star from the right then the first four stars from left to right are highlighted in blue, which signifies that you give the app four stars on a five-star scale. Then you can type your review in the Review window.

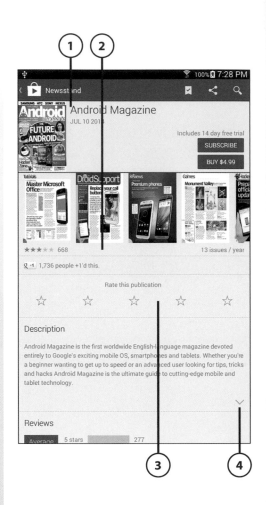

## When I Tap the Rating Star, I See an Information Window Instead

The first time you tap a rating star in Play Newsstand, you see a window telling you that reviews in Google Play are also linked to your Google+ profile and are public, so anyone on Google+ can read your book review. Close the window by tapping OK, and then repeat Step 3 to type your review in the Review window.

4. View the entire description by tapping the down arrow in the Description area.

5. Swipe upward on the screen to view reader reviews, similar magazines, and back issues.

6. Tap More to view more information within a section, such as back issues.

7. Tap the Buy button to begin the purchase process.

8. Tap the price to access more payment options.

9. Tap Payment Options to change or add a credit or debit card, or buy Google Play credits.

10. Tap Redeem to redeem Google Play credits that will pay for the magazine issue in whole or in part.

11. Tap Buy to purchase the issue. After you purchase the issue, you will see the issue in the Play Newsstand app so you can read it as described later in the "Read an Issue" task later in the chapter.

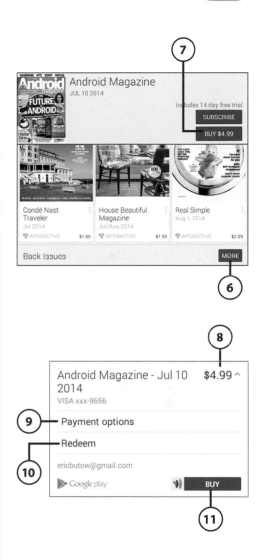

## Subscribe to a Magazine

You can also subscribe to the magazine so you can receive new issues on your Galaxy Tab 4 over a period of time.

1. Open a magazine page as described in the previous section.

2. Tap the Subscribe button to begin the subscription purchase process.

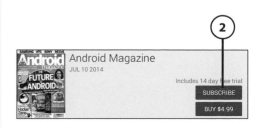

## Can I Preview a Magazine Subscription?

If there is a free trial for your subscription, you will see the length of the free trial above the Subscribe button. Some magazines make it free for you to purchase if you're already a print subscriber. Some magazine subscriptions also offer a limited time free trial, although you have to agree to start paying for the magazine after the trial period. You can cancel the subscription before the trial period is over.

3. Tap the price to access more payment options. If the magazine includes a free trial, you see the date the trial expires.

4. Tap Payment Options to change or add a credit or debit card, or buy Google Play credits.

5. Tap Redeem to redeem Google Play credits that will pay for the magazine subscription in whole or in part.

6. Tap Subscribe to purchase the magazine subscription. After you purchase the subscription, you will see the most recent issue in the Play Newsstand app so you can read it as described in the next task.

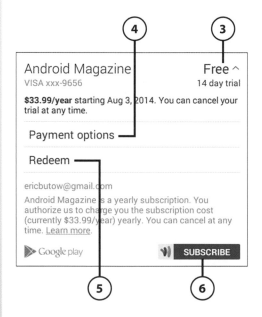

# Read an Issue

1. Open the Play Newsstand app as described earlier in this chapter.

2. Tap Magazines.

3. Swipe down to view the magazine issue you want to read and then tap the cover image.

4. The magazine issue cover appears in the Play Newsstand app. Move to the next page by swiping from right to left on the screen.

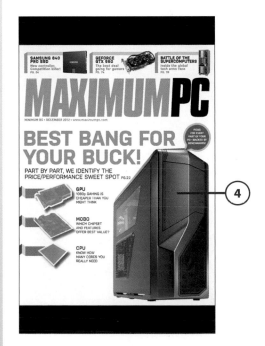

## >>>Go Further

### ADDING AND REMOVING A DOWNLOADED MAGAZINE

When you purchase the magazine, you have the ability to download it to your Galaxy Tab 4 so you can read it even when you're not connected to the Internet. Download the magazine by tapping the Play Newsstand icon in the menu bar, tapping My Library, tapping the Menu icon underneath the magazine cover, and then tapping Keep on Device in the pop-up menu. After you download a magazine, you'll see a blue pushpin icon (a blue circle with a white outline of a pushpin) in the lower-right corner of the magazine cover. You can remove the magazine from your magazine library by tapping the Menu icon and then tapping Keep on Device in the menu.

The Menu icon

The Keep on Device option

## Use Reading Aids

The Play Newsstand app contains several options that make reading a magazine easier for you.

1. Open the Play Newsstand app as described earlier in this chapter.

2. Tap Magazines.

3. Swipe down to view the magazine issue you want to read and then tap the cover image.

4. Tap the right side of the magazine page to progress to the next page. Tap the left side of the page to revisit the previous page. You can also flick left or right to turn pages.

5. Tap the middle of the screen to access reading aid controls.

6. Tap the Contents icon to access the table of contents for the book.

7. The gray area in the center of the screen shows thumbnail images of the magazine. Swipe back and forth to view the article title for the magazine page that appears underneath the black arrow.

8. The article title for the first new article at the top of the page appears above the row of thumbnail images.

9. Tap the Back touch button to close the Contents list.

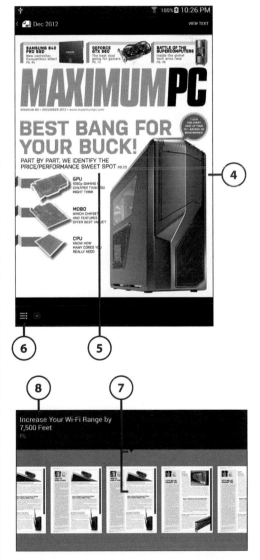

10. Navigate to another page in the magazine by tapping on the right side of the page until you reach the page you want to read.

11. Tap in the middle of the screen to access reading aid controls.

12. Your current location within the magazine is represented by the slider bar.

13. If you're on a page that contains text, you can view the text version of articles on the page by tapping View Text.

14. If there is more than one article on the page, tap the article's title to read in the Flowing Text Articles window.

15. View the entire article by swiping up and down on the screen.

16. Move to the next page in the article by swiping from right to left on the screen. Move to the previous page by swiping from left to right on the screen.

17. View the table of contents by tapping the middle of the screen and then tapping the Contents icon. You can swipe from left to right between magazine pages and then read the article on the selected page by tapping on the thumbnail image of the page.

18. Return to the text article by tapping the Back touch button.

19. The slider icon shows you where you are in relation to the entire article.

20. Return to the magazine page screen by tapping Exit Text.

# Organize Your Magazines

After you have accumulated many titles in your Play Newsstand library, you need a method to the madness of organizing your magazines just as you do with books in the Play Books app. By default, your magazines are ordered by the most recently downloaded on the Play Newsstand home page. You have a couple other sorting options to choose from.

1. Open the Play Newsstand app as described earlier in this chapter.

2. View all the magazines in your library by tapping Magazines.

3. Tap the Menu icon in the menu bar.

4. Tap Refresh to update your library with all of your latest content.

5. Tap Manage Subscriptions to manage your magazine subscriptions on the Google Play Store website within either the Internet or Chrome browser.

6. Tap On Device Only to view only those magazines that have been downloaded onto your device.

7. Tap Sort to sort the list of magazines on the Magazines page by publication date (which is the default selection) or by title.

# Shopping for Book and Magazine Readers

If you prefer to use another book or magazine reader, you can shop the Google Play Store for other cloud storage apps that are optimized for the Android operating system.

1. Tap Play Store on the Home page.

2. Tap Apps.

3. Tap the Search icon in the menu bar.

4. Type **book readers** in the Search Google Play field.

5. Tap the Search button in the keyboard.

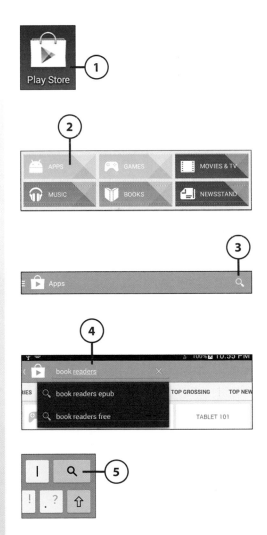

6. Swipe up and down within the list of apps in the search results screen; you also see the Google Play Books app in this list. Tap a tile to view more information about the app. Read more about shopping for apps in the Google Play Store in Chapter 16, "Finding and Managing Apps."

7. Tap the X icon in the Search Google Play field.

8. Type **magazine apps** in the Search Google Play field.

9. Tap the Search button in the keyboard.

**10.** Swipe up and down within the list of apps in the search results screen. Tap a tile to view more information about the app. Read more about shopping for apps in the Google Play Store in Chapter 16.

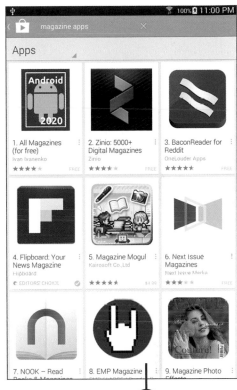

**Store and search all your contacts**

**Track your appointments and events**

**Monitor the weather, news, and stocks from one convenient location**

In this chapter, you find out how to organize your daily schedule, news, and information. You also see how to add and search contacts and calendar events. Topics in this chapter include:

**14**

→ Choosing a weather forecast for your briefing

→ Tracking stocks

→ Selecting your news settings

→ Checking and adding to your personal schedule

→ Setting up contacts accounts

→ Managing contacts

→ Using contacts

→ Creating calendar events

→ Using calendar views

# Using Productivity Apps to Simplify Your Life

Your Galaxy Tab 4 is highly capable of helping you organize your busy life. The preinstalled Contacts and Calendar widgets help you improve your daily efficiency by enabling you to manage personal contacts and schedule important appointments. You can also download free productivity apps from the Google Play Store to get the latest weather forecast, learn what's happening on the stock market, and view the latest news stories. This chapter takes a close look at what these productivity apps, as well as the Contacts and Calendar widgets, can do for you.

# Staying Up to Date

If you want to stay up to date with news, weather, and stock information, there are several well-reviewed free apps available in the Google Play Store.

- AccuWeather, which is an app that enables you to get up-to-the-minute weather conditions and forecasts for your area.

- The Stock Alert Tablet Edition app enables you to view all sorts of information about stocks.

- If you're looking for news, search for News360 for Tablets.

This section gives you a brief look at these three apps so you can get the information you're looking for on your Galaxy Tab 4. Start by downloading the apps. (You can find out how to download apps in Chapter 16, "Finding and Managing Apps.") You can also explore the Google Play Store to see what other apps might meet your needs.

## Choose a Weather Forecast

Follow these steps to display the forecast for a specific city in AccuWeather:

1. On the Home screen, tap Play Store.

2. Tap the Search icon.

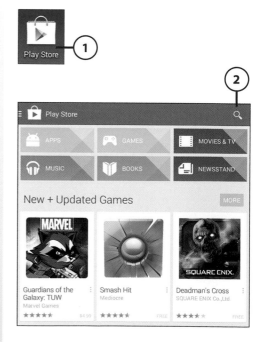

3. Start typing **AccuWeather** in the Address field.

4. Tap AccuWeather in the search list.

5. Tap Install.

6. Tap Accept.

7. After the Galaxy Tab 4 downloads and installs the app, tap Open. Tap I Agree on the Terms of Use page.

8. Tap Next in each of the three steps within the introductory slideshow.

9. Tap No Thanks on the Quick Setup screen.

10. Tap My Current Location in the Choose a Location screen.

11. The current conditions appear on the screen.

12. Swipe from right to left to view the 15-day forecast in the Daily column. Within the list of forecast dates and temperatures, you can scroll down the days to see the forecasted conditions for the next 15 days.

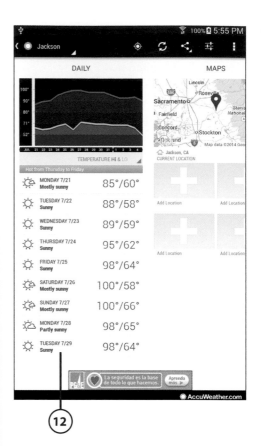

## Adding Additional Forecasts

You can add additional forecasts by tapping your current location at the left side of the menu bar, which is located at the top of the screen. In the drop-down menu that appears, tap Add Location. In the Locations column, type a new city and then tap the Search button on the keyboard. You can navigate among the multiple forecasts by tapping the location at the left side of the menu bar and then selecting the location from the drop-down menu.

## Updating Forecasts and Other Settings

By default, you must manually refresh the weather forecast by tapping the Refresh icon at the right side of the menu bar. You can further customize your forecasts by tapping the Settings icon that appears at the far right of the menu bar. For example, you can change the wind speed units (such as km/h) and time format.

# Track Stocks

You can configure the Stock Alert Tablet app so that you can monitor a desired stock for a company.

1. Tap Play Store on the Home screen.

2. Tap the Search icon.

3. Type **Stock Alert** in the Search field.

4. Tap Stock Alert in the list.

5. Tap More on the Apps screen.

6. Tap Stock Alert Tablet Edition.

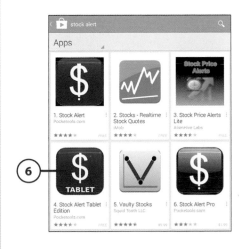

7. Tap Install.

8. Tap Accept. The Galaxy Tab 4 downloads and installs the Stock Alert Tablet Edition app automatically.

9. After the Galaxy Tab 4 downloads and installs the app, tap Open.

10. If this is your first time starting Stock Alert Tablet, tap Accept to accept the End User agreement.

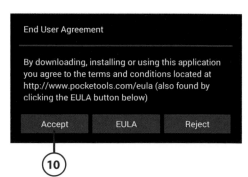

11. Tap the Add Stock icon to add a stock.

12. Type the name of the company with the stock that you want to track. You can also type the stock ticker name.

13. Tap Search to view a list of results for the stock.

14. Scroll down the stock list in the window if necessary. Tap the name of the stock that you just added to view the stock summary.

## Adding Additional Stocks

You can add an additional stock by tapping the Add Stock icon, typing in a new stock ticker in the ticker box directly underneath the Search box, and then tapping Add. You can navigate between multiple stocks by scrolling up and down your list of stocks in the left column and then tapping the stock you want to view.

## Refreshing Stocks

By default, your stock information must be manually refreshed by tapping the Refresh Rates icon above the list of stocks in the left column on the screen.

**Refresh Rates icon**

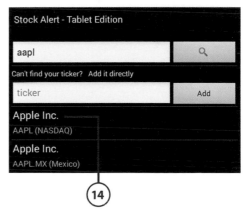

# Select Your News Settings

You can browse the latest world, national, and local news stories by customizing your news settings in News360. However, before you can do so you need to create a News360 account.

1. Tap Play Store on the Home screen.

2. Tap the Search icon.

3. Type **News360** in the Search field.

4. Tap News360: Personalized News in the list.

5. Tap Install.

6. Tap Accept. The Galaxy Tab 4 downloads and installs the News360 for Tablets app automatically.

7. After the Galaxy Tab 4 downloads and installs the app, tap Open.

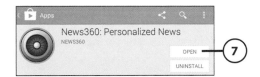

8. Choose how you want to authenticate with News360 by tapping the appropriate social networking icon. You can use your Facebook, Google, Twitter, or email account information. This example uses a connection through a Facebook account.

9. In the Facebook window, type your email account and password, and then tap Log In.

10. Tap OK to give News360 access to your public profile and friend list on Facebook.

11. The opening screen shows you some important features of the News360 screen and how to use the app. Tap Got It, Continue. After you review the information on the screen, tap Start Using News360.

## Learn About Important Features

In the opening screen, you can learn about important features including how to save stories to the Galaxy Tab 4, mark stories as interesting, and sync news stories on other devices and the Web.

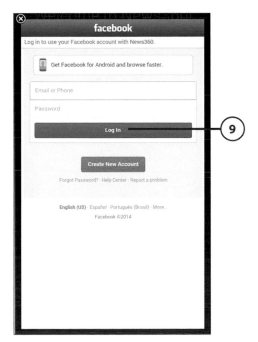

12. Above the default list of stories on the home page, the list of your interest categories appears in the category bar. Swipe left and right within the bar to view all categories in the list. Tap one of the categories to make stories within that category display under the category bar. If there are no stories in the category, News360 invites you to return later.

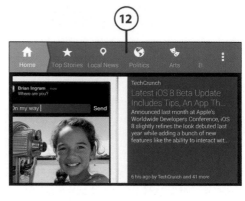

13. Swipe from left to right in the category bar if necessary and then tap Top Stories.

14. The list of top stories appears. You can scroll up and down the list and tap a story title to read it.

## Viewing Subcategories

If a category has subcategories underneath it, then those subcategories appear in the category bar. The category appears at the left side of the bar (to the right of the Back icon) and you see subcategories to the right of that category. For example, in the Science category there are subcategories that include Space, Biology, and Math. Tap the Back icon to view the main categories again.

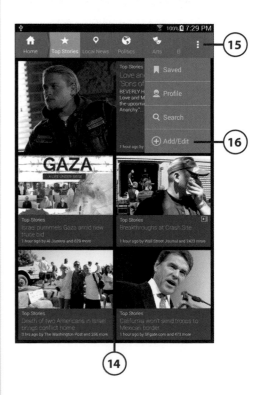

15. You can search for articles or topics by tapping the Menu icon at the right side of the menu bar and then tapping Search.

16. Tap Add/Edit to open the settings page.

**17.** Remove one of your existing categories by tapping the X button to the upper right of the category icon or by tapping a gray topic tile that has a green check mark in the upper-right corner of the tile.

**18.** Add a new section by tapping New Section.

**19.** Type the category name in the Enter Name box.

**20.** Hide the keyboard by tapping the Back touch button below the screen.

**21.** In the Choose Custom Icon section, swipe to the left and right to view all the icons and then tap the icon tile that you want to associate with the category name.

**22.** Tap Done.

23. Swipe back and forth to view a list of categories you can add to the section, and then tap the category tile you want to add. After you add the category tile, a green check mark appears in the upper-right corner of the tile.

24. After you add all the categories you want to add to the section, tap Done.

25. Your new section with the category (or categories) you added appears in the category bar, although you might need to swipe to the left within the bar to see it.

>>>*Go Further*

# HOW DO I REARRANGE MY CATEGORIES IN THE CATEGORY BAR?

If you want to rearrange categories in the category bar, tap the Menu icon in the menu bar and then tap Add/Edit. In the Add/Edit page, tap the category name at the top of the list, such as My Interests. Next tap and hold your finger on the category name you want to move. Drag the category name to the left or right and then release your finger when the category is in your desired location in the menu.

As you move the icon, you'll see where your icon will appear and other icons will move aside to make room for your icon. Release your finger to place the icon in that location. If you want to move your selected icon to a location in the bar that's currently not visible, move the icon to the right side of the bar. Next, swipe to the left within the bar to view the remaining icons in the bar, and then move your selected icon to the right until the icon is where you want it. When you've finished rearranging categories, tap Done.

26. Tap the Menu icon in the menu bar and then tap Profile.

27. Swipe up and down if necessary to view your account information, sign out of News360, change application settings, and learn more about the app. These settings include showing or hiding high-quality images when you're connected to the Internet using a 3G connection and displaying stories in list view instead of as tiles.

28. Return to the News360 home page by tapping Home.

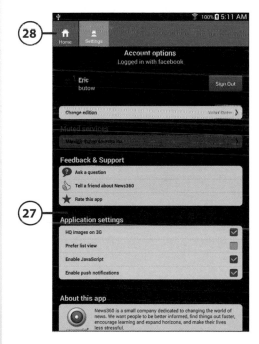

## It's Not All Good

### Refreshing News Stories

By default, News360 refreshes news stories when the app finds new stories to post in your headlines list. If you want to refresh your headlines list manually, tap the category name in the category bar. After a second or two, updated stories appear in tiles on the screen.

# Managing Contacts

The Contacts widget enables you to manage all the important information you receive from colleagues, friends, and prospective business associates. Think of your Galaxy Tab 4 as a virtual filing cabinet or Rolodex where you can store contact information such as names, addresses, emails, and notes. If you collect contacts with other social networking services, you can also configure Contacts to sync information between accounts.

## Set Up Contacts Accounts

The Galaxy Tab 4 can synchronize its contacts information with multiple accounts, such as Google, Corporate Exchange, other email providers, and sites such as Facebook and Google+. Information on your Galaxy Tab 4 is updated when you make changes to information in your accounts. Setting up a contacts account is quite easy.

1. Tap the Apps icon on the Home screen.

2. Tap Settings.

3. Tap General in the menu bar.

4. Tap Add Account.

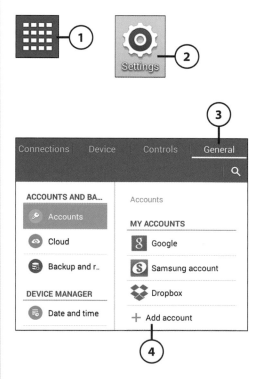

5. Tap an account that you would like to set up.

6. Follow the prompts to set up each account that you would like to add. The accounts you add appear in the Accounts area within the Settings list.

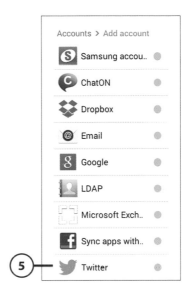

## Add Contacts

Using the Contacts widget, you can store contact information for family, friends, and colleagues for quick access and to send messages.

1. Tap Contacts on the Home screen.

2. A list of all contacts appears. Your own contact information appears listed by default.

3. Tap the New icon to open the Create Contact form window.

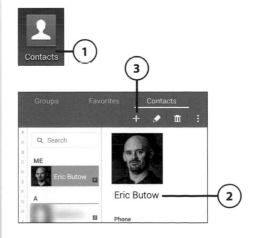

**4.** Tap Device to change the account for which you want to add a contact. For example, you can add a contact in your Google account.

**5.** In the Attention window, tap OK to close it and ensure that you will not see the message about sync being unavailable for contacts you add to your device.

## Why Can't I Sync Contacts I Add to the Tab 4?

The Galaxy Tab 4 can't sync contacts you add to the device itself to any other device to which you connect the Tab 4. If you want to sync to other devices you can add the contact to your online contact database stored in your Samsung, Google, or Microsoft Exchange ActiveSync account.

**6.** Type the first and last name in the Name field.

**7.** If you want to add the first and last name in different fields, tap the arrow icon located to the right of the Name field to add a Name Prefix, First Name, Middle Name, Last Name, and Name Suffix to the contact. There is no need to use the Shift key on the keyboard to capitalize the name because the Galaxy Tab 4 does this automatically.

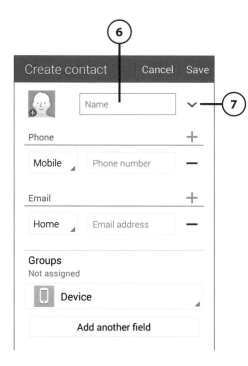

## Don't Worry About Formatting

You don't need to type parentheses or dashes for the phone numbers you enter. The Galaxy Tab 4 formats the number for you.

8. Tap the labels within fields to reveal a pop-up menu with other labels to choose from. For example, tap Mobile to the left of the phone number to open the pop-up menu so you can add other phone numbers such as the person's home phone number.

9. Tap the plus icon in the Phone field to add an additional field, or tap the minus icon to remove a field.

10. Add information in the Email section as you did in the Phone section.

11. Add another field to the contact by tapping Add Another Field. You can add the user's phonetic name, organization, instant messaging address, physical address, any notes about the user, the user's nickname, website, Internet phone number, events related to the contact, and the contact's relationship to you.

12. Tap Events to add events related to the contact, such as the person's birthday, and then tap OK.

**13.** Tap the Birthday label to choose the type of event you want to add.

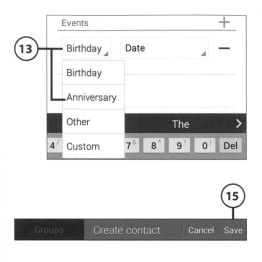

## Assigning Contacts to Groups

You can assign a contact to one of six groups (Business, Co-Workers, Family, Friends, My Contacts, or Starred in Android) by tapping the Groups field located toward the bottom of the New Contact sheet and then tapping a group.

**14.** Add another field to the form by repeating Step 11.

**15.** Tap Save to complete the new contact.

# >>>Go Further

## UPDATING A CONTACT AND DISPLAYING CONTACTS

You can update a contact by first tapping an existing contact in the Contacts list and then tapping the Edit icon located at the upper right of the screen next to the New icon. The contact sheet opens so that you can edit or add information.

You can control how your contacts are listed by setting sorting and display preferences. After you launch the Contacts widget, you can tap the Settings icon located at the upper-right corner of the screen, tap Settings, and then tap Display contacts by. The Display Options menu enables you to list by First Name (which is the default setting) or by Last Name First.

# Search for Contacts

Your list of contacts is sure to grow the longer you have your Galaxy Tab 4. So how do you search your large list of contacts for a specific contact?

1. Tap Contacts on the Home screen.

2. Tap the Search field and use the keyboard to type the name of the contact you are looking for. As soon as you begin to type, the screen displays the contact that most closely reflects what you've typed into the field. Continue typing until you have narrowed the search.

3. View the contact in its entirety by tapping the Back touch button to close the keyboard.

4. Tap the X located in the Search field to clear the Search field of your term. The contact that appears from your search remains visible in the Contacts screen.

# Link Contacts

When you synchronize the contacts on your Galaxy Tab 4 with multiple accounts, such as Facebook, Twitter, and Google, you can have varying numbers and address information for a single contact. You can see all the contacts' numbers and addresses in a single contact entry by linking contacts. Linking contacts can help you keep your contact information up to date.

1.  Tap Contacts on the Home screen. Your contact information appears on the screen.

2.  Scroll down the contact list until you find the contact to which you want to join another contact. Tap and hold your finger on the contact name in the list until a pop-up menu appears.

3.  Tap Link Contact in the menu.

4.  In the Link Contact window, scroll down the list until you see the name of the contact you want to join to the contact you selected in Step 2. The contacts are now joined and the information for both entries in each account has merged.

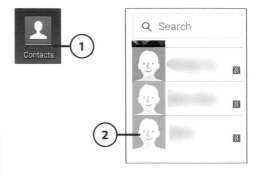

## How Do I Unjoin Contacts?

Unjoin contacts by tapping the contact that has the joined contacts attached to it. For example, if Contact A is joined to Contact B, tap Contact A's name in the list. Then tap the Menu touch button below the screen. In the menu, tap Separate Contact. In the Separate Contact window, tap the minus sign next to Contact B. Tap OK to separate the link. Contact B's information is no longer in the record for Contact A.

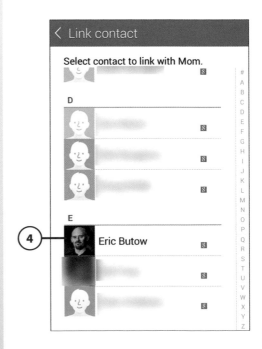

# Use Contacts

After you have entered a contact in your Galaxy Tab 4, you can utilize a few functions and displays directly from the Contacts page. Start by opening a contact's record.

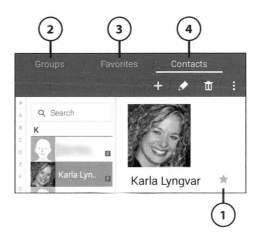

1. Tap the star icon to the left of the contact name to set that contact as a favorite.

2. Tap the Groups tab to view the list of contacts you have assigned to a group.

3. Tap the Favorites tab to view the list of contacts you have designated as favorites.

4. Tap the Contacts tab, and then press and hold your finger on a contact's name in the contact list.

5. Tap Share Via.

6. In the Share Namecard Via window, share a namecard via Bluetooth, the ChatON messaging service, Google Drive, email, Gmail, or Wi-Fi Direct. Think of a namecard as an electronic business card.

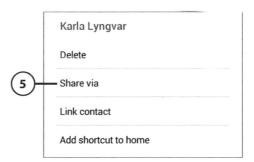

## Managing Contacts

After a contact has been entered into your Galaxy Tab 4, you can manage many of the features of a contact by pressing your finger to it and holding. Options include Join Contact, Add to Favorites, Add to Group, Share Namecard Via, and Print Namecard.

7. Compose a new email to your contact by scrolling down the Contact screen until you reach the Email section and then tap the email icon to the right of the contact's email address.

# Managing Your Busy Schedule

The Calendar app enables you to manage all your appointments and events from one convenient location. Calendar enables you to view a busy schedule in multiple views such as Day, Week, Month, and List. You can also instruct Calendar to send you a little reminder, in the form of an alert, before an event to help ensure that you never miss a meeting and are always on time.

## Create Calendar Events

Your Galaxy Tab 4 was designed for you to be mobile while still enabling you to manage the important stuff, such as doctor appointments, business meetings, and anniversaries. The Calendar enables you to add important event dates to calendars to help ensure that you do not overlook them.

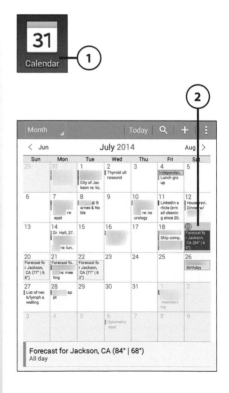

1. Swipe on the Home screen from right to left to move to the second page on the Home screen. Tap Calendar.

2. By default, the calendar opens to the Month view. The current date displays a blue circle around the date.

**3.** Tap the date for which you want to add an event. The date becomes highlighted.

**4.** Tap the + button at the top-right corner of the screen. Note that if you see the New Event window informing you that the calendar cannot sync with Samsung Kies, tap the Do Not Show Again check box and then tap Done.

**5.** The Title field is selected by default. Type a title for the event in the field.

**6.** Tap the date and time in the From field to enter the start date and time of the event. You can also use the controls in the Set Date and Time window to designate an event for a future date and not just the date you specified in Step 3. When you tap the date and time in the From field, a calendar opens, enabling you to select a future date and time.

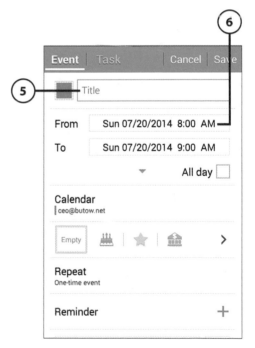

7. The current month appears in the calendar and the date you set for the event in Step 3 is highlighted in the calendar. Change the event date by swiping up and down within the calendar to view months and dates and then tap the date for the event.

8. Tap the controls to enter the start time for the event.

9. Tap Set.

10. Tap the date and time in the To field to bring up the controls and set the date and time for the event as you did when you set the date in the From field.

11. Tap the down arrow icon underneath the To field.

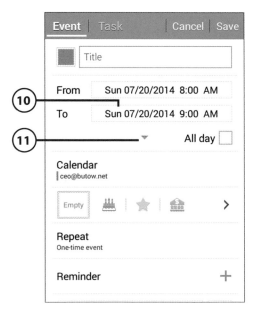

12. Tap the Time Zone button to change the time zone for the event.

13. Tap the up arrow icon to hide the Time Zone button.

14. Tap the All Day check box if the event will happen all day.

15. Tap Repeat if you need to set a repeating cycle for the event. Scroll down to see more options you can set.

16. Tap Reminder to choose an alarm time for the event. You can choose the time you want the reminder to appear as a notification in the Notification bar or you can send the notification to your email account. Tap the plus button at the right of the Reminder field to add another notification that will appear at a different time and/or be delivered in a different manner.

## How Do I View the Reminder in the Status Bar?

When you receive a reminder, you get an audio reminder and also see a reminder icon at the left side of the Status Bar. Tap and hold your finger on the top edge of the screen and swipe down to open the Quick Settings and Notifications screen. The reminder displays at the bottom of the Notifications area.

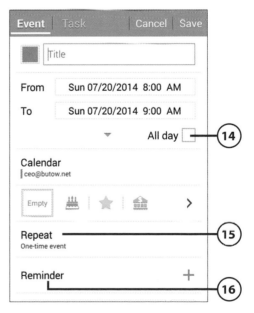

**17.** View more fields in the window by swiping upward within the window.

**18.** Tap the Location field to add a location for the event. If you want to find the location in the Maps app, tap the Maps button to the right of the field. You find out more about using the Maps app in Chapter 10, "Using Maps."

**19.** Tap the Description field to type a description for the event.

**20.** Tap the Participants field to add names from your contacts.

**21.** Tap the Contact button to the right of the field if you want to select names from the Contacts app. In the pop-up window that appears, select one or more contacts by tapping the check box to the left of the contact name.

**22.** Tap the Show Me As field if you want others to see that you're available even during the event. Otherwise, the calendar shows you as busy and blocks out that time so anyone else who views your calendar sees that you're unavailable. Scroll down to set more options.

**23.** Tap the Privacy field and then tap Private in the menu. Otherwise, the event is public so anyone who sees your calendar can view the event.

**24.** Tap Save to complete the event and save it to your calendar.

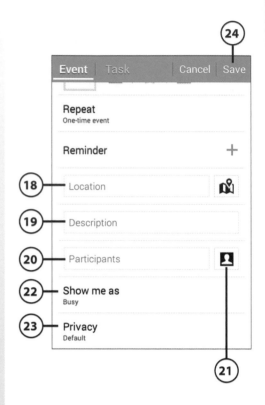

# Use Calendar Views

There are five views in which you can view the contents of your calendar: Year, Day, Week, Month, and Agenda. This section examines each view.

## Accessing Calendar Views

In vertical screen orientation, you access all five views from the calendar view box, and this example shows you how to use the Calendar app in vertical orientation. When you change to horizontal screen orientation, the calendar view box disappears and is replaced by all five calendar view options within the green menu bar at the top of the screen. Tap a view name in the menu bar to display that calendar view.

## Year View

The Year view shows the entire calendar year. Open the Year view by tapping the calendar view box at the left side of the menu bar and then tap Year in the list.

The current year appears above the calendar. Tap the left arrow to the left of the year or the right arrow icon to the right of the current year to view a calendar for the previous or following year, respectively. When you change the year, your selected year appears highlighted in the center. Tap Today in the menu bar to highlight the current date in the calendar.

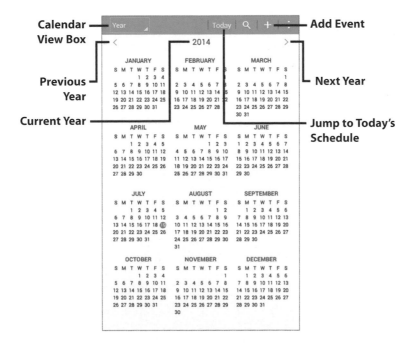

Calendar View Box — Year — Today — + — Add Event

Previous Year — Next Year

Current Year — 2014 — Jump to Today's Schedule

## Day View

The Day view is composed of a list of events blocked for each half hour, with a section at the bottom that enables you to scroll through days and jump to the next or previous month. Open the Day view by tapping the calendar view box at the left side of the menu bar and then tap Day in the list.

You can press your finger to the list and flick up or down to scroll through the list of events. All events scheduled with duration of All Day are located at the very top of the list.

Tap Today in the menu bar to open the calendar for the current date. The timeline located just under the menu enables you to tap specific days during the month. Tap the arrows located at each end of the current date to jump to the previous or next day. Tap Today in the menu bar to return to the current day's schedule no matter where you are in the calendar.

You can tap an event in the list to view notes, edit the entry, delete the event, or send it via Bluetooth, the ChatON messaging service, the Dropbox or Google Drive online file storage services, email, Gmail, or Wi-Fi.

## Week View

The week view is arranged into seven day parts. Open the Week view by tapping the calendar view box at the left side of the menu bar and then tap Week in the list.

Tap the left arrow to the left of the current week or the right arrow to the right of the current week to view the previous and following week, respectively. Tap Today in the menu bar to highlight the current date.

Each event for that week is found in its respective scheduled day block. You can tap an event for any date to view notes, edit the entry, delete the event, or send it via Bluetooth, the ChatON messaging service, the Dropbox or Google Drive online file storage services, email, Gmail, or Wi-Fi.

## More Options in Horizontal Screen Orientation

When you change to horizontal screen orientation while you're in Week View, a section containing the current monthly calendar and the agenda for the selected day of the week appears on the right side of the screen. The current day in the monthly calendar appears inside a blue circle. When you tap a date in the weekly calendar, that selected day appears in the monthly calendar within a blue square and the agenda underneath the monthly calendar is updated to show your events on that day.

## Month View

The Month view provides a broad view of events for a given month. Month view is composed of two sections: the monthly calendar and the day's event schedule. Open the Month view by tapping the calendar view box at the left side of the menu bar and then tap Month in the list.

Each section lists the events scheduled for that particular month. The current day block you are viewing is highlighted within the calendar section. Any event designated as an All Day Event is highlighted in the day block of the Calendar view.

Tap Today in the menu bar to highlight the current date in the calendar. The current month appears above the calendar. Tap the previous month name, which appears to the left of the current month, to view the previous month. View the following month by tapping the following month name to the right of the current month.

You can tap an event to view notes, edit the entry, delete the event, or send it via Bluetooth, the ChatON messaging service, the Dropbox or Google Drive online file storage services, email, Gmail, or Wi-Fi.

## Agenda View

The Agenda view provides a comprehensive view of all scheduled events for an entire year in one list. You can also tap the All button to filter the list by events, tasks, and special occasions. Open the Agenda view by tapping the calendar view box at the left side of the menu bar and then tap Agenda in the list.

Events for the current date or the date with the next event appears at the top of the list. You can tap an event to view notes, edit the entry, delete the event, or send it via Bluetooth, the ChatON messaging service, the Dropbox or Google Drive online file storage services, email, Gmail, or Wi-Fi.

# Add a Task to Your Calendar

You can add a task to your calendar by tapping the Add Event icon in any calendar view. After you tap the icon, note that if you see the New Event window informing you that the calendar cannot sync with Samsung Kies, tap the Do Not Show Again check box and then tap Done.

1. In the window, tap Task in the menu bar.

2. The Title field is selected by default. Type a title for the event in the field.

3. Tap the date in the Due Date field to enter the due date for the task. When you tap the date button, a calendar opens in the Set Date window, enabling you to select a due date.

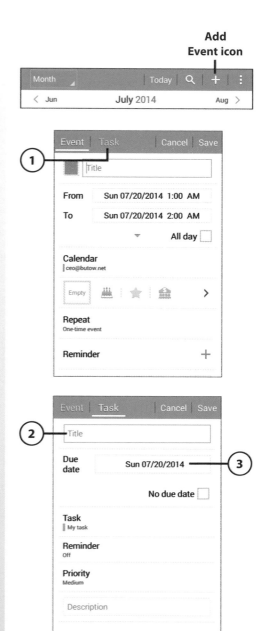

4. Tap the controls to enter the due date for the event.

5. Tap Set.

6. Tap the No Due Date check box if there is no due date.

7. Tap the Task field to open the Task window and save your task to the device or to the Samsung Tasks app. The default selection is to the device.

8. Tap the Reminder field to open the Reminder window and set a reminder type. You can set a reminder on the due date or set a customized reminder, which is on a date of your choosing. The default selection is Off, which means there is no reminder.

9. Tap the Priority field to change the priority level in the menu to High, Medium, or Low. The default priority is Medium.

10. Tap the Description field to type a description for the event.

11. Tap Save to complete the task and save it to your calendar. The task appears on the date within the calendar.

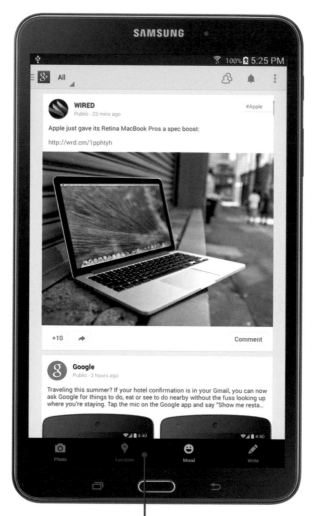

**Use built-in apps on your
Galaxy Tab 4 to enhance
your productivity**

The Galaxy Tab 4 has plenty of preinstalled apps that you can use to stay productive and get the latest information on the go. You can get updates sent to you by the Google Now service and connect with other users through instant messaging and social networking apps. What's more, you can view and create document, spreadsheet, and presentation files. This chapter covers the following:

→ Getting updates from Google Now

→ Using ChatON

→ Connecting to Google+

→ Creating documents and presentations with Hancom Office

# Using Apps for Learning, Creating, and Sharing

## Staying Up to Date with Google Now

Google Now is a new feature that monitors your activity on your Galaxy Tab 4 and shows you features in various tiles, called cards, that Google Now thinks you'll be interested in based on your past activity. For example, you might see cards with your local weather, upcoming appointments, and current traffic conditions where you live.

# Start Google Now for the First Time

You start Google Now by pressing and holding on the Home button for two seconds or by tapping the Google Search box in the lower-left corner of any Home screen.

After you release your finger, the Google Now setup screen appears so you can set up and get more information about the app.

1. Tap Next.

2. Tap Yes, I'm In to continue the setup process as described in the rest of this task. The opening Google Now screen displays.

3. Search Google by tapping the Search field, typing your search term(s), and then tapping the Search button in the keyboard.

4. Tap Customize to change card settings.

5. Delete cards by tapping and holding on a card and then swiping to the left or right.

6. View the current weather information for your city or area by swiping down the screen.

7. Swipe down the screen to see more options.

**The Google Search box**

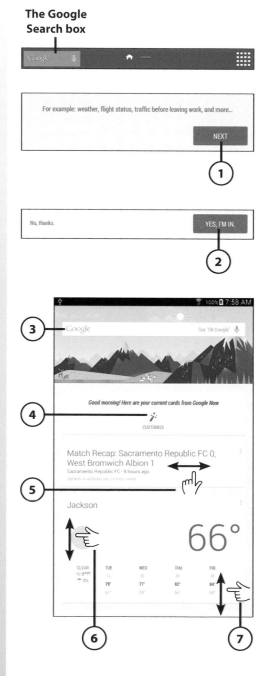

8. Enable location history by tapping Enable Location History.

9. Press the Home button to return to the Home screen.

## Use Google Now

After you finish setting up Google Now, you can access it by tapping the Google Search box in any Home screen. The Google Now screen looks a little different than when you set up the app for the first time.

1. Tap the Google Search box.

2. Type any search term(s) in the Search field. As you type, the first three search results display below the Search field.

3. Tap an item in the result list to open a search result. If you search for a name and/or location, any search results in your Contacts database appears in the list of contacts. View more contact information by tapping the name of the contact. You can also search for more contacts by tapping Search Tablet.

4. View more search results by tapping the Search button in the keyboard.

5. The Search results page appears on the screen. Swipe up and down the screen to view the entire list of results on the page.

6. Tap the Back touch button to return to the Google Now screen.

7. Even if you don't search for anything, Google Now remembers your last three searches on the Google search engine and displays them underneath the Search field.

8. Hide the keyboard by tapping the Back touch button.

9. Swipe up and down the page to view all the other cards on the screen.

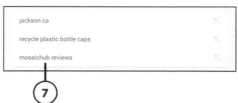

10. Tap the Menu icon within each card's section to change the Google Now settings. The type of card for which you want to change settings determines the available options in the Setting screen. This example uses the Weather card.

11. By default, the Weather card is visible within the Google Now screen. You can hide the Weather card and tell Google Now you're not interested in weather updates for your location by tapping No.

12. Keep the Weather card visible and change more settings by tapping Yes or tapping the right arrow icon.

13. Turn off weather updates in the Weather card by tapping No. Otherwise, tap Yes or the right arrow icon.

14. Change the temperature unit to Celsius by tapping the C icon. The default unit is Fahrenheit as shown by the blue F icon.

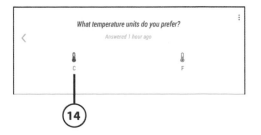

**15.** Return to the Google Now screen by tapping the Back touch button.

**16.** View other cards by swiping up and down in the screen. View more cards by tapping the More button. If no other cards are available, the button says, "Not available" and then the button disappears.

## Can I Add a Widget for Google Now?

There is a Google Now widget on the Widgets screen covered in Chapter 5, "Adding Widgets to Your Home Screens." After you add the widget to your desired Home screen, the widget appears and displays the current weather conditions for your location. Open the Google Now app by tapping on the widget.

Match Recap: Sacramento Republic FC 0,...
Sacramento Republic FC - 11 hours ago

Jackson                                    Tue            Wed
69°

**The Google Now widget
on a Home screen**

# Using ChatON

Samsung's ChatON service is an instant messaging app for the web and mobile platforms that's preinstalled on your Galaxy Tab 4. Instant messaging, better known by its acronym IM, is a category of apps that enable you to chat with one or more people in real time by typing text messages and/or using your webcam to talk with each other. Some IM apps are available on the Web only, such as Google+ Hangouts. Others are proprietary apps such as Microsoft's Skype and Samsung's ChatON.

**1.** Tap the Apps icon on the Home screen.

**2.** Swipe to the second page in the Apps screen and then tap ChatON.

3.  Tap Next.

---

## I See a Window Asking Me to Update My Samsung Account

The first time you start ChatON, you might see a window asking you to update your Samsung account and then download the latest version of ChatON. Update your Samsung account by tapping Yes in the window. After the Tab 4 updates your account, repeat Step 3 to continue using ChatON.

---

## *It's Not All Good*

### What If I Don't Have a Samsung Account or I'm Not Logged Into My Samsung Account?

If you didn't log into or set up a Samsung account when you set up your Galaxy Tab 4, you can't set up ChatON. You will have to close the ChatON app, open the Internet or Chrome app, get an account at www.samsung.com, add a new account by tapping Add Accounts, and then tapping Samsung Account in the Add Account window. Your Samsung account appears in the list of accounts within the Settings screen after you add the account.

If you aren't logged into your Samsung account, open the Quick Settings and Notification screen and then tap the Samsung notification in the Status window. After you sign into your Samsung account successfully, tap the Next button in the ChatON opening screen again.

**4.** The ChatON window opens with the Buddies tab open. (On the Tab 4 7.0, the tab name is Contacts instead of Buddies.) If you don't have any buddies then the buddies list shows only your name.

**5.** Tap the Add Contact button to add a buddy.

**6.** Tap Search by ID in the Add Buddy window.

**7.** Tap in the Email field, type the Samsung account email address of the person you want to add as your buddy, and then tap the Search icon.

**8.** Tap the Add button to add a buddy from the Results list. After a second or two, a pop-up box appears at the bottom of the screen that informs you the app has added the contact. After a few seconds, that pop-up box disappears.

**9.** Tap the arrow at the left side of the menu bar to go back to the main ChatON screen.

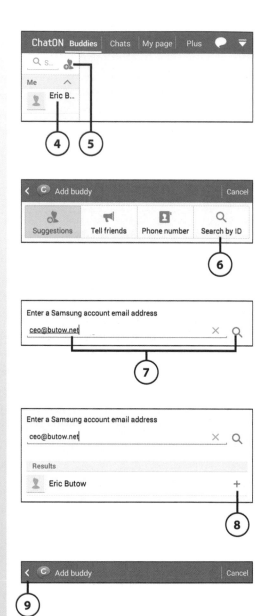

10. Tap the name of your new buddy in the New Buddies list.

11. Tap the Chat button in the contact information that displays on the right side of the screen.

12. Tap in the Enter Message field and type your message.

13. Tap the Send button.

14. Your message appears in the Chat area. Any responses appear below your initial message.

15. Type a response in the Enter Message field.

16. The app saves your chats and displays them in the Chats list. You can view past chats at a later time by tapping Chats in the menu bar and then tapping the chat you want to view in the list. The entire chat appears in the Chat area.

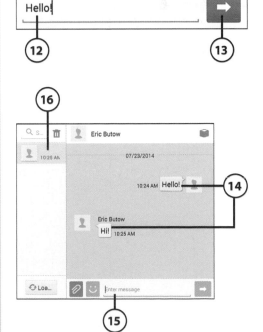

# Connecting to Google+

The Google+ social networking website is the fifth most popular such website in the world with an estimated 120 million monthly visitors as of August 2014 (www.ebizmba.com/articles/social-networking-websites). It might come as no surprise that Google is pushing its social networking service by preinstalling its Google+ apps on the Android operating system, and the same is true for KitKat on the Galaxy Tab 4.

## Set Up Google+

1. Tap the Apps icon on the Home screen.

2. Tap Google+.

---

### What If I Don't Have a Google+ Account?

This book doesn't discuss creating a new Google+ account. You can learn more about the different types of accounts you can create and how to create an account by visiting the Google+ website at https://plus.google.com.

---

3. When you start the Google+ app, it logs you in automatically using your Google account name and password. If you have more than one Google+ account, the Choose Account screen appears so you can tap the button to the right of the account name with which you want to log in, and then tap Next.

4. The Your Contacts screen asks if you want to keep your address book up to date by adding your Google+ connections to your Android contacts. This screen also asks if you want Google to make suggestions about adding new Google+ connections based on who you communicate with most often on your Galaxy Tab 4. The check boxes for these two options are checked by default, which means Google+ enables both of these options. You can disable one or both options by tapping the check box to the left of the option name.

5. Tap Next.

6. The Back Up Your Photos screen appears so you can back up the photos on your Galaxy Tab 4 to a private account on Google+. You can't share this private account with anyone else, and no other Google+ user can see these photos except you. The Over Wi-Fi Only option is checked and highlighted by default.

7. Tap Not Now if you don't want to back up the photos on your Galaxy Tab 4 to your Google+ account.

8. By default, you will also back up any existing photos and videos stored on your Galaxy Tab 4. If you don't want to do this, tap the check box to clear it.

9. Tap Done.

# Use Google+

After you set up Google+, the main Google+ screen appears and the latest message from one of your Google+ friends appears at the top of the screen.

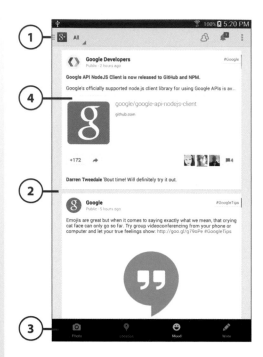

1. The gray menu bar appears at the top of the screen so you can access the menu, change the updates you view, refresh the screen, and also see how many updates you have.

2. The latest updates appear as tiles on the screen. Swipe up and down the screen to read more updates.

3. The black message bar contains four icons so you can share a photo you took on your Galaxy Tab 4, send your current location to your Google+ friends, send a message to your friends about your current mood, or write and post a message to your contacts.

4. Tap a tile to open the post on the entire screen.

5. Tap the Add a Comment field and use the keyboard to type your message to comment on the post.

6. Tap the Send icon.

7. Tap the Google+ icon to return to the Google+ home screen.

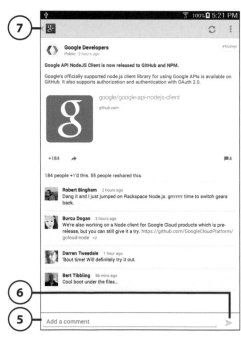

8. Tap the Google+ icon to open the side menu that shows a variety of options for accessing different parts of Google+.

9. Scroll up and down the list to view all of the options. For example, if you want to create a Google+ Hangout that enables you to set up a video chat with several other users, tap Hangouts in the list to open the Hangouts screen. You can learn more about using Hangouts in Chapter 8, "Sending Email and Instant Messages."

10. Tap Home to return to the Home screen.

11. By default, you view posts from all of your "circles", which are groups of your Google+ friends that you can modify. View members of only one circle—for example, only people in the Family category— by tapping All to see the menu of circle categories.

12. Tap the circle that contains users whose posts you want to view. After you tap the circle, the screen refreshes and displays the latest posts from Google+ users in that circle.

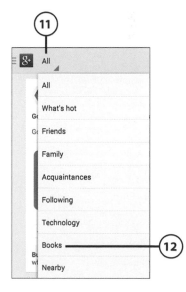

13. Tap the Menu icon and then tap Refresh to refresh the posts on the screen. The icon is blue if there are new posts for you to read.

14. View new and recent notifications in the Notifications list by tapping the Notifications icon. The number of new notifications you have received, such as a new post in a group, appears next to the Notification icon as an orange box with the number of new messages inside it. If there are no new messages, no box appears.

15. New notifications appear at the top of the list. If you see a notification you want to view on the screen then tap it in the list.

16. Close the Notifications list by tapping the Back touch button.

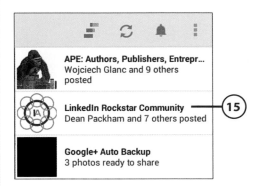

# Write a Post

You can write a new post at any time to transmit to circles of friends that you want to receive the message.

1. Tap Write on the Google+ home screen.

2. Type your message in the Text field.

3. Close the keyboard by tapping the Back touch button.

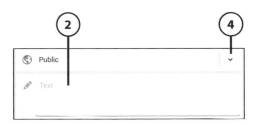

4. Tap the down arrow icon to the right of the list of circles to specify one or more circles with which you will share your post. Otherwise, your message will be sent to all your circles as well as to everyone in the Public circle— that is, all Google+ users.

5. Tap the circle(s) that will view your post from the list. You can also tap Or Pick People and Circles in the menu to open the Share With screen and pick your circles or specific contact name from the list.

6. Tap the Location field if you want to share your location of your post with your viewers.

7. Select your location from the Share Your Location screen. After you select your location, you might see a window reminding you how to delete your location. If you do, tap OK.

8. The location name you selected appears in the Write Post screen.

9. Tap Share when you're finished writing your post. After a second or two the main Google+ screen appears and your post appears as a tile on the screen.

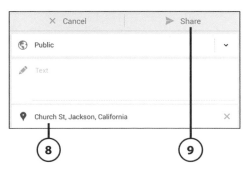

# Creating Documents and Presentations with Hancom Office

Hancom Office Viewer is a productivity app from Hancom that's preinstalled on your Galaxy Tab 4 so you can view Word, PDF, Excel, and PowerPoint files on your Tab 4. You can send those files to yourself and others by email or an online file-sharing service such as Dropbox. You can also print your documents.

If you want to edit your documents, Hancom makes it easy for you to install the full version of Hancom Office for free so you can edit Word, Excel, and PowerPoint files right on your Tab 4.

## Start Hancom Office Viewer for the First Time

1. Tap the Apps icon on the Home screen.

2. Go to the second page of the Apps screen by swiping from right to left on the screen.

3. Tap Hancom Office Viewer.

4. When you start the app for the first time, the app takes a few seconds to install on your Tab 4.

5. The Hancom Office Viewer screen appears and shows that no recent documents have been opened.

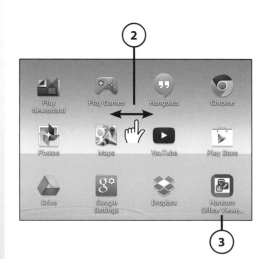

# Open and Close a Document

1. Tap Open.

2. Navigate to the folder that contains the file you want to open. When you find it, tap the filename. In this example, I'm opening a document in Hancom Office Viewer.

3. Scroll up and down the document in the screen to read it.

4. Tap the Menu icon in the menu bar.

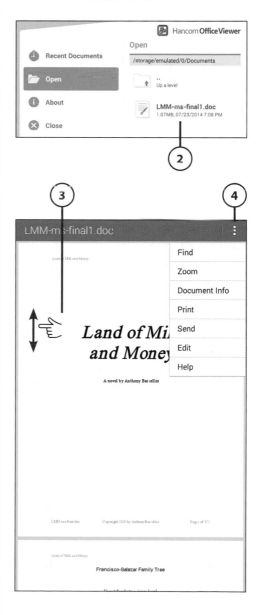

5. Tap to find text in the document that matches your search term(s).

6. Tap to change the view of your file so you can zoom in and get a close-up view of the document or zoom out to see more of the document.

7. Tap to get information about the document including the file size and the last time the file was modified.

8. Tap to print one or more pages in the document.

9. Tap to send the document to your Dropbox or Google Drive account, to someone else in an email or Gmail message, or to another device connected via Bluetooth or Wi-Fi Direct.

10. Tap to edit the document, which you find out how to do later in this chapter.

11. Tap to get online help for the app from the Hancom website or get information about the app.

12. Close the menu by tapping the Back touch button; close the document and return to the main Hancom Office Viewer screen by tapping the Back touch button again.

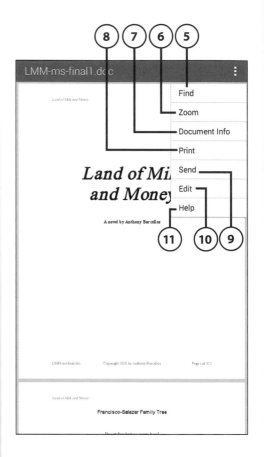

# Install Hancom Office

1. Open a document as described in the previous section.

2. Tap the Menu icon in the menu bar.

3. Tap Edit.

4. If you see a screen telling you a new version of Samsung Apps is available, tap Update. When Samsung Apps finishes updating, you return to the document screen; repeat Steps 2 and 3.

5. Tap Update in the Hancom Office Updater app information screen.

6. Tap Accept and Download in the App Permissions window.

7. After the Tab 4 installs the app, tap Open.

8. In the Hancom Office Updater screen, tap Update to update the Hancom Office widget.

9. Tap the Install button to install the Hword word processing app, the Hcell spreadsheet app, or the Hshow presentation app. This example describes viewing a document so tap the Install button for the Hword app.

10. Tap Free to install the Hword app.

11. Tap Accept and Download in the App Permissions window.

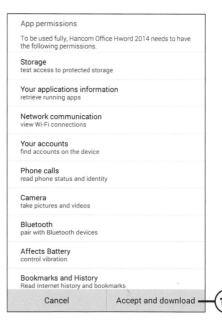

12. After the Tab 4 installs the app, tap Open.

13. The Hword app screen opens documents in the Recent Documents list. As there are no recent documents open, the No Recent Document icon appears in the Recent Documents list on the right side of the screen.

14. Close the app by tapping Close.

---

### Can I Still Use Hancom Office Viewer After I Install Hword?

Installing Hword doesn't remove the Hancom Office Viewer app from your Tab 4. If you want to view a Word or PDF document, you can do so by tapping Hancom Office Viewer in the second page of the Apps screen.

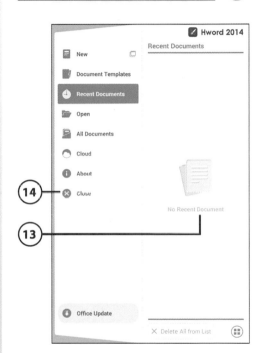

---

# Open a Document in Hword

Now that you've installed Hword on your Tab 4, you can open a document and edit it within the Hword app.

1. Tap the Apps icon on the Home screen and then go to the second page of the Apps screen by swiping from right to left on the screen.

2. Tap Hword 2014.

3. Tap Open.

4. Navigate to the folder that contains the file you want to open. When you find it, tap the filename.

5. Tap a location in the document to open the keyboard and begin editing it; a blue handle appears below the blinking cursor to help show you where you are.

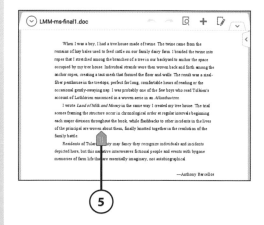

6. Select a word to edit by tapping on the word twice. The word is highlighted and a blue handle appears after the word.

7. Tap an option in the menu to cut or copy the word; select all the text on the page; change the formatting; add a comment; add a hyperlink; share the text with a device, in an email message, or with another app; or spell check the word.

8. Open the formatting toolbar by tapping the Format icon in the menu bar.

9. Close the document by tapping the down arrow at the left side of the menu bar and then tapping Close in the menu.

# Access Files from a Cloud Service

1. Tap Cloud in the Hword home screen to access an online file-sharing service, including Dropbox, Google Drive, or Microsoft OneDrive.

2. Tap the service you use in the menu. After you tap a service, you might be asked to install the cloud service app specifically designed for use with Android. This example uses Dropbox.

3. Allow Hword to access the files and folders in your Dropbox account by tapping Allow.

**4.** Folders within your Dropbox folder appear at the right side of the Hword screen so you can open the file you want within the appropriate folder or subfolder.

**5.** Navigate to the folder that contains your file and then open the file by tapping the filename.

**6.** The first page in the document appears in the Hword screen so you can read through it by swiping up and down on the screen.

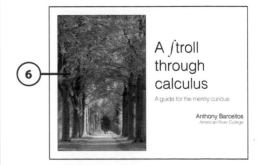

# Create a New Document

Hword makes it easy for you to create a new document. This example describes how to create a Word-format document.

1. Open the Hword app as described earlier in this chapter.

2. Tap Document Templates on the Hword home screen.

3. View all available document templates by swiping up and down in the Document Templates list on the right side of the screen.

4. Tap the New tile.

5.  The new document appears on
    the screen with the keyboard at
    the bottom of the screen. As you
    type, your text appears in the
    default document font.

## What Appears on the Screen When I Choose Another Template?

When you open a template that
isn't blank, the new document
opens with the template layout
and dummy text. You can replace
this dummy text, such as the
name of the fax recipient, with
the actual recipient's name.

6. The default document title name shows Document1, which is the default name of the document.

7. Tap the down arrow icon to the left of the document title name to open the Tasks menu and perform specific tasks including opening another document and changing document and app settings. After you tap the down arrow icon, the icon changes to a white up arrow icon inside a blue button.

8. Close the menu by tapping the Back touch button.

9. Tap the Back touch button to go back to the Hword home screen. If you haven't saved the document, a Close window appears that asks if you want to save changes. If you want to return to editing the document, tap Cancel in the window.

10. Tap Undo to reverse the previous action, such as deleting a word.

11. Tap Redo to reapply the previous action you previously undid. For example, if you tapped the Undo icon after deleting a word, tap the Redo icon to delete the affected word again.

12. Tap the Add Object icon to select an object to add to your document. Objects include a saved image, a table, and a symbol such as a multiplication sign.

13. Tap the Format icon to open the formatting toolbar and change the font size, style, and color; change the appearance and alignment of the selected paragraph; and apply a text style to a selected area of text. For example, you can apply the Title style to a word you want as the document title.

14. Open the Task menu by tapping the down arrow.

15. Tap Save to save the document with its current name in your chosen folder or subfolder.

16. In this menu, you can also assign a password to the document that you're required to enter in Hword before you can open the document, find and replace text, and print your document if you're connected to a printer via a Bluetooth or Wi-Fi connection.

**Run multiple apps in multi-window view**

**Search the Google Play Store for thousands of useful, educational, and entertaining apps**

**Access Google apps from the main Home screen**

**Shop for Galaxy Tab 4 apps in the GALAXY Apps app**

**Get safe and fun content in the Samsung Kids Mode app**

In this chapter, you discover how to expand the capabilities of the Galaxy Tab 4 by finding and installing new apps from both Samsung and Google. You also learn how to access apps from the Home screen, open multiple apps on the screen, and access safe content for your children. What's more, this chapter tells you how to browse and make purchases in the Google Play Store and organize application icons on your Galaxy Tab. Topics covered in this chapter include:

→ Searching for Android applications

→ Purchasing Android applications

→ Rating applications

→ Getting help with apps

→ Arranging app icons on your Galaxy Tab 4

→ Adding and removing Home pages

→ Accessing Google apps from the main Home screen

→ Opening multiple apps on the screen

→ Using the Kids Mode app to find safe content

→ Adding a dictionary and thesaurus

→ Adding an RSS reader

→ Using the Note Everything app

# Finding and Managing Apps

The Galaxy Tab 4 is not just about superior hardware craftsmanship. Your Tab's true strength lies in the incredible software that is developed for it. The Galaxy Tab 4 comes with some truly amazing, preinstalled apps right out of the box, but you can expand its capabilities even further by downloading new apps from the Google Play Store.

You can choose from thousands of innovative apps, ranging from games to productivity apps. The number of apps optimized for use on your Tab is growing rapidly.

Android 4.4, also known by its nickname KitKat, also allows you to access all your Google apps from the first page on the Home screen. KitKat also includes the capability to open multiple apps in one screen so you can switch between open apps easily. What's more, the Tab 4 comes with an app called Kids Mode that makes it easy for you to find suitable content for your children.

# Accessing Google Apps from the Home Screen

The Google icon appears on the main Home screen so you can access any Google app installed on your Tab 4 within a small pop-up window that appears on the screen. You can also remove any Google app icons within the pop-up window as you would with any other app on a Home screen.

1. Tap the Google app on the main Home screen.

2. Open a Google app by tapping on the app within the pop-up window.

3. Move a Google app icon to a different location within the window by tapping and holding on the icon and then dragging the icon to a new location within the window. The other icons in the window rearrange to accommodate your selected icon's new position.

4. Remove a Google app from the pop-up window by tapping and holding on the icon and then dragging the icon to the Remove icon in the menu bar at the top of the screen.

5. Close the pop-up window by tapping the Back touch button.

# Opening Multiple Apps in Multi-Window View

By default, multi-window view is turned on so you can view two open apps at one time on the Tab 4 screen. You can also set up multi-window view in the Settings window so that you can view content in multiple windows when you open files within the My Files or Video apps and when you open attachments from email messages.

After you set up multi-window view, you can only open apps in multi-window view from within the app tray, which you can access from any screen.

1. Tap the Apps icon on the Home screen.

2. Tap Settings.

3. Tap Device in the menu bar.

4. Tap Multi Window. If the Multi Window slider bar is set to Off (a gray O button), turn the feature on by sliding the button to the right; the button changes to a green I button.

5. Tap the Open in Multi Window check box to view content in multiple windows when you open files in the My Files or Video apps and when you view email attachments in full screen mode.

6. Return to the Home screen by pressing the Home button.

7. Tap and hold your finger on the right edge of the screen and then swipe from right to left. The app tray appears on the right side of the screen.

8. Open an app by tapping the app icon. If you don't tap an app icon within a few seconds, the app tray disappears.

# Manage Multiple Windows on the Screen

1. Open the app tray on the Home screen as described earlier in this chapter.

2. Tap Internet.

3. The Internet screen appears and displays the Samsung Galaxy Tab registration website by default.

4. Open the app tray and then tap Gmail.

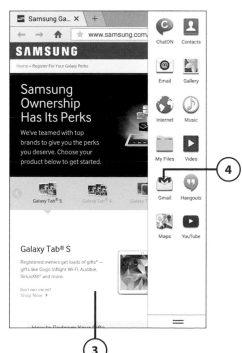

5. The Gmail app window appears on the bottom two-thirds of the screen. It's surrounded by a blue line and has a blue control button at the top center of the window.

6. Resize the Gmail app window by tapping and holding on the blue control button and then swiping up and down in the screen to increase or decrease the window size, respectively. When you've moved the blue control button to your desired window height, release your finger. The Tab 4 resizes the app to the desired size.

7. Open viewing option buttons by tapping the blue control button. A series of four buttons appears in a semicircular pattern below the blue button. Note that if you don't tap one of these four buttons within three seconds, the buttons disappear.

8. Tap to move the Gmail app to the top of the screen and the Internet app to the bottom. After the Gmail app window moves to the top of the screen, the blue control button appears at the bottom center of the window.

9. Tap to drag and drop a paragraph of text or a screenshot image from the Gmail app window into the Internet app window. Tap and hold on the image or text paragraph in the Gmail app window and then drag it into the Internet app window. After you drag the text or image, the Internet app window is highlighted; tap the Gmail app window to continue with Step 10.

10. Tap to view the Gmail app on the entire screen and close multi-window view. You can only view the Internet window again by tapping the Recent touch button and then tapping the Internet screen image in the Recent Apps window; the Internet app also appears on the entire screen.

11. Tap to close the Gmail window.

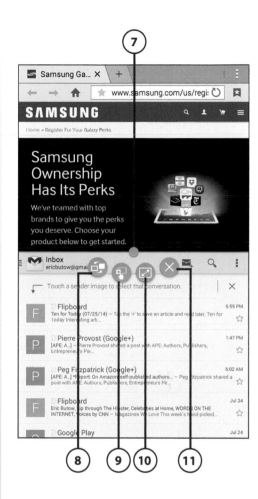

12.  Tap the Internet app window to select it; the Internet app window is highlighted with a blue border and the blue control button appears at the bottom center of the window. Tap the button to perform tasks discussed in Steps 6 through 10.

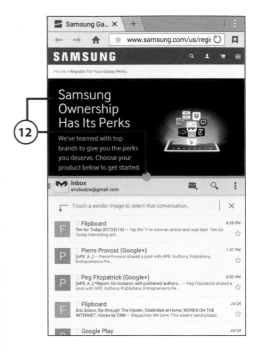

# >>>Go Further

## VIEWING MORE THAN TWO APPS ON THE SCREEN

Though you can only view two apps on the screen at one time in multi-window view, you can open more than two apps within multi-window view. In the example used in this chapter, you have the Internet app window open at the top of the screen and the Gmail app window open at the bottom. When you open the app tray and tap the Contacts icon, the Contacts app window appears at the top of the screen in front of the Internet app. Close the Contacts app window by tapping the blue control button and then tapping the Close button; the Internet window appears again.

# Edit Apps in the App Tray

The app tray shows 12 apps by default, but you can change the apps that you can access in the tray.

1. Open the app tray on the Home screen as you learned to do earlier in this chapter. Tap the Edit button at the bottom of the tray.

2. Tap Edit.

3. Remove apps from the app tray at the right side of the screen by tapping and holding on the app icon and then dragging the icon to the icon holding area on the left side of the screen.

4. Add an app to the tray by tapping and holding the icon in the icon holding area and then dragging the icon to the app tray. If you move an icon next to or between two icons, the other icons in the tray rearrange themselves to accommodate the new icon. You can add an icon after the last icon row by dragging the icon below the last icon row.

5. If you change your mind about editing the app tray, you can reset the app tray layout to its default setting by tapping Reset.

6. When you finish making changes to the app tray, tap Done. The app holding area disappears and the app tray appears with your changes on the right side of the screen. After a few seconds of no activity, the app tray disappears.

# Finding Apps from Samsung

The Tab 4 includes the Kids Mode installation app. After you install the full Kids Mode app you can restrict content for your children and have peace of mind as your kids explore with your Tab.

Samsung also includes the GALAXY Apps app that lets you shop for Android apps optimized for your Tab 4. A great way to become acquainted with GALAXY Apps is just to start browsing. Many reviews of apps and games are available, so you can make an intelligent choice before downloading.

## Set Up the Kids Mode App

1. Tap the Apps icon on the Home screen.

2. Swipe to the second page of the Apps screen and then tap Kids Mode.

3. In the Install Application window, tap OK.

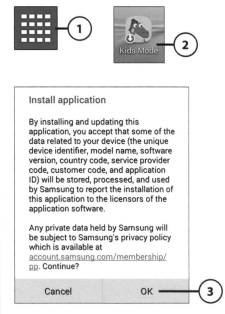

**4.** Install the complete Kids Mode app by tapping Install.

**5.** After the Tab 4 installs the app, the second page of the Apps screen appears again; tap Kids Mode.

**6.** Swipe back and forth on the screen to get more information about the Kids Mode app.

**7.** Set the PIN for the app by tapping Set PIN. When you enter the PIN, you can set parental controls as well as close Kids Mode so you can return to normal usage.

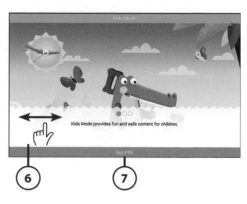

8. Tap a four-digit PIN in the keypad.

9. Confirm the PIN by tapping it again in the keypad.

10. Type a password you can use in case you forget your PIN. The password must have at least four characters.

11. Tap Continue.

12. Confirm the password by typing it in again.

13. Tap OK.

14. Create the kid's profile by typing the name of the child in the Name field.

15. Tap Next in the keyboard.

16. Enter the child's birthdate by tapping the up and down arrows above and below the month, date, and year.

17. Tap Set.

18. Tap Next.

19. Tap Accept in the Disclaimer window.

20. Tap the check box(es) next to the apps the child can use. The Kids Mode app determines how many apps the child can use by the child's age. In this example, tap the check box next to Peel Smart Remote.

21. After you tap the check box, tap Next at the bottom of the window.

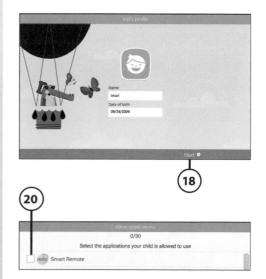

**22.** Tap Finish.

**23.** Tap the Close icon; you can hand the Tab 4 to your child to let him or her play with the device.

**24.** Your child can play with apps in the main Kids Mode screen by tapping the appropriate icon on the screen. For example, the child can take pictures on the Tab 4 by tapping the green camera icon. Your kids can also swipe back and forth on the screen to view more animations and features.

**25.** Access the Parental Control screen by tapping the Parental Control icon and then typing your PIN in the keypad that appears on the screen.

**26.** Close Kids Mode by tapping the Exit icon and then typing your PIN in the keypad that appears on the screen. The next time you start the Kids Mode app, you see the main Kids Mode screen.

## Pressing the Home Button After You Exit Kids Mode

After you exit Kids Mode, every time you tap the Home button you see a Complete Action Using window that asks if you want to complete the action using Kids Mode or TouchWiz Home. Tap the Kids Mode icon to return to the main Kids Mode screen or tap TouchWiz Home to return to the main Home screen. If you just want to return to your selected screen this one time, tap Just Once. If you want to return to your selected screen every time from now on, tap Always.

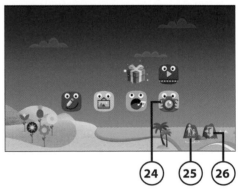

# Shop in the Galaxy Apps Store

1. Tap the Apps icon on the Home screen.

2. Tap GALAXY Apps.

3. A page of featured apps displays. Scroll up and down the page to review groups of apps as well as individual apps. You can view more apps in a group by tapping See More.

4. Tap the Category icon in the menu bar, swipe up and down the category list if necessary to view all the categories, and then tap a category to browse the list of results for that category.

5. If you know the name of the app, book, magazine, or movie you want, tap the Search icon to specify a search term.

6. Type a search term into the Search field. Possible matches for your search appear in the list below the field.

7. Tap the app in the list if the product you want is listed as an option.

8. Swipe up and down the list of apps in the Results page and then tap the title of the app you want more information about.

9. Read more about the product. You can purchase—or download, if the app is free—the app on the description page. In this example, install Fraction Calculator Plus Free by tapping Free.

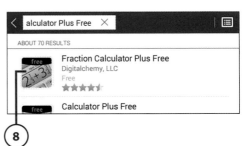

## More About Product Descriptions

The description page for an app is chock-full of useful information so you can make an educated decision about whether you want to purchase the app. Sample screenshots of the app are featured on this page along with customer reviews and information about the developer.

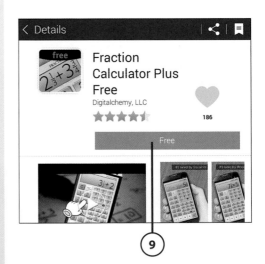

# Getting Apps in the Google Play Store

The Google Play Store makes it easy for you to browse apps and games that you can download to your Galaxy Tab 4. If this is your first time shopping in the Google Play Store, you will find the interface quite intuitive. A great way to become acquainted with the Google Play Store is just to start browsing. Many reviews of apps and games are available, so you can make an intelligent choice before downloading. A Google, Bing, or Yahoo! search for "Best Android apps for Galaxy Tab 4" can help you identify the most popular apps. Tab 4 users from around the world are writing articles about their experiences with apps that you might find useful. After you download and try out an app, consider giving your feedback so that new Tab 4 users can learn from you.

## Search for Android Applications

To access the Google Play Store for the first time, you must use your Google account to sign into the Google Play Store. After you launch the Google Play Store app, there are several ways for you to search apps from the home page. The home page search options change position on the page, depending on which orientation you hold your Tab 4: vertical or horizontal.

1. Tap Play Store on the Home screen.

2. Tap Accept if you see the Google Play Store Terms of Service.

### Terms of Service
The Terms of Service appear only the first time you launch the Google Play Store.

3. Tap Apps on the Google Play Store home page. A page of featured apps displays.

4. Scroll up and down the page to review groups of apps as well as individual apps. You can view more apps in a group by tapping More.

5. Tap a category to browse the list of results for that category.

6. If you know the name of the app, book, magazine, or movie you want, tap the Search icon to specify a search term.

7. Type a search term into the Search Google Play field. Possible matches for your search appear in the list below the search field.

8. Tap the app in the list if the product you want is listed as an option.

9. Swipe up and down the list of apps in the Results page and then tap the title of the app you want more information about.

10. Read more about the product. You can purchase—or download, if the app is free—the app on the description page. In this example, install Where's My Perry? Free by tapping Install.

## Other Ways to Search for Apps

Your Galaxy Tab 4 also has the Samsung Apps application prein-stalled on the Home screen. You can find many popular free and paid apps for your particular Tab 4 with Samsung Apps. You access Samsung Apps by tapping the Samsung Apps icon on the main Home screen.

# Find Great Apps

There are thousands of apps that you can download to your Galaxy Tab 4, so use your storage space wisely by finding the great ones. Finding the best apps might be the biggest challenge of all as you wade through your many options. This task gives you some tips on how to locate the highest-performing apps.

1. Tap Apps in the Google Play Store app.

2. Take a look at the featured apps on the Play Store home page. Keep in mind that large companies, usually with well-established names, tend to dominate the featured list. Lesser-known developers are also producing outstanding apps, so look deeper.

3. Some apps have trial versions you can test drive before purchasing. Look for Lite or Free versions of applications to test before you buy.

4. Tap an app in the Apps list that you want to learn more about.

5. Scroll down to check out customer reviews for products, but don't trust everything you read. Some reviews might not be in-depth or unbiased, and therefore they are less helpful.

6. Scroll to the bottom of the page and take a look at the Similar Apps list. You see apps that are similar along with their ratings next to them. You might find a higher-rated app that you want to look into.

# >>>Go Further
## USING OTHER RESOURCES TO FIND APPS

You can use other solid resources outside the Play Store for finding great apps.

**Perform a Google search**—For example, if you are looking for an app suited for taking dictation, type "Galaxy Tab 4 App Dictation."

**Search for sites that feature and post reviews for apps**—Be aware that some of these sites are sponsored by the developers and might not convey completely objective views.

**Find a Galaxy Tab forum**—There are many of these popping up every day. In a forum, you can post questions to other Galaxy Tab 4 owners regarding apps. Be aware that experienced Tab users might not moderate all of these forums, and the advice you receive can be questionable.

## Purchase Android Applications

Software developers from around the world have developed thousands of apps for you to take advantage of with your Galaxy Tab 4. You can choose from many free apps in the Google Play Store, and you can also purchase a variety of more sophisticated apps for a fee. The process for downloading free apps and paid apps is similar, but you need to designate a payment method to make purchases.

1. Tap Play Store on the Home screen.

2. Locate and then tap the app that you want to download. The product description page opens.

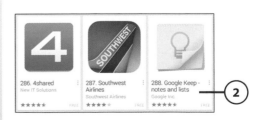

3.  Tap the price of the app to see the permissions for this app. If this app is free, as in this example with Google Keep, tap the Install button. A page that lists the permissions the app is requesting opens.

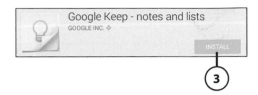

4.  Tap Accept to begin installing the app.

## Accepting Permissions

If the application you have selected requires control of your Tab or access to data, the Google Play Store displays the information in this area. The list of permissions changes from app to app. When you accept permissions, you are essentially allowing the application you are purchasing to access your Galaxy Tab 4, including Internet access.

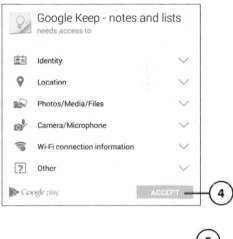

5.  Tap Open to launch the application.

>>>Go Further

## UPDATING APPS

The Google Play Store periodically searches for updates for apps that have been downloaded to your Galaxy Tab 4. If an update has been found, a notification appears in the Status Bar. You can open the Quick Settings and Notifications screen and then tap the item in the Notifications list to be taken to the Google Play Store so you can begin the update. You can learn more about opening the Quick Settings and Notifications screen in Chapter 3, "Setting Up the Galaxy Tab 4."

## >>>*Go Further*
### DISABLING UPDATE NOTIFICATIONS

If you prefer to manually check for updates, you can configure the Google Play Store to stop notifying you about updates. Just launch the Google Play Store app and then tap the Menu icon in the right side of the menu bar at the top of the screen. Select Settings in the menu, and then deselect the Notifications option. You can tap the Download icon in the top-right corner of the Apps Bar to view a list of installed apps in the My Apps screen. The list of installed apps also lets you know which apps have an update that is available. You can also enable the Allow Automatic Updating setting within this list.

## Rate Applications

Rating content you have purchased on Google Play Store helps others make educated decisions about their purchases. The Google Play Store uses a five-star rating system to rate all content. Much of the content on the Google Play Store features reviews that you can read to see how others like the product.

1. Tap Play Store on the Home screen.

2. Tap the Google Play Store icon.

3. Tap My Apps.

4. Tap the app that you want to rate.

5. Tap a rating star on a scale from one to five. For example, if you tap the second star from the right the first four stars from left to right are highlighted in blue, which signifies that you give the app four stars on a five-star scale.

6. Tap OK if you see a window with information about Google Play reviews using Google+.

7. Tap the rating star again as you did in Step 5.

8. Enter a title for your review in the Title field.

9. Enter your comments in the Description field.

10. Tap Submit.

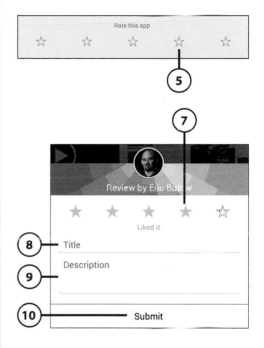

## Get Help with Apps

Many new apps are being added to the Google Play Store daily from well-known companies, small companies, and individual developers. Bugs and other problems are likely to arise in such a fast-moving market. There are ways for you to contact developers so that you can ask questions.

1. Tap Play Store on the Home screen.

2. Tap the Google Play Store icon.

3. Tap My Apps.

4. Tap the app for which you need help.

5. Tap the down arrow icon to view the entire description.

6. Scroll down and then tap Visit Webpage in the Developer section to visit the developer's site and search for information.

7. Tap Send Email to compose an email message asking your question(s).

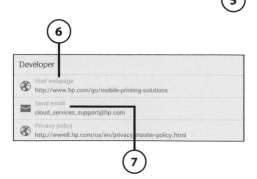

# Managing Apps Through Your Home Pages

You begin many of your activities on the Home screen of the Galaxy Tab 4. As you purchase new apps, the number of icons in your Applications menu multiplies, which might prompt you to rearrange them according to the ones you use the most. You can manage your apps through your home pages by creating new home pages, deleting existing home pages, and grouping and arranging apps as you see fit on respective pages.

By default, when you download an application from Google Play Store, a shortcut is placed in the Applications menu, which is accessible from any Home screen. You can easily move shortcuts from the Applications menu to a Home screen and then rearrange them.

1. Tap the Apps icon on the Home screen.

2. Swipe from right to left on the screen to view the app you added on the second page of the Apps screen.

3. Locate the application shortcut, or widget, that you want to use, and then press and hold your finger on it. An overlay of the main Home screen appears on the page and overlays of both Home pages display below the main Home screen overlay.

**4.** Move the shortcut to the desired Home screen overlay. Your selected Home screen appears as an overlay on the screen.

**5.** Move the shortcut to your desired location on the Home screen.

**6.** Release your finger. The shortcut is placed on the Home screen.

**7.** Repeat Steps 2 and 3 to move more App shortcuts from the Applications menu to the Home screen.

**8.** By default, your Galaxy Tab has three Home screens. Press your finger on a shortcut on a Home screen (in this example, Home screen 2) that you would like to move to another Home screen.

## >>>Go Further
### ADD TO HOME SCREEN

A quick way to add widgets, apps, folders, and new pages is to use the Add to Home feature. Press your finger on an empty space on a Home screen and hold until the Home screen menu pops up. Tap Add to Home screen and then choose the options that you want and follow the prompts to complete the task.

9. Drag the icon with your finger to the edge of the screen to move to another Home screen (in this example, Home screen 2).

10. Remove your finger from the shortcut when you reach the spot where you would like to leave the shortcut.

## >>>*Go Further*

### CUSTOMIZING HOME SCREENS

Each Galaxy Tab 4 can be customized as unique as its individual owner. You can arrange your icons on any Home screen for shortcuts or widgets that you frequently use. For example, you can arrange all your games on one Home screen panel and all your productivity apps on another. You can even create new panels by tapping the Menu touch button located on your Galaxy Tab, from any Home screen, and tapping Edit.

**11.** When you hold your finger on a shortcut and after it pulsates once, the Remove icon (a trash-can) appears in the top-right of the screen. Drag a shortcut to the Remove icon to remove it from a Home screen.

### Removing Shortcuts and Widgets

When you remove a shortcut or widget icon, it does not delete or uninstall the app from your Galaxy Tab 4; it simply removes it from that panel. If you want to create a shortcut for that application again, it is still located in the Applications menu, or you can use the Add to Home Screen function.

## >>>*Go Further*

### UNINSTALLING APPS FROM YOUR TAB

After you purchase an app from the Google Play Store, you own it forever. You can uninstall a paid app from your Galaxy Tab 4 and then choose to reinstall it later (at no additional charge) in the future. To uninstall an app, tap the Apps icon on a Home screen and then tap Settings. Tap Applications Manager, and choose All to view a list of your applications. Tap the app that you want to uninstall to open the App Info screen and then tap Uninstall. You can also uninstall apps by using the Uninstall option for the application on the Google Play Store.

# Adding Useful Apps

The true power of the tablet revolution lies not only in the simplification of computing, but also personalization. Apps enable you to optimize your Galaxy Tab for your unique lifestyle. Your Galaxy Tab 4 can be a virtual dictionary or thesaurus. Add an RSS reader and transform your Tab into a news-gathering device so that you are always up to date on current news and events. Many practical apps on the market enhance the capabilities of your Galaxy Tab 4, freeing you from having to purchase and carry a second device such as a digital audio recorder or scanner. There are too many options to list them all here, but let's explore a few practical apps that you might want to consider.

## Use the Merriam-Webster Dictionary App

Adding a simple dictionary app to your Galaxy Tab 4 is a very handy and practical solution for having to lug around an actual paper reference book.

The Merriam-Webster Dictionary app is free on the Google Play Store and delivers content that is trusted. The following steps presume you have already downloaded the Merriam-Webster Dictionary app from the Google Play Store.

1. Tap the Merriam-Webster app on the Home screen.

### Use Any Dictionary App

There are many other free options for dictionary and thesaurus reference apps. If you prefer another, don't hesitate to use it. This is just a recommendation for the usefulness of such a reference to exist on your Galaxy Tab 4. The Dictionary.com app is also a great application and gets the job done.

2. Tap in the Search field and enter a word to look up. Search suggestions appear in the list beneath the field.

3. Tap the correct word in the list. The definition(s) for the entry appear.

4. You can tap the speaker icon to hear the pronunciation of the word.

5. Tap the star to add this word to your Favorites.

6. Tap to view all words you have marked as Favorites.

7. Tap to view a list of recently searched words.

8. Tap to open the app menu.

9. You can learn a new word every day. Tap to view the word of the day.

10. Tap to get a list of apps recommended to you by Merriam-Webster, such as the Britannica Encyclopedia.

11. Tap to provide Feedback to the developers of this app.

12. Tap to rate this app in the Play Store.

13. Tap to share information about this app in an email message, on social networks, on cloud storage services, in other apps such as Memo, or to other devices.

14. Tap to learn about and purchase the premium version of the app in the Play Store.

15. Tap to get information about Merriam-Webster.

16. Tap to get copyright information for the app.

# Use the LinkedIn Pulse RSS Reader

If part of your daily routine includes reading news websites and blogs, adding an RSS reader can help you manage your news sources from one app in the form of feeds instead of visiting multiple websites. LinkedIn Pulse is a free RSS feed reader that you can download from the Google Play Store; it enables you to acquire and manage multiple news feeds as an interactive mosaic. The following steps presume you have already downloaded the LinkedIn Pulse app from the Google Play Store.

1. Tap Pulse on the Home screen.

2. Tap Get Started.

3. If you don't have a LinkedIn account, tap Join LinkedIn. This example presumes you already have a LinkedIn account.

4. Type your LinkedIn username and password in the Email and Password fields.

5. Tap Continue.

6. Pulse is loaded with predefined news feed channels to get you started. Each tiles represents an individual feed channel. Flick down on the screen to view the rest of the channels.

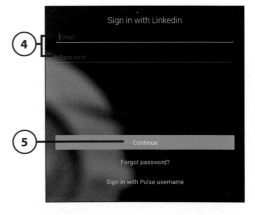

7.  Tap to choose a new feed to add to the page.

8.  After you tap the topic(s) you want, tap Start Reading.

9.  Tap a news story to open it. The story opens.

## Refreshing Automatically

You can choose an automatic refresh option by tapping the Pulse icon on the menu bar at the top of the screen. Next, tap All Channels. Pulse automatically refreshes the news feeds for all Pulse channels including the ones in your list.

10.  Open a menu to change your viewing options by tapping the Menu icon.

## Landscape or Portrait Orientation

The Pulse interface options change, depending on whether you hold your Tab in landscape orientation or portrait orientation as shown in these steps. Try holding your Tab in various orientations to see which you prefer.

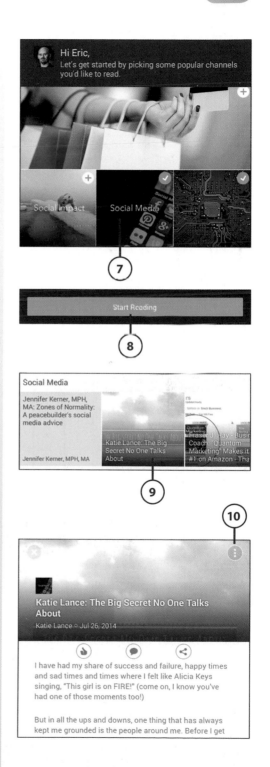

11. Tap to save the article as a favorite.

12. Tap to select a new font size and style for the article text as well as the brightness level for the page.

13. Tap to open the article in the Internet or Chrome browser.

14. Tap to open the article on the main website where the article is found.

15. Tap to like the article and share that with the website that contains the article and on your LinkedIn profile. The number of likes already posted appears to the right of the icon.

16. Tap to comment on the article and share that with the website that contains the article and on your LinkedIn profile. The number of comments already posted appears to the right of the icon.

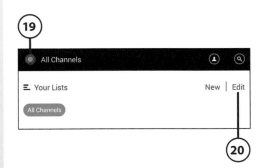

17. Tap to share the article on Linked, Facebook, Twitter, and/ or Google+; you can also share the article with other apps including email, Gmail, ChatON, and Dropbox. The number of times the article has been shared appears to the right of the icon.

18. Tap the Close button in the upper-left corner of the screen to return to the category news feed page.

19. Tap the Pulse icon in the menu bar.

20. Tap Edit.

**21.** Press your finger to the name of a news feed and drag it to reorder feeds.

**22.** Remove a feed from your list by tapping the check mark icon and then tapping Remove in the window.

**23.** Tap Done when you finish editing your feeds list.

**24.** You can add a new content list category into which you can place feeds by tapping the Pulse icon in the menu bar and then tapping New.

**25.** Type the new list category name in the Create List field.

**26.** Tap Okay.

27. Search the feed you want to add in the category and then tap the button to the right of the feed name you want to add.

28. The feeds you add appear above the All Channels list.

29. Tap Done when you finish editing your feeds list.

30. Your new list appears on the screen.

31. Add more categories to the list by tapping either the Search icon in the menu bar or the Find More to Follow button at the bottom of the feed list.

32. Search new categories and then tap the feed you want to add in the What's New section or the category name in the Categories section. This example uses the Technology category.

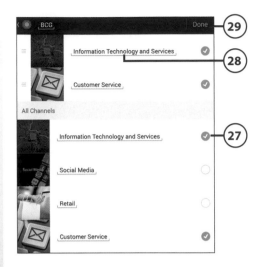

## Multiple Pages of News Feeds

You can add 50 pages of news feeds within Pulse with 12 feeds per page for a maximum total of 600 feeds. If you choose to populate a new page with feeds you can access the new pages by tapping the various page numbers at the top of each page.

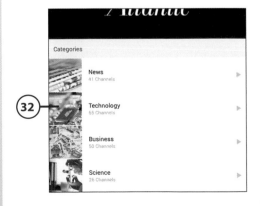

**33.** Search the feed you want to add in the category and then tap the plus icon to the right of the feed name you want to add.

**34.** Tap the Back touch button twice to return to the feeds page.

**35.** The feed you added appears at the top of the list.

**36.** View an article in the new feed by tapping the tile.

**37.** Tap to view your profile, change your profile settings, and view a list of your saved stories.

# Use Note Everything

A digital voice recorder can be a priceless tool if you ever need to record some notes for yourself. Or have you ever wished you had the capability to scan barcodes on a product so that you could store the information?

Note Everything is a free app that can do all of this and more, including taking handwritten notes and tucking information away neatly in folders. This section presumes you have already downloaded the Note Everything app from the Google Play Store.

**1.** Tap Note Everything on the Home screen.

## Receiving Help

When you first use certain functions, a help screen appears and provides you with tips.

2. Tap Close in the What's New screen.

3. Tap to add a new note.

4. Tap Textnote to leave a note using the keyboard. This is similar to how the preinstalled Memo widget works on your Tab, but you might find it more beneficial to have all your notes in one location.

5. Tap Paintnote to leave a note using your finger as a pen. You can tap the Menu button on your Galaxy Tab and change the color of ink, erase marks, change stroke width, clear colors, work full screen, and more. This is a great option for jotting down a quick visual note.

6. Tap Voicenote to record voice memos. Each recording is stored as an individual file that you can play back on your Galaxy Tab.

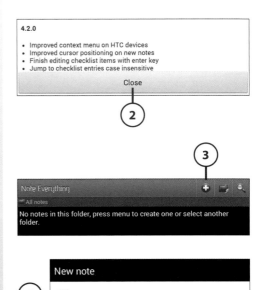

7. Tap Note from Barcode to use your Galaxy Tab 4 camera to read barcodes and note the barcode for later reference. This option requires you to install another free app named Barcode Scanner for it to work. The installation process is streamlined within the Note Everything app and takes only a few moments.

8. Tap Note from Google Docs to import and export text notes from Google Docs. This option requires you to install another free app named Note Everything (NE) GDocs. These two apps can work seamlessly together or independently.

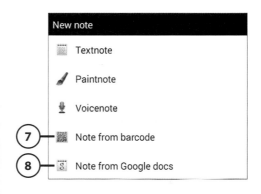

## Recording Voice Notes

After each recording, you can choose whether to use or discard the recording. If you choose to keep it, you are taken to a page with a notepad where you can play back the voice memo and take text notes at the same time.

## *It's Not All Good*

### Not Always Accurate

Be advised that not all barcode scanners on your Galaxy Tab 4 are 100% accurate. That goes for any product, not just the one featured here. Sometimes these scanners might not recognize the product, or the price they provide for the product might be way off the mark. Use all these apps with caution. If you don't like this app, you can choose from many other free options.

9. After you write a note, tap the Back touch button. The note is placed in the main (root) menu. Tap and hold your finger on any note that you would like to move to a different folder, and a pop-up menu appears.

10. Tap Move to Folder.

11. Tap Close after you read the help screen. Help screens appear when you access a function for the first time.

12. Tap to create a folder.

13. Type the name in the Foldername field.

14. Tap OK to move the note to the new folder.

**Pair Bluetooth devices
with your Galaxy Tab 4**

**Manage a
MicroSD card**

This chapter covers how to get the most from your Galaxy Tab 4 using hardware accessories such as the optional Multimedia Desk Dock, the Keyboard Dock, and memory card options. Accessories covered in this chapter include:

→ Bluetooth keyboards

→ Other Bluetooth devices

→ MicroSD cards

# Adding New Hardware

Your Galaxy Tab 4 is fully capable of providing an amazing multi-media experience right out of the box, but whether you are viewing movies, capturing photos and video, or composing a long email, you want your Galaxy Tab to be versatile. Accessories such as Bluetooth headsets, desk docks, Bluetooth keyboards, and extra memory cards can offer some much needed practical support for your Tab use.

You can find accessories for the 7", 8", and 10.1" Galaxy Tab 4 models in electronics stores such as Best Buy, or you can try your local electronics store. Online stores, such as Samsung.com and Amazon.com, are also great places to find hardware accessories for the Galaxy Tabs. Always make sure that you pick the right accessory for your Galaxy Tab model. As of this writing none of the previous Galaxy Tab accessories work with the Tab 4.

### Limited Accessories to Date

This section covers accessories that were available as the book was written for the Galaxy Tab 4 10.1" device. It's likely that shortly after this book finds its way onto shelves there will be new accessories for all three Tab 4 models that are not mentioned in this chapter. For example, Samsung does not offer a multi-media desk dock or keyboard dock for the Galaxy Tab 4. We encourage you to keep up to date on what is available for your device by periodically checking the Samsung website, Amazon.com, and tech forums.

# Bluetooth Keyboards

Your Galaxy Tab 4 comes with Bluetooth 4.0 technology, which enables you to use devices such as wireless headphones and wireless keyboards. There are limited third-party companies that produce accessories such as the Bluetooth keyboard for the 10.1" Tab 4 devices. (One such company is Logitech.) A Bluetooth keyboard provides the convenience of typing with a physical keyboard, which makes it easier to write a lengthy message. This accessory provides a typing experience similar to using a computer keyboard, so inputting information is easier than using the onscreen keyboard. Users who perform extensive writing tasks might find the more ergonomically pleasing Bluetooth keyboard a better alternative to the onscreen keyboard. This accessory is usually in a 2-in-1 package, which means that it serves both as a QWERTY keyboard and also a folding leather case to protect your keyboard. A Bluetooth keyboard case not only protects your Galaxy Tab, but it is also very travel-friendly. You can find Logitech accessories by performing a product search on Amazon.com.

# Pairing Bluetooth Devices

Along with the many other comfort features and conveniences found with the Galaxy Tab 4, your Tab gives you the capability to connect some external hardware devices wirelessly. The Tab 4 is equipped with Bluetooth 4.0 technology, enabling you to connect cable-free with Bluetooth-capable keyboards and headphones. By default, Bluetooth is disabled on your Tab. If you have already played with this setting, you can tell if Bluetooth is turned on by verifying that the Bluetooth symbol is visible in the Status Bar at the top of the screen.

# Pair a Bluetooth Device

You can easily connect your Tab 4 to
a Bluetooth device in two phases:
discovering and pairing.

1.  Turn on the wireless device that
    you want to pair with your Galaxy
    Tab and make it discoverable.

## Discoverability

Bluetooth devices broadcast their
availability only after you instruct
them to do so. If necessary, refer
to your device's manual to learn
how to make it discoverable.

2.  Tap the Apps icon on the Home
    screen.

3.  Tap Settings on the Apps screen.

4.  Tap Bluetooth to view the
    Bluetooth options to the right of
    the screen.

5.  Swipe the Bluetooth slider to the
    right to place the Bluetooth set-
    ting in the On position. The switch
    turns green and any detectable
    Bluetooth devices are listed to the
    right.

6.  Tap your Bluetooth device in the
    list. (If you don't see your device,
    tap Scan in the menu bar above
    the list.) Your Tab attempts to pair
    with the device.

7.  The device then appears under a
    newly created Paired Devices list.

### Paired Bluetooth Device Settings

After you have successfully paired your device to your Tab 4, a Settings icon appears next to the name of the Bluetooth device within the Paired Devices list. Tap that Settings icon to rename, unpair, or further configure your device.

### When Paired

When a device is paired with your Galaxy Tab, you never have to configure the devices again.

# MicroSD Cards

Your Tab supports MicroSD and MicroSDHC memory cards that come in the following sizes: 4GB, 8GB, 16GB, 32GB, and 64GB. (You can only use 64GB MicroSD and MicroSDHC cards on the Tab 4 8.0 and Tab 4 10.1 models.) Increasing the storage capacity of your Galaxy Tab 4 is a convenient way to store more music, photos, videos, and other files.

## Formatting MicroSD Cards

If you buy a new card, you need to format it for your Tab 4. Whether you are upgrading a MicroSD card or adding a new card, follow these steps to format your new memory card:

1. Tap the Apps icon on the Home screen.

2. Tap Settings on the Apps screen.

3. Tap General in the menu bar.

4. Tap Storage.

5. Insert the MicroSD card into your Tab 4. All of the MicroSD Card information appears under the SD Card category to the right.

6. Tap the Format SD card option located at the bottom of the SD card category.

7. Read the warning and then tap Format SD Card.

8. If you type a password to log into the Tab 4, type the password in the Confirm Password screen.

9. When you finish typing the password, tap Continue.

10. Read the warning and then tap Delete All. The SD card is formatted and becomes instantly available for use.

## Unmount Before Removing

It is very important that you first unmount the MicroSD card before removing it from the slot. Failing to do so can result in damage to the MicroSD card. Simply tap Unmount SD Card in the SD Card category.

**Unmount the MicroSD card by tapping Unmount SD Card**

Available space
14.79GB

Unmount SD card
Unmount SD card to safely remove it.

Format SD card
Deletes all data on SD card, including music and photos.

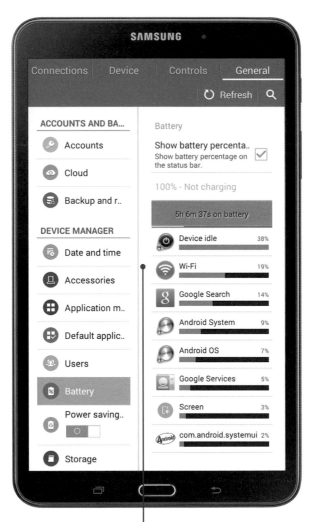

**Troubleshoot Galaxy Tab software, hardware, and accessories**

This chapter covers ways that you can properly maintain your Galaxy Tab 4 and troubleshoot basic software or hardware problems. Topics covered in this chapter include:

→ Maintaining your Galaxy Tab 4

→ Updating the Galaxy Tab software

→ Backing up and restoring your Galaxy Tab 4

→ Extending battery life

→ Solving Galaxy Tab issues

→ Troubleshooting connected devices

→ Getting help

# Troubleshooting Your Galaxy Tab 4

Although problems concerning the Galaxy Tab 4 software, hardware, and accessories are rare, on occasion you might experience incidents where your Tab does not perform properly. There are a few fixes you can try if you experience the occasional glitch that can occur with any hardware device.

Although your Galaxy Tab 4 is a sophisticated piece of hardware, it is less complex than an actual computer, making any issue that might arise more manageable.

## Maintaining Your Galaxy Tab 4

Regular maintenance of your Galaxy Tab 4 not only helps extend the life of your Tab, it also helps ensure peak performance. It's important that you make sure your Galaxy Tab 4 software is up to date and understand basic troubleshooting concepts. Properly cleaning and protecting your Tab's body can be equally important. The Galaxy Tab was designed to be sturdy, but, like any other electronic device, it can collect dust, and a simple drop on the sidewalk can prove disastrous. The first step in maintaining your Galaxy Tab is prevention. You can start by purchasing a protective case.

A sturdy case designed for the Galaxy Tab 4 is important for the overall protection of your device. A number of companies have created a variety of cases for the Tab, so search the Internet or go to Amazon.com to see what's out there. The more padded the case, the better it can absorb a shock if you happen to drop your Tab. A case can also help protect your Tab from dust and keep it dry if you happen to get caught in the rain. Make sure that you keep the inside of your case clean. Dust and sand can find its way into even the most well-constructed cases. Instead of using your sleeve to wipe off your Galaxy Tab's display, invest in a microfiber cloth; you can find them in any office supply or computer store.

Your first instinct might be to wet a cloth to clean your Galaxy Tab touch-screen. Don't use liquids to clean the touchscreen, especially if they include alcohol or ammonia. These harsh chemicals can cause irreparable damage to the touchscreen, rendering it difficult to see. Consider purchasing a screen protector at a local store or your favorite online retailer to keep the touch-screen dust and scratch free. Some screen protectors also come with a micro-fiber cleaning cloth.

# Updating Galaxy Tab 4 Software

Every so often, Google releases software updates for your Galaxy Tab's Android operating system. To get the most from your Galaxy Tab 4, it is good practice to update soon after an upgrade has been released. When an update is available, you receive a notification that indicates that you can download a system upgrade. At that point, you have the option to initiate the software update. You can also check for system updates manually by tapping Settings in the Apps screen, tapping General in the menu bar at the top of the screen, tapping About Device in the Settings list, and then choosing Software Update. You are given an option to Check for Updates. If your system is up to date, your Tab alerts you to this fact. If an update is available, follow the provided directions to upgrade your software.

The Android operating system is not the only software you need to update on your Galaxy Tab. Your Tab also uses software, called *firmware*, to run its internal functions. When an update is available, use your own discretion as to whether you want to update right away, just in case there are any issues with the update.

# Backing Up and Restoring Your Galaxy Tab 4

Backing up the contents of your Galaxy Tab 4 is a good practice for securing your important information and multimedia content. You can ensure that your contacts, photos, videos, and apps are copied to your PC or Mac in case something happens to your Tab.

## Ensure Automatic Google Account Backup

Your Google account information—such as your Gmail inbox, Contacts list, and Calendar app appointments—automatically sync with Google servers, so this information is already backed up for you. To ensure that your Google account information is being automatically backed up, follow these directions.

1. Tap the Apps icon on the Home screen.

2. Tap Settings on the Apps screen.

3. Tap General in the menu bar.

4. Tap Google in the list.

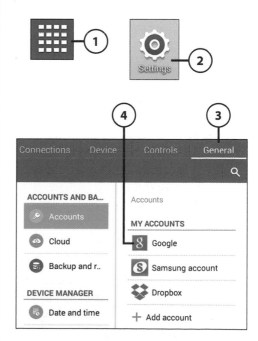

5. Tap the Google email account in the list of accounts.

6. Ensure that all the account settings in the list have a green check mark to the right. If they don't, tap the box to place a green check mark within the box.

## Multiple Google Accounts
If you have multiple Google accounts, repeat Steps 1 through 6 for each account.

7. Tap Backup and Reset.

8. Ensure that a green check mark appears next to Back Up My Data and Automatic Restore. If not, tap the box in each field to place a green check mark within the box. The information associated with your Google address is now automatically backed up.

9. Tap Backup Account to immediately begin backing up your Google account data.

## The Automatic Restore Option
When checked, the Automatic Restore option ensures that any data or settings placed on third-party apps are restored when you restore those apps to your Galaxy Tab.

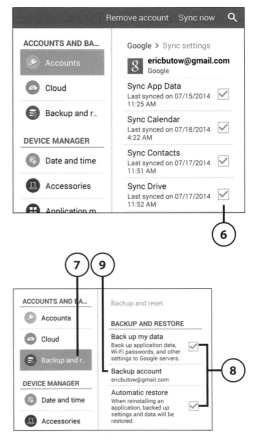

# Syncing and Using Manual Backup

There are multiple ways for you to back up content that is outside of your Google account information on your Galaxy Tab 4, such as your apps and multimedia content, onto your computer. Connect your Galaxy Tab 4 to your PC as a mass storage device and manually drag and drop files. You can use the Samsung Kies software to transfer data, synchronize files, and update firmware while connected to a PC or Mac.

When connected to your PC as a mass storage device, you can view all of the data on your Tab's internal storage and optional MicroSD card. The content is categorized into specific folders that you can copy from your card and internal storage such as DCIM, Download, Music, Pictures, Movies, Podcasts, and more. You can also copy all folders with the names of apps installed on your Galaxy Tab 4.

You can also use the Samsung Kies software for PCs and Macs to sync your content. See Chapter 12, "Playing Music and Video," to learn how to exchange content between your Galaxy Tab 4 and your computer by connecting as a mass storage device and by using Samsung Kies.

# Extending Battery Life

Your Galaxy Tab 4 is capable of up to at least 7.5 hours of battery life depending on the model you have. Battery life can also vary depending on how you use the Galaxy Tab. Strenuous tasks, such as playing HD video, dramatically lower your battery life more than surfing the Web does. You can monitor your battery power at the top of the screen in the Status area. The green battery status icon located in the lower right of the Status Bar lets you keep an eye on how much battery power you have left. When the battery gets low, a warning appears, informing you of the percentage of battery power you have left and instructing you to connect the charger. When the battery is too low, your Tab automatically shuts down. There are a few things you can do to extend the life of your Tab's battery.

# Monitor Power Usage

On the Galaxy Tab 4 you can use the Battery Usage screen to see which of the apps you use consumes the most power, and then you can reduce the use of those apps. Your battery power savings are small, but if you're running low on power with no way to recharge, every little bit counts. Follow these directions to access the Battery Usage screen.

1. Tap the Apps icon on the Home screen.

2. Tap Settings on the Apps screen.

3. Scroll down the Settings list (if necessary) and then tap Battery. The screen displays the items that are consuming the most battery power. In this example, 19 percent of the battery power has been used for the Wi-Fi hardware to communicate with the Internet.

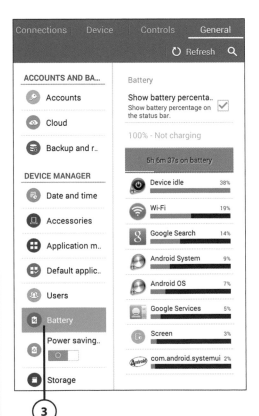

# Adjust Screen Brightness

The high-quality touchscreen of the Galaxy Tab 4 can consume plenty of battery power. The higher the brightness level set on your Galaxy Tab 4 the more power the touchscreen uses. If you are viewing the screen in very bright conditions, you probably do not need a very high brightness setting. Consider dimming the screen to extend the battery life.

1. Tap the Apps icon on the Home screen.

2. Tap Settings on the Apps screen.

3. Tap Device in the menu bar.

4. Tap Display.

5. Tap Brightness.

6. Slide the slider to the left to lower the brightness level or to the right to increase the brightness level.

7. Tap OK.

## Quick Settings for Brightness

The Galaxy Tab 4 offers a quicker way for you to access the brightness controls by providing quick settings in the notification panel. Open the Quick Settings and Notifications screen and then use the slider below the Wi-Fi, Location, and Sound buttons to adjust screen brightness.

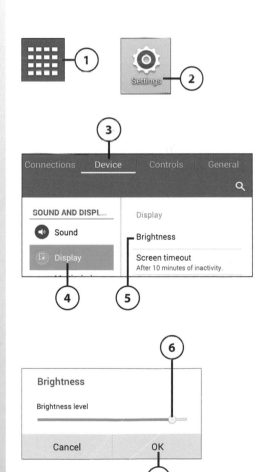

## Utilize Sleep Mode

Your Galaxy Tab 4 goes to sleep after a specified period of inactivity, but you don't have to wait for it to fall asleep; you can put it to sleep manually. When your Tab is awake, it is consuming battery power. Press the sleep button on the side of your Tab when you have finished using the device to conserve battery power.

## Conserve Power by Turning Off Wi-Fi

When the Wi-Fi antenna is activated on your Galaxy Tab, your device is incessantly looking for available Wi-Fi networks to join, which uses battery power. To see if Wi-Fi is turned on, check the Status Bar in the top-left corner of your Galaxy Tab for the Wi-Fi symbol. If you do not need a Wi-Fi connection, turn it off to conserve battery power. If you are not wandering and are using Wi-Fi in a single location, look for a power outlet and plug in your Tab.

1. Tap the Apps icon on the Home screen.

2. Tap Settings on the Apps screen.

3. Tap Wi-Fi to view Wi-Fi networks available to you.

4. Turn off Wi-Fi by sliding the Wi-Fi slider to the left. The slider button displays an O (for Off) with a gray background, and the right side of the screen asks you to turn on Wi-Fi to see available networks.

## Quick Settings for Wi-Fi

The Galaxy Tab 4 offers an even quicker way for you to access the Wi-Fi setting by providing quick settings in the notification panel. Simply tap in the far-right corner of the Status Bar located at the bottom right of your Tab's screen and tap the green Wi-Fi setting to turn it off.

# Conserve Power by Turning Off Bluetooth

When Bluetooth is activated on your Galaxy Tab, your device is constantly checking for other Bluetooth devices, which drains battery power. To see if Bluetooth is turned on, check the Status Bar in the top-left corner of your Galaxy Tab for the Bluetooth symbol. If you are not using a Bluetooth device, turn this function off. There are also security reasons why you should turn off Bluetooth when you are not using it, so get in the habit of turning Bluetooth off as soon as you finish using a wireless device with your Galaxy Tab. You can easily deactivate Bluetooth in the Notifications panel.

1. Tap the Apps icon on the Home screen.

2. Tap Settings on the Apps screen.

3. View all Bluetooth devices to which the Galaxy Tab 4 is connected by tapping Bluetooth.

4. Turn off Bluetooth by sliding the Bluetooth slider to the left. The slider button displays an O (for Off) with a gray background, and the right side of the screen asks you to turn on Bluetooth to see available devices.

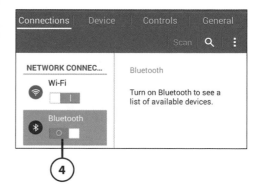

## Quick Settings for Bluetooth

The Galaxy Tab 4 offers an even quicker way for you to access the Bluetooth set-ting in the Quick Settings and Notifications screen. Turn off Bluetooth by simply tapping the green Bluetooth tile in the far-right corner of the Status Bar located at the top right of your Tab's screen.

# Solving Random Galaxy Tab Issues

The occasional hardware or software glitch happens to even the best of electronic devices. You might encounter an issue, although rare, where an app you are using freezes, a wireless device proves difficult to pair with your Galaxy Tab 4, the touchscreen becomes unresponsive, or landscape orienta-tion is not available at all times. Fortunately, it is not very difficult to trouble-shoot some of these issues. If you should happen to come across a problem that you can't solve yourself, there are plenty of channels for you to find tech-nical support.

## Difficulty Turning Your Tab On or Off

On rare occasions, you might find that your Galaxy Tab 4 is stubborn when you try to turn it on or off. It might appear that the device has locked or become unresponsive. If this happens to you, hold the Power button for 8 seconds to see if the Tab 4 responds. If this does not work, you might need to let your Tab sit for a few seconds before you again try holding the Power but-ton for 8 seconds.

## Touchscreen Becomes Unresponsive

This tip assumes that your Galaxy Tab 4 and any app you are using is respon-sive, but the touchscreen is not responding to your touch. If you attempt to use your Galaxy Tab 4 touchscreen while wearing conventional gloves, it does not work. This can prove inconvenient on a very cold day, so you might want to consider a capacitive stylus for your Galaxy Tab.

Your Tab uses a capacitive touchscreen that holds an electrical charge. When you touch the screen with your bare finger, capacitive stylus, or special static-carrying gloves, it changes the amount of charge at the specific point of contact. In a nutshell, this is how the touchscreen interprets your taps, drags, and pinches.

The touchscreen might also be unresponsive to your touch if you happen to have a thin coat of film on your fingertips. So no sticky fingers, please.

## Force Stop an App

Sometimes an app might get an attitude and become unruly. For example, an app might provide a warning screen saying that it is currently busy and is unresponsive, or it might give some other issue warning to convey that a problem exists. If an app is giving you problems, you can manually stop the app.

1. Tap the Apps icon on the Home screen.

2. Tap Settings on the Apps screen.

3. Scroll down the Settings list (if necessary) and then tap Application Manager.

4. In the heading area above the list of apps, swipe right to left until you see the Running header. The Running list appears under the Running header and shows only the apps that are currently running.

5. Swipe down the list of apps if necessary and then tap the problem app.

6. Tap Stop. The app stops running.

7. Tap Report to send a problem report to the app's developer.

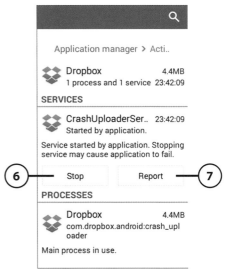

# Battery Does Not Charge

If you find that your battery is not charging, first start with the power outlet. Is the outlet supplying power? Is the power strip turned on? Plug something else into the outlet to see if it works, or try another outlet.

Make sure that everything is connected properly. Is the adapter secure on both ends? If the outlet supplies power and the cables are connected properly, but the battery still does not charge, try another cable. If this does not solve the issue, your battery might be defective. Contact Samsung technical support. (See the "Getting Technical Help" section later in this chapter for more information about how to contact Samsung.) There is no way for you to remove the battery yourself.

## Overheating

Overheating is rare, but if your Galaxy Tab becomes too hot and regularly turns itself off, you might need to replace the battery. You can tell if your Tab is getting too hot by holding it in your hands. Use caution.

# Landscape Orientation Does Not Work

The orientation setting on your Galaxy Tab 4 could be set so that your Tab stays in either portrait or landscape mode, regardless of how you hold the device. If your Tab no longer utilizes landscape orientation, first check the setting for screen orientation.

The Galaxy Tab 4 has an Auto-Rotate setting that must be selected for the screen to adjust from portrait to landscape mode, depending on how you hold the device. You can easily confirm that the Auto-Rotate setting is selected from the Settings menu.

1. Open the Quick Settings and Notifications screen from the Home screen by tapping and holding on the top edge of the screen and then swiping downward.

2. Locate the Screen Rotation setting button and confirm that the button above the Screen Rotation text is green. If the icon is gray, activate the setting by tapping the button. Your Galaxy Tab screen should now adjust to the orientation in which you hold the device.

### Changing Orientation on the Tab 4 10.1"

For the 10.1" Tab, you need to go into the settings under Screen and ensure that the Auto-Rotate Screen option is enabled. A green check mark next to this setting means that it is enabled.

### Landscape Orientation and Apps

Not every app on the Android Market was developed to take advantage of the landscape orientation of your Galaxy Tab. If you notice this issue while using an app, close the app and then see whether your Tab can situate itself in landscape orientation.

# Troubleshooting Wi-Fi Accessibility Problems

Your Galaxy Tab 4 provides you the convenience and flexibility of wireless Internet access via Wi-Fi connectivity. Along with this convenience and flexibility comes the potential for connectivity issues regarding wireless networks. If you are unable to access a Wi-Fi network, or if your connection is sporadic, there are some troubleshooting tips you can use to pinpoint basic accessibility options.

## Make Sure Wi-Fi Is Activated

First and foremost, make sure that the Wi-Fi antenna is on. You can determine this by looking in the right corner of the system bar at the top of your Galaxy Tab screen to see whether the Wi-Fi icon is visible. If it is not on, you can open the Quick Settings and Notifications screen and then activate Wi-Fi by tapping the Wi-Fi button.

**Wi-Fi Antenna**

# Check Your Range

If Wi-Fi is activated on your Galaxy Tab 4 and you still cannot connect, take note of how far away you are from the Wi-Fi access point. You can be only 115 feet from a Wi-Fi access point before the signal becomes weak or drops altogether. Structures such as walls with lots of electronics can also impede a Wi-Fi signal. Make sure you are close to the access point or turn on the access point's range booster, if it has one, to improve your connection.

## Reset Your Router

The issue might not be your distance from the Wi-Fi access point, a signal-impeding barrier, or your Galaxy Tab 4. As a last resort, you might need to reset the router. After you reset your router, you have to set up your network from the ground up.

# Reset the Galaxy Tab 4 Software

If all else fails and your technical problems still persist, as a last ditch effort you might need to reset the Galaxy Tab software. Resetting your Galaxy Tab software restores your Tab to the factory defaults, just like when you took it out of the box for the first time. Consider contacting support before you reset your Tab, but if you must, follow these directions to reset the device.

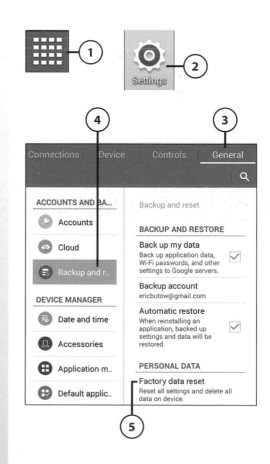

1. Tap the Apps icon on the Home screen.

2. Tap Settings on the Apps screen.

3. Tap General in the menu bar.

4. Tap Backup and Reset.

5. Tap Factory Data Reset.

6. Tap the Reset Device button.

7. If you use a password to log into your Tab, type the password in the Confirm Password field.

8. Tap Continue.

9. Tap the Delete All button to confirm. Your Tab is returned to its factory state.

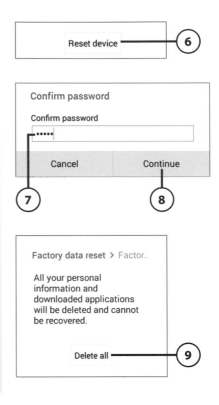

# Getting Technical Help

There are many outlets available where you can find help if you run across a Galaxy Tab technical problem that you can't seem to beat. Although limited, the user's manual is a good place to start. You can download the correct manual for your Galaxy Tab model online from the Samsung website (www.samsung.com), in the form of a PDF, and scan the table of contents or perform searches in the document for words that pertain to your problem. In most user manual PDFs, topics in the Table of Contents are often linked to the section they pertain to within the document, so when you find what you are looking for, click the topic and jump to the page.

Websites and Galaxy Tab forums are also a great way for you to get support for your device. Type a search phrase, such as "Galaxy Tab Google Calendar sync problem," into Google. Chances are there are plenty of people who are experiencing the same issue. Doing some online research of your own could save you a few minutes on the telephone with technical support and help you solve your problem more quickly.

# Contact Your Cellular Provider or Samsung

The Samsung website is a great resource for getting help with technical issues with your Galaxy Tab 4. The Samsung website (www.samsung.com/us/support/) offers support via Twitter, Facebook, Google Plus, as well as by phone (1-800-726-7864). Before you call, you need to have your device's model number so that you can give it to the technical support representative.

## Locate Tab Model Number

You can find the model number on the box that your Tab shipped in, and you can also find it in the Settings menu.

1. Tap the Apps icon on the Home screen.

2. Tap Settings on the Apps screen.

3. Tap General in the menu bar at the top of the screen.

4. Scroll down the Settings list and then tap About Device.

5. Locate your Tab's model number in the About Device field on the right of the screen.

This appendix offers options on how to accessorize your Galaxy Tab 4 with protective cases, screen protectors, chargers, and adapters. It also covers ways to maximize the longevity of your Galaxy Tab 4. Accessories covered in this appendix include:

→ Protective cases
→ Screen protectors
→ Chargers and adapters

# Finding Galaxy Tab 4 Accessories

There are many accessories available for the 7", 8", and 10.1" models of the Galaxy Tab 4, ranging from those that increase its usability to those that protect your Tab 4 or enhance its style. You can start on the Samsung website to explore which accessories are right for you, but don't stop there. Many other companies create high-quality accessories for the Tab 4. Amazon.com is a great place to browse the many offerings for the Tab 4 and read product reviews from other buyers. Let's take a look at a variety of accessories to see how they can benefit you.

## Protective Cases

Perhaps the most fundamental duty you have as a Galaxy Tab 4 owner is to protect your Tab from becoming damaged. There are many cases on the market to choose from, and all provide some degree of protection for your Tab. It is important to note that as of this writing, Samsung does not offer cases for either of the Galaxy

Tab 4 devices on their website. Fortunately, there are many third-party vendors you can browse on Amazon.com and other electronics stores that offer an assortment of options for your 7", 8", or 10.1" Tab 4.

Skins are stylish and provide a thin layer of protection around your Galaxy Tab 4, which can be effective for protecting your Tab against dust, nicks, and scratches. A skin by itself is less effective for absorbing shock, such as from a drop, than a padded case that remains on your Tab at all times.

Some padded cases, such as the Poetic SlimBook Leather Case for all three Tab 4 models as well as the Moko Slim-Fit Cover Case for the 8.0" and 10.1" Tab 4 models, also act as stands.

1. Fold the front cover of the case underneath the Tab 4.

2. Set the Tab down on a flat surface so the screen is in landscape orientation.

3. Angle the Galaxy Tab 4 display so that it is easy to view. This is a great orientation in which to watch videos or movies.

4. Set the Galaxy Tab 4 up in portrait orientation by positioning the folded cover behind it.

## >>>Go Further
### ALTERNATIVES TO CASES

Protective cases aren't the only way to keep your Galaxy Tab 4 safe from the elements and damage. Protective pouches, sleeves, or slipcases are other alternatives. If you prefer the tactile experience of the Galaxy Tab 4 body in your hands while you use it, you can use a pouch when you're carrying your Tab and then slip the device from the pouch when you're ready to use it. A leather or cloth pouch can also act as an extra layer of protection for that stylish skin you have been eyeing for your Tab.

# Screen Protectors

Most cases, skins, and pouches do not include a protective screen cover to keep your high-resolution screen from getting scratched, so you might have to purchase one separately. You can choose from a variety of protective screens; the most popular are clear (invisible), mirrored, and antiglare.

A clear protective screen performs the basic duty of preventing your Galaxy Tab's glass screen from being scratched or collecting dust. A protective film offers three layers of protection after you apply one using its self-adhering surface, and it's barely noticeable. Some screen protectors, such as the ArmorSuit Military Shield, even protect against moisture and self-heal (minor scratches to the shield's surface repair themselves over time). To remove the protector, just peel off the film.

A mirrored screen does exactly what it says. When your Galaxy Tab 4 screen is off, the screen reflects as a mirror. When the Galaxy Tab 4 screen is on, the mirror goes away. This option not only protects your screen but also adds a stylish aesthetic to your Tab. One thing to keep in mind when choosing this option is the glare factor when using your Tab in the sun. A substantial glare can impede screen visibility.

Antiglare screen protectors make it easier for you to view your Galaxy Tab display indoors or outdoors in direct sunlight. While protecting your screen, they also help to reduce annoying surface glare caused by bright indoor lighting.

When you clean your screen, be sure to use a microfiber cloth. You can order one or more microfiber cloths online or pick them up at any office supply store. Then you can use the dry cloth to gently wipe smudges, dust, and lint that accumulate as you use the Tab 4. Never use paper towels because they can scratch your screen.

If you have bigger stains on your screen, such as food, you can dampen the cloth lightly and gently wipe the screen. Dry the screen with a dry microfiber cloth. (This is a good reason why you should get at least two cloths.) Never use window cleaners to clean the screens as the chemicals in those cleaners can permanently damage the screen.

# Chargers and Adapters

The Galaxy Tab 4 was designed for a person who is on the go. Put your Tab 4 7.0" in your back pocket or tuck your 8.0" or 10.1" Tab under your arm and go. Many accessories are available to the power user, including additional power chargers and adapters. For example, you might want to charge your Galaxy Tab at the office as well as at home. Instead of remembering to transport a single cable, wall jack, or dock, why not invest in two? You can also have the convenience of charging your Galaxy Tab while in a car.

- **Galaxy Tab USB Charging/Data Cable**—You can use this data cable to connect your Tab to a PC, Mac, or Samsung charger. This offers a two-in-one solution for charging power and transferring data simultaneously via USB data sync cable. You can also use it to connect your Tab to your computer.

- **Galaxy Tab 40-pin Vehicle Power Adapter with Detachable Cable**—The Samsung Car Adapter, with data cable, enables you to charge your Galaxy Tab while in your car. You can plug it into your car's 12-volt cigarette lighter socket. If you have to transfer data from your Galaxy Tab to your laptop, or vice versa, this car charger provides a detachable USB cable that enables you to connect to your laptop and make the transfer. You can also simultaneously charge your Galaxy Tab through the same connection to your laptop.

- **Galaxy Tab 40-Pin Travel Adapter with Detachable Cable**—Charge your Tab while on the go or at home with this adapter that plugs into any standard wall outlet. This adapter includes a USB port for universal charging and a 2A charger.

## >>>Go Further
## OTHER CHARGERS AND ADAPTERS

When it comes to accessories, perhaps the biggest decision to make is choosing from the variety of available manufacturers' products. There are many options for the power user, such as worldwide travel plug adapters, mini surge protectors, and dual cigarette lighter sockets. Always make sure that the accessories you use are compatible with your Galaxy Tab 4. Not all manufacturers' accessories are of equal quality.

This appendix provides definitions of terms discussed in this book. Terms are listed in alphabetical order.

B

# Glossary of Terms

There are a number of terms listed throughout this book, and if you want to read a list of definitions before you start reading the book—or just need a quick refresher—this appendix is for you. Though this book contains all the important definitions you should know about, this list isn't exhaustive. Other definitions appear throughout this book and may also appear on the book web page on the Que Publishing website (http://www.quepublishing.com).

**adapter**   A device that connects two different pieces of equipment that cannot be connected directly.

**Airplane mode**   A setting on the Galaxy Tab 4 that enables you to quickly turn on and off wireless connectivity.

**Android**   An operating system for smartphones and tablets produced by Google.

**apps**   Short for applications. Apps are programs that are written to perform different tasks on the Galaxy Tab 4.

**Apps screen**   A screen that contains icons for all apps installed on your Galaxy Tab 4.

**backup**   The process of copying and archiving computer data, usually to another device or remote file storage service.

**Bluetooth**   A technology standard to connect computers, smartphones, tablets, and other computing devices (for example, printers) wirelessly over short distances.

**book reader**   An app that enables you to read ebooks on your Galaxy Tab 4. The Google Play Books reader app is preinstalled on the Tab 4.

**bookmark**   In a browser app, this is a favorite website saved in the app so you can access it easily. In a book reader app, a bookmark is a page in your book that you can tag so you can go back to that page easily.

**brightness sensor**   A sensor that measures the ambient light around the Galaxy Tab 4 so the Tab 4 can automatically adjust the light level of the screen to help you see the screen clearly.

**browser**   An app that enables you to view websites and web pages. The Internet and Google Chrome browser apps are preinstalled on the Tab 4.

**button bar**   An area that contains icons for performing specific tasks within an app.

**ChatON**   Samsung's instant messaging app that is preinstalled on the Galaxy Tab 4.

**cloud storage**   A service that enables you to upload files onto its server computers. Cloud storage services make it easy for you to share large files with others.

**contact**   A file that stores contact information such as names, addresses, emails, and notes.

**contact account**   A contact file for a specific person that contains all the information associated with that person.

**drag**   View content on the screen by touching the top of the screen and moving your finger to drag content the length of the screen. You can also drag from left to right within an app screen if the app allows it.

**Dropbox**   A remote file storage service that is preinstalled on the Galaxy Tab 4 so you can back up your Tab 4 data to the Dropbox server and share files with other Dropbox users.

**ebook**   An electronic version of a book designed specifically for reading in a book reader app.

**email**   A method for distributing messages to one or more people on a computer network.

**episode**   A separate program that is part of a larger video or podcast series.

**Exposure Level**   A feature in the Camera app for adjusting the lighting levels in your photo or video to account for the lighting conditions in your environment.

**feed**   A data format for providing you with regularly updated content that you subscribe to, such as news headlines.

**flick**   The method of scrolling up and down the screen in the Galaxy Tab 4. After you touch the top (or bottom) of the screen, move your finger quickly down (or up) and then lift your finger at the last moment so the content scrolls after you lift your finger.

**force stop**   Manually stop an app that is no longer working correctly.

**Galaxy Tab**   The name for Samsung's line of tablets that run the Android operating system.

**Google**   A multinational computing company founded in 1998 that's head-quarted in Mountain View, California. Google is most popular for its web search engine and for its Android operating system.

**Google Chrome**   A Web browser app that is preinstalled on your Galaxy Tab 4.

**Google Cloud Print**   A web-based service that allows any web-enabled device, including the Galaxy Tab 4, to access a printer that is connected to the Cloud Print service. Access the Google Cloud Print website at www.google.com/cloudprint/learn.

**Google Drive**   A cloud storage app that is preinstalled on your Galaxy Tab 4.

**Google Hangouts**   The instant messaging app for the Galaxy Tab 4. If you have the Messaging app installed, which is Google's obsolete instant messaging app, the Tab 4 will ask you to upgrade to Google Hangouts the first time you launch the Messaging app.

**Google Now**   An intelligent personal assistant app that's preinstalled on your Galaxy Tab 4. Google Now can perform tasks for you based on your location and how you're using your Tab 4.

**Google Play Store**   A preinstalled app on the Galaxy Tab 4 that enables you to shop for apps, purchase an app, and download the app to your Tab 4 so you can use it.

**Google+**    A social networking website designed and operated by Google for sharing updates, multimedia files, and chatting with other Google+ users.

**GPS**    An acronym that stands for Global Positioning System, which makes it possible for specific apps (such as Google Maps) to use GPS satellites so those apps can find out where you are and provide location-specific information.

**HD**    An abbreviation that stands for High Definition video, which is typically 1,280 × 720 (720p) or 1,980 × 1,080 (1080p) pixel resolution.

**history list**    A list of all web pages you've visited during your browsing session stored in the browser app.

**Home screen**    The screen that appears by default after you either swipe on or enter your password, PIN, or pattern in the Lock screen. There are also two other home screens that you can access by swiping back and forth; these other two home screens show the Flipboard, Game Hub, and Video Player widgets by default.

**hypertext**    Text or images in a web page that are linked to text or an image on another web page. Tap the linked text or image on the page to open the linked page that contains the other text and/or image.

**icon**    An image on the screen that represents a specific application, file, folder, or option.

**IMAP**    An acronym for Internet Message Access Protocol, which makes the server the place where all messages are stored. Therefore, your Galaxy Tab 4 and computer display all email messages on the server.

**instant messaging**    Real-time transmission of text messages between two or more users.

**Internet**    A global system of interconnected networks that you can use to access websites as well as other services such as email.

**IR blaster**    An infrared device that allows you to control devices (such as a television and cable box) that accepts infrared commands from a mobile device such as a remote control or your Galaxy Tab 4.

**iTunes**    A media player and media library app that enables you to download, play, and organize audio and video files. iTunes is available for both the Windows and Mac OS platforms.

**Jelly Bean**    The nickname for Android versions 4.1.x, 4.2.x, and 4.3.

**Kies**   An application produced by Samsung for Windows and Mac OS that makes it easy for you to sync your music, movies, and photos between your computer and your Galaxy Tab 4.

**KitKat**   The nickname for Android version 4.4.x, which is named after the Nestlé candy bar. The Galaxy Tab 4 uses Android 4.4.2.

**Lock screen**   The default screen that appears on the Galaxy Tab 4 when it first boots. This screen shows the current date and time as well as the Wi-Fi connectivity status, battery charge status, and Smart Stay feature status in the upper-right corner of the screen.

**magazine reader**   An app that enables you to read online versions of magazines on your Galaxy Tab 4. The Google Play Magazines reader app is preinstalled on your Tab 4.

**Maps**   A preinstalled app on your Galaxy Tab 4 that gives you the capability to get directions and pinpoint locations.

**megapixel**   One million pixels, where a pixel is the smallest component of a digital image. A megapixel is the standard measure of the resolution of digital cameras; the higher the megapixels, the higher the resolution.

**Metering**   A setting in the Camera app that determines how the camera factors light in a scene to achieve the proper exposure.

**MicroSD**   An acronym for Micro Secure Digital, a standard memory card format for portable devices like the Galaxy Tab 4.

**mount**   Insert the MicroSD card into the MicroSD slot on your Galaxy Tab 4.

**multi-touch screen**   A screen that recognizes gestures using multiple finger touches to perform certain tasks, such as enlarging the size of text within a document.

**network**   A system of connected computing devices that enable users to share data and resources such as printers.

**news reader**   An app that enables you to view news stories from a variety of sources within the app.

**notifications**   Messages that appear in the Status Bar at the top of the screen. You can also view notifications in the Quick Settings and Notifications screen, which you can open by tapping and holding your finger on the top edge of the screen and swiping your finger down.

**parental controls**    Set usage restrictions for one or more users on your Galaxy Tab 4. For example, you can restrict the apps a user can shop for in the Google Play Store based on the maturity level setting for that app.

**password**    A secret string of characters or a word that you must enter on your Galaxy Tab 4 to gain access to the resources on your Tab 4.

**pinch**    A gesture where you touch the screen with both your thumb and forefinger and bring them together in a pinching motion.

**playlist**    A list of favorite songs that you can access easily in either the Music Hub or Music Player app. You can also add songs to and delete songs from your playlist.

**podcast**    An episodic series of multimedia files (such as audio and/or video) that users can download to their computer, tablet, or smartphone.

**POP**    An acronym that stands for Post Office Protocol. POP retrieves and removes email from a server. Therefore, the server acts as a temporary holding place for email.

**protective screen**    A protective film that keeps the glass screen on your Galaxy Tab 4 from being scratched or collecting dust.

**Quick Settings**    Settings you can turn on and off within the Quick Settings and Notifications screen, which you can open by tapping and holding your finger on the top edge of the screen and swiping your finger down.

**reset**    Restore the Galaxy Tab 4 to its factory defaults so it's just like it was when you took the Tab 4 out of the box for the first time.

**router**    A small physical device that connects computers and devices to the Internet and to each other through a wired and/or wireless connection.

**RSS**    An abbreviation for Rich Site Summary that is a standard format for publishing frequently updated information, such as news stories.

**Scene mode**    One of several options in the Camera app that enables you to optimize your camera for special shooting situations.

**screen capture**    A photo you create of the Galaxy Tab 4 screen interface. Take a screen capture by holding down the Power and Home buttons simultaneously.

**screen orientation**    The way features on a page appear on the screen for normal viewing. By default, the Tab 4 screen orientation is vertical—that is, higher than it is wide. However, features on the page change when you rotate the unit 90 degrees so the screen is horizontal (wider than it is high).

**SD**   An abbreviation that stands for Standard Definition video, which is either 720 × 486 or 720 × 576 pixel resolution.

**server**   A computer and software designed to manage requests for network services, such as a data repository.

**sharing**   Making files available on your Galaxy Tab 4 for others to download and view on their smartphones, tablets, or computers.

**shortcut**   An icon placed on a home screen so you can access an app or widget easily.

**signature**   Text that you can save to the Email or Gmail app and use when you want to place this text at the end of your email message.

**skin**   A thin cover around your Galaxy Tab 4 that can help protect your Tab 4 from dust, nicks, and scratches.

**Sleep mode**   The screen turns off after a period of inactivity to conserve battery power.

**Slider**   A horizontal line with a button, you can hold your finger and move the button along the line to change the setting level, such as the level of brightness on the screen.

**Smart Stay**   A new feature in the Galaxy Tab 4 that uses the camera to track your eye movements. If the Tab 4 recognizes that your eyes are looking at the screen then the Tab 4 screen will remain on and won't go into sleep mode.

**social aggregation**   An app or website that combines all your social networking feeds onto one screen so you can view all your updates at a glance.

**social network**   A dedicated website or app that enables users to exchange information with each other.

**spam**   An inappropriate or irrelevant email message sent to you (and usually a large number of other recipients).

**swipe**   Move elements on the screen by sliding your finger across the screen and then lifting your finger off the screen.

**sync**   Synchronize a single set of data between two or more devices. For example, you can back up data on your Galaxy Tab 4 to your desktop or laptop every time you sync both devices, so if you lose your data on the Galaxy Tab 4 (or lose the Tab 4 itself) you can restore the data from the backed up copies on your computer.

**tab area**   An area on the screen with buttons that enable you to perform specific functions within an app.

**tablet** A mobile computer that contains the display, battery, and circuitry in a shape that resembles a stone or paper tablet.

**Timer** A feature in the Camera app that enables you to determine how long the Tab should wait before the camera takes a picture.

**touch screen** A screen on a device that enables users to control by touching areas on the screen with one or more fingers.

**unmount** The instruction you give the Galaxy Tab 4 to prepare to remove the MicroSD card from its slot.

**URL** An abbreviation that stands for Uniform Resource Locator, which can be a website name or a specific page in a website—for example, http://www.quepublishing.com.

**USB** An abbreviation that stands for Universal Serial Bus, which is an industry standard for cables and connectors that enable computing devices to communicate with each other.

**user account** A small file that contains information about you so you can authenticate yourself on the Galaxy Tab 4 and gain authorization to access various files and services on the Tab 4.

**VPN** The abbreviation for Virtual Private Network. A VPN enables users in a public network (such as the Internet) to transfer private data by making it appear to the users that they're in a private network of their own.

**wallpaper** An image that appears in the background on your Home, Apps, and/or Lock screens.

**Web** Short for World Wide Web, which is a system of interlinked hypertext documents you access through the Internet.

**web page** A document that is suitable for viewing on a browser app (usually written in Hypertext Markup Language, or HTML) that is stored on the Web.

**website** A location on the Internet that manages one or more web pages.

**White Balance** This feature in the Camera app helps accurately reproduce colors when you are recording in various lighting situations so that neutral colors, such as white and gray, are truly neutral and all colors are rendered without undesired color casts.

**widget** A small, portable piece of code that you can interact with like a miniature application. There are dozens of widgets preinstalled on your Galaxy Tab 4.

**Wi-Fi**    The technology standard by which computers and devices can connect to the Internet and/or one another wirelessly.

**Wi-Fi Direct**    A wireless connectivity standard that allows devices to communicate with each other wirelessly without having to use a wireless access
point, such as a wireless router.

**Windows Media Player**    The default multimedia player app for Microsoft
Windows that you can use to sync audio, photo, and video files between your
connected Galaxy Tab 4 and Windows computer.

**YouTube**    A website for storing, sharing, and playing videos. You can access
YouTube videos within the preinstalled YouTube app on the Galaxy Tab 4.

# Index

# C

# D

## Y-Z